WORD AND PRESENCE

INTERNATIONAL THEOLOGICAL COMMENTARY

Fredrick Carlson Holmgren and George A. F. Knight
General Editors

Volumes now available

Forthcoming in 1992

WORD AND PRESENCE

A Commentary on the Book of

Deuteronomy

IAN CAIRNS

WM. B. EERDMANS PUBLISHING CO., GRAND RAPIDS

THE HANDSEL PRESS LTD, EDINBURGH

First published 1992 by William B. Eerdmans Publishing Company,
255 Jefferson Ave. S.E., Grand Rapids, Michigan 49503
and
The Handsel Press Limited
58 Frederick Street, Edinburgh EH2 1LS

Printed in the United States of America

Library of Congress Cataloging-in-Publication Data

Cairns, Ian.
Word and presence: a commentary on Deuteronomy / Ian Cairns.
p.   cm.   — (International theological commentary)
Includes bibliographical references.
ISBN 0-8028-0160-9 (pbk.)
1. Bible. O.T. Deuteronomy — Commentaries.   I. Title.   II. Series.
BS1275.3.C35   1991
222'.1507 — dc20   91-41819
CIP

Handsel Press ISBN 1 871828 17 1

CONTENTS

ABBREVIATIONS

ANET	*Ancient Near Eastern Texts*, ed. James B. Pritchard, 3rd ed.
CH	Codex Hammurabi
D	The Deuteronomic strand of material in the Pentateuch
E	The Elohistic strand of material in the Pentateuch
J	The Yahwistic strand of material in the Pentateuch
JB	Jerusalem Bible
JE	Material conflated from the Yahwistic and Elohistic strands
LXX	Septuagint
MT	Masoretic Text
NEB	New English Bible
NJB	New Jerusalem Bible
NJV	New Jewish Version
P	The Priestly strand of material in the Pentateuch
RSV	Revised Standard Version

EDITORS' PREFACE

The Old Testament alive in the Church: this is the goal of the *International Theological Commentary*. Arising out of changing, unsettled times, this Scripture speaks with an authentic voice to our own troubled world. It witnesses to God's ongoing purpose and to his caring presence in the universe without ignoring those experiences of life that cause one to question God's existence and love. This commentary series is written by front-rank scholars who treasure the life of faith.

Addressed to ministers and Christian educators, the *International Theological Commentary* moves beyond the usual critical-historical approach to the Bible and offers a *theological* interpretation of the Hebrew text. Thus, engaging larger textual units of the biblical writings, the authors of these volumes assist the reader in the appreciation of the theology underlying the text as well as its place in the thought of the Hebrew Scriptures. But more, since the Bible is the book of the believing community, its text has acquired ever more meaning through an ongoing interpretation. This growth of interpretation may be found both within the Bible itself and in the continuing scholarship of the Church.

Contributors to the *International Theological Commentary* are Christians — persons who affirm the witness of the New Testament concerning Jesus Christ. For Christians, the Bible is *one* scripture containing the Old and New Testaments. For this reason, a commentary on the Old Testament may not ignore the second part of the canon, namely, the New Testament.

Since its beginning, the Church has recognized a special relationship between the two Testaments. But the precise character of this bond has been difficult to define. Thousands of books and articles have discussed the issue. The diversity of views represented in these publications makes us aware that the Church is not of one mind in expressing the "how" of this relationship. The authors of this commentary share a developing consensus that any serious explanation of the Old Testament's relationship to the New will uphold the integrity of the Old Testament. Even though Christianity is rooted in the soil of the Hebrew Scriptures, the biblical interpreter must take care lest he or she "christianize" these Scriptures.

Authors writing in this commentary will, no doubt, hold varied views concerning *how* the Old Testament relates to the New. No attempt has been made to dictate one viewpoint in this matter. With the whole Church, we are convinced that the relationship between the two Testaments is real and substantial. But we recognize also the diversity of opinions among Christian scholars when they attempt to articulate fully the nature of this relationship.

In addition to the Christian Church, there exists another people for whom the Old Testament is important, namely, the Jewish community. Both Jews and Christians claim the Hebrew Bible as Scripture. Jews believe that the basic teachings of this Scripture point toward, and are developed by, the Talmud, which assumed its present form about 500 C.E. On the other hand, Christians hold that the Old Testament finds its fulfillment in the New Testament. The Hebrew Bible, therefore, belongs to both the Church and the Synagogue.

Recent studies have demonstrated how profoundly early Christianity reflects a Jewish character. This fact is not surprising because the Christian movement arose out of the context of first-century Judaism. Further, Jesus himself was Jewish, as were the first Christians. It is to be expected, therefore, that Jewish and Christian interpretations of the Hebrew Bible will reveal similarities *and* disparities. Such is the case. The authors of the *International Theological Commentary* will refer to the various Jewish traditions that they consider important for an appreciation of the Old Testament text. Such references will enrich our understanding of certain biblical passages and, as an extra gift, offer us insight into the relationship of Judaism to early Christianity.

An important second aspect of the present series is its *inter-*

national character. In the past, Western church leaders were considered to be *the* leaders of the Church — at least by those living in the West! The theology and biblical exegesis done by these scholars dominated the thinking of the Church. Most commentaries were produced in the Western world and reflected the lifestyle, needs, and thoughts of its civilization. But the Christian Church is a worldwide community. People who belong to this universal Church reflect differing thoughts, needs, and lifestyles.

Today the fastest growing churches in the world are to be found, not in the West, but in Africa, Indonesia, South America, Korea, Taiwan, and elsewhere. By the end of this century, Christians in these areas will outnumber those who live in the West. In our age, especially, a commentary on the Bible must transcend the parochialism of Western civilization and be sensitive to issues that are the special problems of persons who live outside of the "Christian" West, issues such as race relations, personal survival and fulfillment, liberation, revolution, famine, tyranny, disease, war, the poor, and religion and state. Inspired of God, the authors of the Old Testament knew what life is like on the edge of existence. They addressed themselves to everyday people who often faced more than everyday problems. Refusing to limit God to the "spiritual," they portrayed God as one who heard and knew the cries of people in pain (see Exod. 3:7-8). The contributors to the *International Theological Commentary* are persons who prize the writings of these biblical authors as a word of life to our world today. They read the Hebrew Scriptures in the twin contexts of ancient Israel and our modern day.

The scholars selected as contributors underscore the international aspect of the series. Representing very different geographical, ideological, and ecclesiastical backgrounds, they come from over seventeen countries. Besides scholars from such traditional countries as England, Scotland, France, Italy, Switzerland, Canada, New Zealand, Australia, South Africa, and the United States, contributors from the following places are included: Israel, Indonesia, India, Thailand, Singapore, Taiwan, and countries of Eastern Europe. Such diversity makes for richness of thought. Christian scholars living in Buddhist, Muslim, or Socialist lands may be able to offer the World Church insights into the biblical message — insights to which the scholarship of the West could be blind.

The proclamation of the biblical message is the focal concern of the *International Theological Commentary*. Generally speaking, the authors of these commentaries value the historical-critical studies of past scholars, but they are convinced that these studies by themselves are not enough. The Bible is more than an object of critical study; it is the revelation of God. In the written Word, God has disclosed himself and his will to humankind. Our authors see themselves as servants of the Word which, when rightly received, brings *shalom* to both the individual and the community.

— George A. F. Knight
— Fredrick Carlson Holmgren

INTRODUCTION

"THE FIFTH BOOK OF MOSES, CALLED DEUTERONOMY"

Such was the heading given Deuteronomy in older versions of the English Bible. Precritical tradition quite simply regarded Moses as the author, but modern research has shown that the matter is not so simple. The book itself does indeed state that Moses "wrote the words of this law in a book" (Deut. 31:9, 24), and that he "spoke" certain parts of the contents "in the ears of all the assembly of Israel" (1:5; 4:45; 31:30). But the framework as a whole is certainly from another hand. Moreover, there are clear indications that the material in general reflects a situation long after Moses' time:

- The account of Moses' death (ch. 34) is obviously not from his hand.
- The writer is clearly already living in Western Palestine. In 1:1 he describes Moses as speaking "beyond the Jordan," meaning specifically the southeastern corner of the land (similarly 1:5; 3:8; 4:46).
- For the writer, the Hebrew occupation of Palestine is already history (2:12).
- The material of Deuteronomy represents a middle stage in the development of OT law. For example, the Deuteronomic regulation prescribing one only centralized place of sacrifice for all Israel (12:13) is more "advanced" than Exod. 20:24-25, which envisages a plurality of legitimate altar sites (Exod. 20:24-25 is from the earlier JE strand of the Pentateuch). On

1

the other hand, Deut. 18:6-8, which grants rights of priesthood to all Levites, is a prior stage of development compared with Exod. 28:1, which limits priesthood to "Aaron and his sons" (Exod. 28:1 belongs to the later P strand of the Pentateuch). As the intermediate stage of a centuries-long development, then, the Deuteronomic legal material obviously locates itself long after the time of Moses.

- The language style of Deuteronomy differs markedly from that of the earlier strands of the Pentateuch, but has strong affinities with seventh-century Hebrew (Jeremiah and the Lachish Letters).

- The block of torah (law) in Exodus (the "Book of the Covenant," Exod. 20:23-23:33) and the corresponding block in Deuteronomy (the "Deuteronomic code," Deut. 12-26) both show concern for social justice. But the concern is much more developed in the Deuteronomic code. The same strong stress appears also in the preaching of the eighth-century prophets, and indeed strong links are apparent between their social concern and that expressed in Deuteronomy. This points to the conclusion that possibly the Book of the Covenant and certainly the Deuteronomic code were still in process of formation at the time when the eighth-century prophets were active.

THE STRUCTURE OF THE BOOK OF DEUTERONOMY

As we shall see, the structure of Deuteronomy is complicated, but in broad outline it is as follows:

I. First Speech of Moses (1:1-4:43): An introduction to the exhortation section (6:1-11:32)

   A. The speech proper, relating Israel's journey from Mt. Horeb to the plains of Moab (1:1-3:29)

   B. An addendum to the speech: plea for Israel to live faithful to the will of God as declared at Horeb (4:1-40)

   C. Appended notes (4:41-43)

II. Second Speech of Moses (4:44-28:68)

A. Prelude to Second Speech of Moses (4:44–5:33): The theophany at Horeb. The Ten Commandments, given in the context of God's self-revelation, are the kernel of God's will for God's people.

B. The speech proper (6:1–11:32): Exhortation material, consisting of sermon fragments: "God's people must love their LORD with all their heart, remembering the great love that their LORD has lavished on them"

C. The Deuteronomic code (12:1–26:15): Continuation of Second Speech of Moses

D. The Solemnization of the Covenant (26:16–28:68)

   1. The Formula of Covenant Solemnization (26:16-19): Doubles as the conclusion to Second Speech of Moses

   2. Liturgy of Covenant Solemnization, with sanctions in the form of blessings on the obedient and curses on the covenant breakers (27:1-26)

   3. Series of blesses and curses, which once formed the sanctions attached to a variant solemnization liturgy (28:1-68)

III. Third Speech of Moses (29:1–30:20): The stuff of the "speech" can also be viewed as material derived from a liturgy solemnizing a covenant renewal in the plains of Moab

A. Exhortation (29:1-15)

B. Series of curses (29:16-28)

C. Exhortation (29:29–30:20)

IV. Addenda (31:1–34:12)

A. Successor to Moses

   1. Joshua designated and appointed (31:1-8, 14-15, 23)

   2. Torah document entrusted to the Levites, to be kept alongside the ark of the covenant and read periodically at the great festivals (31:9-13, 24-29)

B. Song of Moses

      1. Introduction (31:16-22, 30)
      2. Song of Moses (32:1-43)
      3. Conclusion (32:44-47)
    C. Moses blesses Israel (33:1-29)
    D. Moses' death
      1. Foretelling Moses' death (32:48-52)
      2. Moses' death (34:1-12)

Examination of the outline above confirms the impression that the structure of Deuteronomy is by no means simple. Indeed, it can be said that in the process of its development the book of Deuteronomy has successively been presented in several different formats and frameworks. All of these successive stages and structures have left their trace behind them, so that the present stage of the book constitutes a composite structure of great complexity.

As an aid, then, to the study of the book, let us distinguish these elements in the composite structure:

1. Deuteronomy as a code, or collection, of laws and regulations
2. Deuteronomy as a Covenant Document
3. Deuteronomy as Moses' Farewell Speech
4. Deuteronomy as the final volume of the Pentateuch ("The Five Books")

Deuteronomy as a Legal Code

Research has shown that the Deuteronomic code (or block of torah), Deut. 12–26, is closely related to the so-called Book of the Covenant, Exod. 20:23–23:19. In fact, a careful comparison of the two reveals that (apart from one long section, Exod. 21:18–22:15, which has its own separate history) only four short sentences in the Book of the Covenant (Exod. 20:26; 22:28, 29b, 31) are not reflected or expanded in the Deuteronomic code. So in practical terms, the Deuteronomic code may be said to be an expanded edition of the Book of the Covenant.

The Deuteronomic code, then, is rooted in the Book of the Covenant. But let us go back a step further and ask where the Book of the Covenant came from.

In its present context within the book of Exodus, the Book of the Covenant is put forward as a summary of Moses' conversation with God on Mt. Horeb (= Sinai). The content of that conversation was reported to the people (Exod. 24:3), then written down (v. 4) to become the Book of the Covenant (vv. 7-8). But it would be very difficult to maintain that the entire content of this "book" was literally conveyed directly to Moses on Horeb. Why? The regulations contained in the "book" generally assume an agrarian background, and that not in a predictive kind of way ("this is how your descendants are to behave when eventually they occupy their God-promised homeland"). On the contrary, the impression is that those agrarian conditions are current actuality for the original hearers. In other words, Israel is already living in Palestine.

There is more. Many points of similarity emerge when the contents of the Book of the Covenant are compared with other ancient Near Eastern legal codes. Indeed, it can be said that every single provision in the Book of the Covenant is paralleled in one or other of the ancient Near Eastern codes. Certainly it can be pointed out that Israel is part of the Semitic linguistic grouping and therefore shares in the common cultural heritage of the Semites. On that basis, it could very well be that some of the ancient Semitic laws were already known before Moses' time, by the tribes which eventually came together to form Israel.

It is noteworthy, however, that the points of similarity noted above are not confined to the content of individual sentences, but extend to the arrangement and sequence of the sentences within paragraphs and chapters. It is therefore more convincing to conclude that much of the Book of the Covenant's content was taken over from the Canaanites (inheritors of the ancient Babylonian and Assyrian culture), after Israel entered Palestine.

Most OT scholars believe that the Book of the Covenant is part of the Elohist (E) source and therefore belongs to the tradition developed in northern Israel, united with the southern or Yahwist (J) strand only about the 6th cent. B.C. As to its development within northern Israel, it may be assumed that from the time of Israel's settling in Palestine, the great core events of the nation's birth — liberation from Egypt, meeting with God at Horeb, occupation of the land — were periodically commemorated and celebrated in festivals at the worship centers of Shechem, Bethel, and so forth. In the ceremonial or liturgy of those recurrent commemorations, the proclamation of torah played an important role. Those torah sentences were presented as the content of the divine voice once heard on Horeb and now echoing in the contemporary liturgy.

The continuing repetition of the liturgy at successive festivals would result in a polishing and expansion of the torah sentences that were read. It was a natural process that legal sentences and formulations from the surrounding Canaanite culture were adopted and worked into this constantly repeated celebration torah.

The Book of the Covenant is the product of this expansion process at a certain stage. The Deuteronomic code represents a later stage in the same process.

If it is true that much of this torah material was taken over from "outside" in the course of a long development, is it appropriate to say that the Book of the Covenant (and the Deuteronomic code in turn) is the direct speech of God heard by Moses on Mt. Horeb and painstakingly recorded (Exod. 24:3-4)? Is it appropriate that the writer of Deuteronomy should claim (Deut. 31:9) that "Moses wrote this law"?

We miss the point when we interpret these words with bald literalism. Let us not stick at the surface meaning but penetrate to the thrilling theological intent of these formulations. It should be remembered that in the ancient Near East every legal code was regarded as a divine gift. Statutes were not simply promulgated as the decrees of this or that Great King, but as the demands of the god under whose mandate the Great King ruled. For example, the law code of the eighteenth-century Babylonian king Hammurabi was regarded as a revelation from the sun-god Shamash, who had entrusted his laws to the administration of Hammurabi. For Israel to state, therefore, that the Book of the Covenant (cf. the Deuteronomic code) was

6

received as a totality from God at Horeb was to make a twofold confession.

First, this expressed the conviction that all wholesome law in Israel was a gift from Yahweh their God — even though in fact a large proportion of that law came to Israel through the mediation of their Canaanite neighbors. Second, Israel was convinced that Yahweh's self-revelation on Horeb in the time of Moses was the foundation event which determined all their subsequent history as the people of God.

So, on the basis of these two convictions, Israel reached the conclusion that the whole body of law (which in fact was the end product of a centuries-long development) had been given in embryo in the few short sentences which were indeed revealed to Moses by Yahweh on that historic occasion at Horeb–Sinai. For that reason also the totality of Israelite law came to be bound up with the name of Moses. It was he who mediated the original covenant at Horeb in the 13th century. So he came to be regarded as the human source of every sentence which in process became incorporated in the body of law constituting the covenant conditions.

Deuteronomy as the Text of a Treaty

We have already noted that the laws and regulations of Deuteronomy were not originally exclusive to Israel, but exhibited points of similarity with the common store of ancient Near Eastern law. We noted also that in its process of development the Deuteronomic code was greatly influenced by Israel's international setting.

Now we note another point of comparison with ancient Near Eastern traditions. At a certain stage in its development, a treaty text structure was imposed on Deuteronomy. This structure was common to international treaties throughout the ancient Near East, in particular those between the Great Kings and their vassals.

Building on the pioneering work of George E. Mendenhall (*Law and Covenant in Israel and the Ancient Near East*), scholars have adduced a convincing parallel between the structure of a typical ancient Near Eastern vassal treaty and that of Deuteronomy.

1. *Preamble* introducing the Great King by his name and titles (Deut. 5:1-2)
2. *Previous history,* tracing the background relationship between Great King and vassal up till the moment of treaty making (5:2-6)
3. *Covenant Stipulations* constituting the core of the treaty (5:7-33)
   a. *Basic principles* (chs. 6:1–11:32)
   b. *Detailed stipulations* (12:1–26:15)
4. *Provisions for ratification of the treaty* (26:16-19)
5. *Requirement that the treaty text be kept safe and reread periodically* (31:9-13, 26)
6. *Citing of witnesses to the treaty* (30:19-20)
7. *Treaty sanctions:* curses on violation and blessings on faithful keeping of the treaty (27:1–30:18)

The closeness of the parallel is convincing evidence that the Deuteronomic material has been deliberately conformed to the ancient pattern. A parallel also exists between the vassal treaty pattern and the structure of Exod. 19–24 (the Book of the Covenant and its setting), but the parallel with Deuteronomy is much more marked and complete. Why should this be so?

The reason is probably to be found in the political situation of the times. During the 8th cent. the power of Assyria peaked, then declined during the 7th century. It is precisely in this period that the book of Deuteronomy was taking definitive shape. Faced with the power and decline of Assyria, the Great King's treaty demands and guarantees would be very much in the minds of the smaller powers throughout the ancient Near East. To cast the emergent book of Deuteronomy therefore in the form of such a treaty would be to make a powerful theological statement; whatever the ebb and flow of international politics, the truly definitive guidelines for Israel are the guarantees and demands of the nation's Great King, Yahweh. Faithfulness to *this* treaty covenant is the only and sufficient ultimate security.

Deuteronomy as the Farewell Speech of Moses

As well as exhibiting the structure of a legal code and a treaty text, Deuteronomy also presents itself as a series of three speeches spoken by Moses in the plain of Moab shortly before his death. This speech structure seems to have been imposed on Deuteronomy at a rather late stage in the development of the material.

In general, OT scholars have adopted Martin Noth's suggestion that about the middle of the 6th cent. Deut. 5–31, already in the form of a treaty text, was taken over and integrated into a longer historical work which Noth calls the "Deuteronomistic history." According to Noth, Deut. 1–31; Josh. 1–23; Judges; and 1 Sam. 1–2 Kgs. 25 originally formed a single composition which was only subsequently divided into the books as we have them in our present canon. The original method of dividing the material into blocks was by means of speeches. The end of each significant period was marked by a speech, usually delivered by the outstanding figure of that period. The list of speeches is as follows:

Deut. 1:1–4:40	Moses' first speech
Deut. 5:1–28:68	Moses' second speech
Deut. 29:1–31:13	Moses' third speech
Josh. 23	Joshua's speech
1 Sam. 12	Samuel's speech
(1 Kgs. 2	David's speech)
1 Kgs. 8:12-61	Solomon's speech
2 Kgs. 17	"Speech" or comment of the author, on the collapse of the kingdom of northern Israel
2 Kgs. 25:1-7	"Speech" or lament of the author on the collapse of the kingdom of Judah

It is worth noting that this "speech" element is in fact not foreign to the vassal treaty tradition described in the previous section. The connection has been spelled out by Klaus Baltzer in his book *The Covenant Formulary*. According to Baltzer, the people of God were presented with the text of the Yahweh-Israel covenant on three types of occasions:

9

1. The text was read periodically (in shorter or longer form) in the context of worship at Israel's festivals.
2. It was read in times of covenant renewal, after the nation's faithlessness had caused a cancellation of the covenant.
3. At the death of the nation's leader, the covenant was renewed, to signify that the new leader pledged obedience to its requirements and was confirmed in the role of covenant mediator.

It is clear that the speeches in the Deuteronomic history belong to Baltzer's third category. The covenant mediator, as he lays down office, reviews his period of service and urges both the people and his successor to remain faithful for the future.

We should note too that in the ancient Near East the death of the Great King automatically cancelled the treaties made with his vassals, so that they would need to enter into a fresh agreement with his successor. Similarly, the death and replacement of a vassal required the renewal of the treaty.

It is interesting that whereas Joshua, Samuel, David, and Solomon each make a single speech, Moses makes three. Perhaps this is connected with the Hebrew custom that words of particular importance are uttered three times, to give them their due weight. Thus Moses is portrayed as delivering a three-in-one speech of farewell to stress that the torah mediated by Moses is the all-important foundation of Israel's existence. Because of that, the person of Moses, as the first purveyor and interpreter of that all-important torah, deserves to be highlighted in this special way.

Deuteronomy as the Closing Volume of the Pentateuch

In the final stages of its development, the book of Deuteronomy, which had been incorporated as the opening volume of the Deuteronomic (Deuteronomistic) history (see the preceding section), was detached from that work and united with what scholars call the Tetrateuch (Genesis, Exodus, Leviticus, Numbers). Thus was formed the Pentateuch ("five books") which Jews regard as *hattorah*, the word of God par excellence.

At the time of Deuteronomy's incorporation into the Pentateuch,

Deut. 31:16-22 and 31:30–34:12 were added. This additional material includes the Song of Moses, Moses' blessing on Israel, and the death of Moses. The function of these three additions is to strengthen the ties between Deuteronomy and the Tetrateuch.

The Song of Moses in Deut. 32 forms a parallel with the Song of Moses in Exod. 15. The difference between the two is that the Song of Exod. 15 is optimistic in tone, whereas Deut. 32 is in a somewhat minor key. This contrast reflects the different sociopolitical climates in which the two were composed. Exodus 15 (probably 12th or 11th cent.) represents a period of Israel's growing strength, whereas Deut. 32 is from the period of collapse (possibly even exilic).

In the theology of the Deuteronomic school, strength and prosperity are Yahweh's blessings on obedience, whereas decline and collapse are Yahweh's curse on disobedience. Together then, the two songs form a poignant frame for the exposition of the law: blessings if Israel obeys, disaster if Israel turns away.

Moses' blessing on Israel in Deut. 33 obviously constitutes a companion piece to Jacob's blessing on the tribes, Gen. 49. Jacob's blessing on the twelve tribes is at the time when they have just left the promised land and commenced their stay in Egypt. Moses' blessing, on the other hand, is given after they have left Egypt and are about to reenter the promised land. So the pairing of these two blessings links together the opening and closing volumes of the Pentateuch.

By describing the death of the mediator, the account of Moses' death in Deut. 34 rounds off the story of the giving of the torah which began in Exod. 19.

THE CHARACTERISTICS
OF DEUTERONOMY'S MATERIAL

Having examined the structure of Deuteronomy, we turn now to its contents.

In discussing Deuteronomy as a legal code (see above, 4-7), we stressed the close connection between the Deuteronomic code (Deut. 12–26) and the Book of Covenant (Exod. 20–23). Almost everything in the Book of the Covenant is repeated and expanded in the Deuteronomic code.

From another angle, our understanding of Deuteronomy is enhanced if we examine the Deuteronomic material which is *not* found in the Book of the Covenant. This material falls into two categories:

(1) Material which, though not in the Book of the Covenant, is nevertheless paralleled in the ancient Near Eastern legal codes. For example: Deut. 21:18-21 is paralleled in CH 168-69; Deut. 22:13-27 is paralleled in CH 127-131.

We assume that this material had long been widely known in the ancient Near East, hence probably in Israel as well (whether in oral or written form), and only at a relatively late date incorporated into the legal copies by the Deuteronomic school and adapted to their theology.

(2) Material in the Deuteronomic code for which there is no extant parallel, either in the Book of the Covenant or in the ancient Near Eastern legal codes. Gerhard von Rad suggests (*Deuteronomy*, 15-23) that it is precisely in examining this uniquely Deuteronomic material that we shall gain our clearest insights into the theology of Deuteronomy and into the sources of its tradition.

This specific material is as follows:

1. Exhortations to Israel to "cleave to the LORD" and love him with all the heart.
2. Regulations designed to preserve the status and welfare of the Levites.
3. Rules regulating the role of prophecy in Israel.
4. Emphasis on social justice.
5. Regulations concerning the "holy war" or "Yahweh's war."
6. Regulations defining the office of kingship.
7. Insistence that there is only one legitimate shrine where Israel may worship Yahweh.

Let us consider these points in turn.

"Cleave to the Lord"

Both in the Deuteronomic code (Deut. 12–26) and in the preceding exhortation section (chs. 6–11), the primary law of "loving the LORD your God with all your heart" is continually stressed. Indeed, this "love" is not simply a matter of command, but rather a theme of exhortation, reflection, and homily.

Examples of this from the Deuteronomic code are Deut. 13:1-4, 10; 14:1-2; 26:1-11. Examples from the exhortation section are 6:4; 7:6-16; 8:5-6.

Who are these preachers who persuade and exhort their people with such urgency? In seeking to answer this question, Gerhard von Rad (*Studies in Deuteronomy,* 13-14) cites Neh. 8:1-9:

> Ezra read from the book of the law of Moses . . . and . . . the Levites helped the people to understand the law. They read from the book . . . clearly (RSV mg "with interpretation"); and they gave the sense, so that the people understood the reading.

The implication seems to be that Ezra read the classical Hebrew text while the Levites paraphrased, expanded, and expounded it in the common Aramaic. Von Rad acknowledges that the time gap between Ezra (5th-4th cent.) and the period when the Deuteronomic material was being shaped (9th-7th cent.) is a large one. Nevertheless, he is attracted by the possibility that the preaching task which the Levites obviously fulfill in Ezra 8:1-9 had for centuries previously already been part of their role. Thus, von Rad concludes there is a strong possibility that it is the voice of the Levites which we hear in the exhortatory sections of Deuteronomy.

Concern for the Status and Welfare of the Levites

The suggestion just outlined becomes stronger when we consider the clear concern of Deuteronomy for the well-being of the Levites (cf. Deut. 12:18b-19; 14:27-29a; 18:1-8).

Most OT scholars agree that the position of the Levites must have deteriorated following the centralization of Israel's worship at the one shrine (King Josiah's reform inaugurated ca. 621). Before the centralization, the Levites had constituted the priesthood at the local shrines. But with the abolition of this plurality of worship centers, many local Levites became redundant. So to relieve the suffering of these unemployed, Deuteronomy provides for them to share in the proceeds of the harvest offering and so forth.

This concern for the Levites suggests that the compilers of Deuteronomy had close connections with the Levite class.

Rules Concerning Prophecy

Besides the Levites, the prophets also attract special attention in Deuteronomy. Deuteronomy 18:14-15 is pivotal:

> For these nations, which you are about to dispossess, give heed to soothsayers and to diviners; but as for you, the LORD your God has not allowed you so to do. The LORD your God will raise up for you a prophet like me from among you, from your brethren — him you shall heed. . . .

Every form of soothsaying is a human effort to prize open the divine secrets. God forbids such efforts by God's people precisely because God's self has opened up the true way of access to such divine secrets as may legitimately be known by humankind. That way is the revelation of God's own will in the torah, while the torah in turn is clarified by the prophetic word. When God gave the torah on Horeb, God also instituted the office of mediator in Israel, so that the mediator might explain and apply the torah in all developing situations which Israel would encounter down the generations. Moses himself was appointed first mediator, so that every authentic prophet down the generations becomes the successor of Moses.

Thus according to Deuteronomy, the role of the prophets is twofold. On the one hand, the prophet is subservient to the torah. He or she is charged with explaining the torah, and the prophet's total message and behavior are to be measured and assessed against the torah as standard (13:1-5).

On the other hand, the prophet also has an active and dynamic role. The task is not limited to a bald repetition of already-existent sentences of torah, but also includes the apprehension of new words from God (18:18-20).

In principle, then, the Deuteronomic school regards prophecy as the extension of the mediator role first occupied by Moses. It is noteworthy that of all the collections of law in the OT, it is only the Deuteronomic code that is concerned to lay down guidelines regarding the role of prophecy.

Emphasis on Social Justice

As mentioned above, the emphasis on social justice, already apparent in the Book of the Covenant, is highly characteristic of Deuteronomy. The same emphasis is found also in the eighth-century prophets. Indeed, we get the impression that the Deuteronomic school and the preexilic writing prophets breathe the same atmosphere and have exerted a mutual influence. The rights of those at risk (the poor, foreigners, widows, orphans, women) are of common concern to the Book of the Covenant and the Deuteronomic code, on the one hand, and the prophets Amos, Micah, Hosea, and Isaiah, on the other. Similarly, the concern that the processes of the judiciary should be impartial, humane, and free from extortion and corruption is shared by both.

From these four points so far discussed, then, we draw the conclusion that the Deuteronomic school had strong ties both with the Levites and with those who highly regarded the prophets. This prophetic-levitic combination, interestingly enough, does not appear as the background of Deuteronomy alone, but also of the prophet Hosea. Hans Walter Wolff's suggestion ("Hoseas geistige Heimat") is apposite here, that during the 8th cent. in northern Israel it was an underground levitic-prophetic alliance which preserved authentic Yahwism, at a time when the official cultus had been adulterated with paganism. (We will pick up the northern Israelite connections of the Deuteronomic school later.)

Regulations Concerning the "Holy War" or "War of Yahweh"

The following passages reflect the "holy war" tradition:

20:1-9	Kindling the fighting spirit (cf. Judg. 7:1-3)
20:10-18; 21:10-14	Treatment of prisoners

15

23:1-8	Categories barred from participation, lest the ritual purity of the army be compromised
23:9-14	Preserving the ritual purity of the encampment
24:5	The newly-married exempted
25:17-19	Command to annihilate the Amalekites

The older sources embodied in Exodus, Numbers, Joshua, and Judges indicate that the "war of Yahweh" had its historical setting in the period from the Exodus until (basically) the end of the Conquest.

As the term implies, Israel believed that it was Yahweh's self who subdued their opponents and gave the promised land into their power. Israel's role was confined to that of humble obedience to Yahweh's instructions.

The forces involved were very much a people's army, zealous volunteers banding together to become the instrument of Yahweh's victory. In its historical setting, the action was at the local level. But as the tradition passed into literature, the scope of the action widened to embrace "all Israel." "Yahweh's war" was an important factor through the period of the Judges. But during the reigns of David and Solomon volunteers were increasingly replaced by hired, professional militia, and the ancient tradition fell into disuse.

Why then does the tradition of "Yahweh's war" reemerge in Deuteronomy? Undoubtedly there are both political and theological reasons for this.

Gerhard von Rad (*Studies in Deuteronomy,* 45ff.) accounts for the political dimension in the following way. About the year 701, Sennacherib of Assyria smashed the political power of Judah and took over their mercenaries. Eighty years later, therefore, when King Josiah wished to reassert political independence, he had to face the reality that Judah's professional army no longer existed and an empty treasury precluded hiring replacements. In such circumstances, then, Josiah reverted to the ancient practice of mustering a people's army. His action was endowed with mana by linking it to the old "holy war" tradition.

Theologically, this renewed appeal to "Yahweh's war" strengthens the Deuteronomic call for repentance and covenant obedience. The land is Yahweh's gift, and the gift is conditional on the covenant people's continued faithfulness to the will of God as expressed in the covenant document (the Deuteronomic code).

We may note in passing that the Levites, as discussed above, have a strong connection with the "Yahweh's war" tradition. In the ancient sources the Levites are portrayed as aggressive and militant Yahwists. In Gen. 34:25-26 Levi and his brother defend the honor of Jacob's family. (There are indications that originally this action was regarded positively, though in its present context [cf. Gen. 34:30] it comes to have a negative assessment.)

Similarly, in Exod. 32:26-29 the Levites are portrayed as defending authentic Yahwism with the sword.

With these verses compare:

Deut. 20:2-4	A levitical priest is charged with rousing the fighting spirit.
Deut. 33:8-9	It is the Levites' zeal in defending Yahwism that earns for them the priestly status.

Attitude Toward Kingship

The rules governing kingship (17:14-20) reflect an awareness of the dangers inherent in the institution. The Deuteronomic school acquiesce in the kingship, but with conditions which serve to limit the royal power. This same cautiousness as regards the office of king appears also in northern Israelite traditions:

1 Sam. 8, 12 (According to Hans W. Hertzberg, *I and II Samuel*, 74, 96, this material is probably from the "Mizpah source," which has affinities with the theology of the Elohist source)

Judg. 9, especially vv. 7-15 (A Shechem source which highlights negative aspects of the institution of kingship)

Hos. 5:1; 8:4; 10:15; 13:10-11 (The kings become a symbol of Israel's rebellion against Yahweh)

The similarity in tone between these northern traditions and Deut. 17:14-20 strengthens the impression that the Deuteronomic school had its origins in the north. When the tradition moved south (see below, 20-21), the Deuteronomic school were faced with the reality that the office of kingship played a very important role in the covenant tradition as it had developed in the kingdom of Judah. In the process of "indigenizing" the Deuteronomic theology in the south, therefore, kingship was (hesitantly) acknowledged as a legitimate covenant institution. But there was an effort to neutralize its inherent dangers by laying down strict rules to control its functioning.

Centralization of the Cultus

This emphasis forms the background to several sections of Deuteronomy: 12:1-28; 14:22-29; 15:19-23; 16:1-17; 17:8-13; 18:1-8; 19:1-13.

Clearly, the final edition of Deuteronomy identifies that "one place" with Jerusalem. But was it always so? When the tradition was still developing in northern Israel, could the reference have been to one of the northern shrines, for example, Shechem or Bethel? It is hard to be certain on such matters. What is sure, however, is the prime motive for this centralization of worship. It stems from a desire to control the worship and faith of Israel, and so safeguard its authenticity and purity.

HISTORY OF THE COMPILATION OF DEUTERONOMY

Connection with Northern Israel

We have already touched on several factors which suggest that the Deuteronomic tradition is rooted in northern Israel:

1. The Deuteronomic code is basically an expansion of the Book of the Covenant, which is embedded in the Elohistic source and presumably originates in the north.
2. Deuteronomy and Hosea share a common background and common prophetic-levitic influence. Since Hosea is from

the north, the impression strengthens that the Deuteronomic school is also.
3. The Deuteronomic attitude to kingship seems to be connected with the "anti-kingship" strand of northern tradition.

Later, in the Commentary, we shall come across several further
correspondences. But in principle the northern provenance of
Deuteronomy seems certain.

Dating the Deuteronomic Code and the Book of the Covenant

We have already noted that on the one hand there is a close
connection between the Deuteronomic code and the Book of the
Covenant, whereas on the other hand there is presumably a con-
siderable time gap between the compilation of the two. The
material in the Deuteronomic code is much more "spelled out"
than that in Book of the Covenant. Such a development would
require a time span of fifty to one hundred years (continual
polishing and restating, probably in the liturgies of the great
festivals; see below, 20). So a date for the completion of the Book
of the Covenant would help us calculate the probable period for
the compilation of the Deuteronomic code.

Most OT scholars subsume the Book of the Covenant within
the Elohistic source, which they would date toward the end of
the 9th cent. or the beginning of the 8th. It may be taken as
certain, of course, that the Book of the Covenant had its own
separate history before its incorporation into the Elohistic material. Nevertheless, this does not greatly affect our consideration
here, for the precursor of the Deuteronomic code which concerns
us here is not the Book of the Covenant detached from context,
but the Book of the Covenant in the context of the Elohistic
source.

In that case, there is fair likelihood that the compilation of the
Deuteronomic code was well on the way to completion by 750-
700.

The Crucible in Which the Material Was Shaped

There is general agreement that both the Deuteronomic code (Deut. 12–26) and the exhortatory material (chs. 6–11) was shaped in the worship ceremonies that took place during the recurrent festivals in northern Israel. In Deuteronomy itself (31:10-13) there is provision that once in seven years the complete Deuteronomic code should be read to Israel assembled in festival at "the place which Yahweh will choose." We may guess that "the chosen place" was originally Shechem (27:4, 12, 13), which in earliest times seems to have been northern Israel's leading shrine. (Later on, as we have mentioned, "the chosen place" was identified as Jerusalem.)

In the process of continued rereading, the torah became fuller, and increasingly approximated to the form of the Deuteronomic code as we have it today.

It can be taken as certain, too, that the reading of the law was accompanied by sermons which underlined the essence of the torah and urged Israel to savor the covenant relationship which Yahweh was offering them (see above, 12-13). Memorable fragments of these sermons were preserved by the Levites and are now incorporated in chs. 6–11 and perhaps also chs. 28–30.

The festival at "the chosen place" was first and foremost a remembrance and reaffirmation of the covenant between Yahweh and the people. In this context, therefore, the torah which was read functioned as the text of the covenant. Further, the reading of the text was accompanied by an account of Yahweh's gracious actions which form the basis of the covenant (cf. 5:1-6), and reinforced by a recital of blessings or curses on those who honor or despise the covenant stipulations. So then, from the overall liturgy of the festival — reading of the law, recital of Yahweh's gracious deeds, solemn reiteration of blessings and curses, homilies and exhortations — there emerged the framework (see above, 7-8) which was used by the compiler of Deuteronomy.

The Deuteronomic School Moves South

We have already mentioned the likelihood that for the last sixty years or so before the collapse of the northern kingdom authentic

Yahwism survived as a kind of "underground movement," the core of which was a prophetic-levitic alliance.

In 722 the northern capital Samaria fell to the king of Assyria. We may guess that at that time Levites and other guardians of the sacred traditions fled south, carrying the Deuteronomic materials with them. It is difficult to say whether the text of chs. 5–26 (or chs. 5–30) was basically complete at that time. But we can at least be sure that the process of compilation was already far advanced.

On reaching Jerusalem, efforts would be made to establish the Deuteronomic tradition in the southern milieu. We have already (see above, 17-18) met one example of this, namely, the "acclimatizing" of the attitude of kingship (17:14–20).

The Influence of the Deuteronomic Material in the South

The Deuteronomic material was probably influential in the thinking of King Hezekiah of Judah and in the religious reformation which he undertook ca. 705 (see 2 Kgs. 18). But in 697 Hezekiah was succeeded by his son Manasseh. Throughout the reign of Manasseh (696–642) and his son Amon (641-640) the Deuteronomic school seems to have worked secretively. We can imagine that during those fifty-five years they concentrated their efforts on rounding out the written form of their precious traditions.

With the accession of Josiah in 639 the Deuteronomic school gained their opportunity. Indeed, it is likely that several of their leading figures were among the officials who guided the young king during his minority. On assuming full authority, Josiah began the process of reforming the worship in Jerusalem by banning various forms of paganism and reinstituting the Yahwistic cultus. The reformation probably began ca. 627 (cf. 2 Chr. 34:3).

Then, in the process of cleaning and restoring the Jerusalem temple in 621, the workers came across a text of the Torah. It may be debated whether the manuscript had been really lost and forgotten or artfully planted by members of the Deuteronomic school, so as to be conveniently "discovered" at the appropriate time. However that may be, the finding of the manuscript undoubtedly gave strong impetus to the reform movement which was already under way.

We read in 2 Kgs. 22:11-13 that Josiah and his advisers were deeply disturbed by the contents of the text, and reacted by taking drastic action. When we examine in detail the actions they took, we are struck by the parallels between those actions and the requirements written in the book of Deuteronomy. A list of the parallels is as follows:

Deuteronomic Command		Josiah's Action
Break down their altars, pillars, Asherim, carved images	Deut. 7:5; 12:3 (cf. 16:21)	2 Kgs. 23:4, 6, 7, 14
Prohibition of worshipping "the host of heaven"	Deut. 17:3	2 Kgs. 23:4, 5
Destroy the high places and other pagan shrines	Deut. 12:2	2 Kgs. 23:13
Prohibition of worshipping sun and moon	Deut. 17:3	2 Kgs. 23:5, 11
Prohibition on cultic prostitution	Deut. 23:17	2 Kgs. 23:7
Prohibition on worship of Molech	Deut. 12:31; 18:10	2 Kgs. 23:10
Prohibition on worshipping foreign gods and goddesses	Deut. 12:29-30	2 Kgs. 23:13
Prohibition on calling up the dead	Deut. 18:11	1 Kgs. 23:24
Passover to be celebrated at a single location	Deut. 16:1-8	2 Kgs. 23:21-23
Curses of God on covenant violators	Deut. 27:15-26; 28:15-68; 29:20-28; 30:17-18	2 Kgs. 22:11-13, 17

The number and closeness of these parallels is clear indication that the Torah text discovered was a version of Deuteronomy (perhaps chs. 5–30).

From Josiah's Death to the Fall of Judah

The results of Josiah's reform were not long-lasting. The process of decline which negated the reform is perhaps reflected in Jeremiah's evolving attitude to the reform movement:

> Jer. 11:1-8 (These words are probably not from Jeremiah himself but from the Deuteronomic redactors of his work. Nevertheless, we may take them as an accurate reflection of his attitude in the years 621-608):
>
> Cursed be the one who does not heed the words of this covenant. (v. 3)

Seemingly in this period Jeremiah acknowledged and supported the reform movement. Little if any of his extant preaching is from those years. Probably his "silence" reflects his belief that the reform has been largely successful.

> Jer. 8:8 (The precise dating of this verse in difficult. It fits most naturally in the reign of Jehoiakim, 608-598, or in the last years of Josiah):
>
> The false pen of the scribes has made it [the Torah] into a lie.

This sentence is usually interpreted as meaning that Jeremiah is experiencing disquiet over the way the Torah is being expounded and applied. The Torah is being handled in a narrowly-literalistic and superficial way, so that its true meaning is distorted and the obedience offered by the people correspondingly shallow and ineffectual.

> Jer. 31:31-33 (This passage is probably from about the time of Josiah's death):

Jeremiah is aware that "they broke my covenant" (v. 32), so he longs for a new covenant based on a torah "within them, written on their hearts" (v. 33).

This passage mirrors Jeremiah's conviction that adherence to a torah regarded merely as a chain of commands and prohibitions cannot produce genuine obedience. Thus implicitly he judges

Josiah's reform to have been basically unsuccessful. The failure of official reform creates in him a longing for authentic reform based on a deep personal appropriation of torah.

After the death of Josiah, Israel's condition continued to deteriorate, until Jerusalem finally fell to Babylon; and in the years 597, 586, and 581 three successive groups of leading citizens were deported to Babylon.

Causes of Israel's Collapse

After the fall of Jerusalem, the Deuteronomic school sought to analyze the reasons why God rejected God's "chosen people." In exploring this bitter reality, they reviewed the whole process of Israel's history, from Sinai–Horeb to the fall of Samaria and of Jerusalem. In their literary composition which we call the Deuteronomistic history, they draw their conclusion. It is Israel's disobedience to the torah, as the core of God's covenant with them, which has brought about Israel's exile.

Within the framework of the Deuteronomistic history as a whole, the book of Deuteronomy is highlighted as the primary volume. For Deuteronomy is the definitive text of torah, and torah provides the measuring stick for Israel's history. The word given at the beginning of the process is definitive for every successive stage.

The concluding verses of the Deuteronomistic history (2 Kgs. 25:27-30) allude to an incident which is to be dated 560. We may assume, therefore, that the history itself was completed shortly afterwards, that is, 550.

The Conclusion of the Pentateuch

When did this happen — Deuteronomy's being detached from the Deuteronomistic history and attached to the Tetrateuch to form the "Five Volumes"?

The decisive clue in this is that the Samaritans acknowledge the Pentateuch as the definitive Torah, but deny equivalent status to the remaining books of the Deuteronomic history.

According to Josephus, the break between Jews and Samaritans occurred during the time of Alexander the Great (336-323). Stated so baldly, this is simplistic. Yet the dating is sufficient for our purposes. If the Samaritans at the end of 4th cent. were able to accept the Pentateuch (i.e., including Deuteronomy) as a unitary whole, then obviously Deuteronomy had already been solidly established for some time as an integral part of the whole Torah. This establishment process would require at least fifty years. So we may assume that by 400-380, at the latest, Deuteronomy was attached to the Pentateuch. It was at that time, then, that Deut. 32–34 were added as a rounding out of the definitive narrative.

THE FIRST SPEECH
OF MOSES

Deuteronomy 1:1–4:43

In the Introduction we have already suggested that Deut. 1–4 was added to the code (chs. 12–26) and exhortatory section (chs. [5] 6–11) of Deuteronomy by the Deuteronomic historian, at the time when Deut. 5–26 (27–30) was set in place as the opening section of the overall Deuteronomic history.

PREFACE TO
MOSES' FIRST SPEECH
Deuteronomy 1:1-5

These verses are at pains to give an accurate geographical (1:1-2) and chronological (v. 3) setting for the speech. In the case of the geographical, the impression of clarity is deceptive, in that seemingly two distinct locations are described. On the one hand, the final editor obviously regards "the Arabah" as referring to the lower Jordan Valley "opposite Beth-peor" (4:46), a site on the northeastern corner of the Dead Sea. On the other hand, "Arabah" is also linked with Kadesh-barnea "between Paran and Tophel" (1:1-2), some 120 km. southwest of the Dead Sea. Just possibly this duality of location has some connection with the dual tradition of Israel's entry into Canaan: the "Judah tribes" entering from the south (Kadesh-barnea?) in the 15th cent. B.C. and the "Joseph tribes" from the southeast two centuries or so later.

The meticulous dating in v. 3 is typical of the Priestly (P) school and may originate from the period when Deuteronomy was first attached to the Tetrateuch to form the Pentateuch.

Whatever strands are represented, the Deuteronomic historian stresses that the unitary message is for "all Israel" (v. 1) — a brave statement of faith at a time when the northern kingdom had already been swallowed by a foreign empire 160 years previously.

It is important at the outset to remember that in reading Deuteronomy we need to wear bifocals (if not "trifocals"!). One focus is on the covenant promises and conditions seen through the thirteenth-century eyes of Moses. A second looks from the retrospect of the sixth-century Deuteronomists' nostalgic "might have been" and urgent call to repentance. Focus three (and even four) presents us with the perspectives of the Deuteronomic school at intermediate stages between these two poles. There is a "word" of God to be "seen" (paradox!; cf., e.g., Amos 1:1) through each of these foci.

THE SPEECH PROPER
Deuteronomy 1:6–4:43

MOSES REVIEWS THE JOURNEY
FROM HOREB TO MOAB (1:6–3:29)

The review comprises three major points:

1. 1:6-46   The generation that failed to enter Canaan
2. 2:1–3:20   The generation that succeeded in entering Canaan
3. 3:21-29   Why the covenant leader is debarred from entering Canaan

On closer inspection, the three-phase story resolves itself into nine episodes:

1. 1:6-18   Assistants for Moses
   1:19-46   The survey scouts report back
2. 2:1-7   Israel traverses Edomite territory
   2:8-15   Israel traverses Moabite territory
   2:16-25   Confrontation with the Ammonites is forbidden
   2:26-37   Sihon king of Heshbon is defeated
   3:1-11   Og king of Bashan is defeated
   3:12-22   Territory of Heshbon and Bashan is allocated to the Transjordanian tribes
3. 3:23-29   Moses is debarred from crossing the Jordan

A comparison with Exodus-Numbers reveals that, with the exception of 2:16-25; 3:23-29, all these units are paralleled in the older Yahwistic-Elohistic (JE) source. The Deuteronomic handling of the material highlights three emphases in particular:

31

- God's guiding hand is strongly in evidence throughout the conquest process.
- Moses' dignity and authority as servant of God and leader of Israel is highlighted.
- The responsibility for following the revealed will of God is laid squarely on the people.

Traditional material that does not directly serve these emphases, or that may have weakened their cogency is bypassed.

It is impossible to be certain whether the Deuteronomist used JE directly as a source, or drew on the stock of common tradition. On balance, however, the evidence would seem to support the second of these alternatives.

Assistants for Moses (1:6-18)

1:6-8   These verses form a suture, fastening the preface (vv. 1-5) to the new section (vv. 9-18): "The LORD our God said to us in Horeb." The word "us" is a feature of ch. 1 and indeed of the whole of Deuteronomy. The Deuteronomist is well aware of the six hundred-year gap between Moses and the exilic generation he is addressing. He uses "us," therefore, to insist that the ancestors' meeting with God at Horeb is not bare historical fact, but an open continuing possibility in the present. Each generation must contemporize the historical experience, making it "our own." In all the changing circumstances the historical word continues valid; the true well-being of each generation consists in their/our being "not disobedient to the heavenly vision" (Acts 26:19).

"You Have Stayed Long Enough"

The people are understandably reluctant to let go of their security. They regard Horeb, the mountain of revelation, as God's home. What guarantee have they that the Horeb presence will continue to be accessible in the hazardous unknown of the desert? But the call is inexorable. God's self-revelation is in order that Israel may possess the land. To stick at the revelation experience and not allow it to energize and lead us forward is to falsify it.

"Swore to Your Ancestors"

The Deuteronomist envisages Moses harking back a further five hundred years to trace the beginnings of God's promise. Even the definitive Horeb covenant does not emerge unprepared from the blue. With infinite patience God has in Moses' day brought a five hundred-year process to maturity. Did God not undertake a binding oath of faithfulness? The generation seven hundred years after Moses may take comfort from the long perspective!

1:9-18 In this section vv. 9-12 should be compared with Exod. 18:13-26, and Deut. 1:13-18 with Num. 11:14-17.

Scholars have suggested that Exod. 18 reflects a social structure from a later age, perhaps that of David-Solomon or Jehoshaphat, which has been back-dated into Mosaic times. On the other hand, Num. 11 represents the endeavor of a prophetic and charismatic movement at some indeterminate point in Israel's history to trace their inspiration back to Moses and claim him as their fountainhead.

The Deuteronomist links the two in this way in order to portray Moses as the source of all "decency and order" in Israel, whether in the military, civil, or religious spheres. Therefore the torah of which Moses was the mediator is definitive in all these areas, encompassing and enlivening every aspect of the people's life.

1:9-12 It is noteworthy that Moses' frustration, which in Num. 11:10-15 boils over in angry reproach of God, is here softened, and addressed no longer to God but to the people. Moses exudes calm capability, and his mana is correspondingly enhanced. In the same way the initiative for the organizational reform comes not from Jethro (Exod. 18) but from Moses himself. So it is a sense of inherent appropriateness rather than an urgent need for assistance which inspires Moses' sharing of "clerical" responsibility with the "laity"!

1:13-18 A comparison with other texts where "heads of thousands, hundreds, fifties" are mentioned (1 Sam. 8:12; 17:18; 22:7; 2 Kgs. 1:9, 11, 13; Isa. 3:3) makes it plain that these were military leaders. Thus Deut. 1:13-18 seems to reflect a period of Israel's history when military and judicial functions coincided. According to v. 15 the new "commanders" are selected from existing heads of tribes (the phrase is lacking in the LXX), thus suggesting a continuity between the old order under tribal elders and the new system of government by numerical groupings. The word for "officer" (*shoter,* v. 15b) literally means "drawer-up of lines" (organizer); hence the LXX translates it "secretary" (drawer-up of lines of writing, keeper of civil lists).

The little "Guideline for Judges" in vv. 16-17 has its parallels in the ancient Near Eastern codes (e.g., CH 5), as well as in the Book of the Covenant (Exod. 23:1-3, 6-9) and the Deuteronomic Code (Deut. 16:18-20). It is difficult to determine the point at which the material entered the Israelite tradition. It may already have been part of the pre-Mosaic tribes' inheritance in nomadic days. Or it may have been a borrowing from Canaanite neighbors following the Settlement. According to 1:16-17 the Guideline was given to Moses after the Horeb-Sinai covenant-theophany, immediately prior to setting out for Canaan. In the Book of the Covenant, however, it is part of the actual Word heard on the mountain.

In v. 16 we have the first of many references throughout Deuteronomy to the "alien" (*ger*). The *ger* is the foreigner taking long- or short-term refuge in Israel. Far from the protection of his own family group, he would place himself under the protection of a local clan. Such a person was peculiarly vulnerable to exploitation. Israelite tradition states that he is specially under the protection of God, precisely because of his vulnerability.

The case that is "too hard" (v. 17) is one that has no precedent. No "decision" (*mishpat*) therefore exists in regard to it. The "assistant" judge would normally be guided by such precedent-decisions, and therefore needs help when they are absent.

The Survey Scouts Report Back (1:19-46)

The comparable JE material is in Num. 13:17–14:25 and 14:39-45. A general comparison of the two versions reveals some interesting differences.

In Numbers it is Moses who takes the initiative in sending out the scouts, whereas in Deuteronomy the suggestion comes from the people. The effect is to stress Moses' implicit trust in Yahweh's promises. He accedes to the people's request for reassurance, but does not need it himself.

In Numbers Caleb and Joshua seek to quiet the people's fears and strengthen their faith. In Deuteronomy this role is fulfilled by Moses.

In Numbers the scouts' report is a mixture of positive and negative factors, so that the people's fear is to some degree "understandable." In Deuteronomy, however, the basic report is positive. The negative aspects emerge only secondarily, as the people adduce them to justify their reluctance and disobedience. The effect is to place responsibility for the people's attitude to Yahweh squarely on the people themselves.

1:19-21 The people have now reached the threshold of promise: "this is the land, which God is giving us" (v. 20) — present continuous tense. Promises five hundred years old are at the point of fruition. Note the patient faithfulness of God! The summons to faith, "do not fear or be dismayed" (v. 21), is typical Deuteronomic language (cf. 31:8; Josh. 1:9; 8:1; 10:25).

1:22-25 That the reconnaissance party consisted of "twelve men, one man for each tribe" (Deut. 1:23) is a stylization of history. It seems fairly certain historically that prior to their entry in Canaan "Israel" did not yet constitute an orderly league of twelve clearly-defined tribes, but a rather loose federation of groups originating from various tribal backgrounds.

Nevertheless, in the sixth-century situation which the Deuteronomist was addressing, the "each tribe-one representative" slogan was theologically important. In seeking to regalvanize the trembling faith of Israel, the Deuteronomist was stressing "one people, worshipping one God, whose will is expressed in one Torah." That stress is spelled out here by saying to each tribe-member: "You were personally represented there at the beginning; and you are personally responsible today for your obedience to the declared will of God."

1:26-28 Fear is born out of failure to trust, and when allowed to flourish unchecked erodes the very foundations of faith — to the point where reality is turned upside down, and the loving purpose of the Redeemer-God is construed as vindictiveness and "hate" (v. 27). It is ironic that the jibes of their opponents (9:28b) thus find an echo on the lips of God's people!

The Anakim (1:28) are historically attested as an ancient Near Eastern people, but in the earliest OT sources they have assumed mythological proportions. (Num. 13:33 identifies them with the Nephilim — "giants" — of Gen. 6:4.)

To the despairing cry that "the enemy is of superhuman proportions," Moses replies that the superhuman Power fighting for us is more than a match for the most horrendous opponent (Deut. 1:30).

1:29-33 Verse 30 constitutes an allusion to the "Yahweh war" tradition (see Introduction, 15-17). Miraculous intervention inducing numinous panic was part of the armory of the divine warrior ([Exod. 14:24-27]; Judg. 7:22). The plagues of Egypt and the debacle of the Red Sea happened "before your eyes," for you were present in the persons of your ancestors. Be assured, then, that what Yahweh did then, Yahweh can still do for those who trust.

The spectacular intervention of Deut. 1:30 is continued in the calm providential dealings of v. 31. Both the drama and the routine are evidence of Yahweh's presence. "God bore you. . . in all the way" — sustained you at every stage of the journey (cf. Exod. 19:4; Deut. 32:11; Hos. 11:3; Isa. 46:3).

Interestingly, the reproach of failure to "believe" (Deut. 1:32) is expressed by means of a Hebrew participle, thus stressing the continuous process: "You did not exert yourself to maintain the attitude of constant dependence."

Fire and cloud mark the path taken by the God who goes on

ahead (v. 33). This fire and cloud is the extension of the theophany
on Mt. Horeb. The people were understandably reluctant to leave
the mountain where God had revealed Godself so vividly. For
Horeb was regarded as Yahweh's home on earth. What guarantee
was there of an abiding presence on the ongoing journey far
beyond the sacred borders? God's reply is to vouchsafe a "fragment" of the Horeb fire and cloud, going ahead to mark out the
road — tangible assurance of Yahweh's constant presence. Faith
consists in quitting the security of past experience and committing
oneself to the God out there ahead.

1:34-36 The reference to Caleb (v. 36) may be a later addition
to bring the passage closer into line with Num. 14. However that
may be, the phrase used of him is an evocative one. A rather
literalistic rendering would be: "He filled the cup of his following
to the brim." "Following" and "believing" are presented as two
sides of one coin: to venture one's safety on the basis of one's
convictions.

1:37-38 Deuteronomy 1:37 links with v. 34: "Yahweh was
angry with you"; "Yahweh was angry with me also on your
account."
    The anger aroused by the blameworthy people's rebellion over-
flows to include their blameless leader. (The thought is repeated in
3:26; 4:21.) There is nothing in the JE tradition to suggest that
Moses' dying outside the promised land was a punishment or an
expression of God's displeasure. Deuteronomy 34:1-6 (which probably is a Deuteronomic reworking of JE material) simply records
that God drew Moses' life to a close in the land of Moab, ostensibly
because his work was complete.
    The Priestly (P) writing, however, compiled more than one
hundred years after the Deuteronomic history, does contain a
tradition that Moses was debarred from entering Canaan because
of disobedience (32:48-52; Num. 20:12). This tradition reflects
the postexilic sensitivity to the divine wrath on sin, and wishes to
stress that no sin is a matter of indifference, even if committed
by the most revered servant of God the nation had known.
    The insight enshrined in the Deuteronomic phrase "on your

account" is of a different quality. The writer senses that there is a problem in the great leader's not being granted the sweet taste of the fruit of his forty-year mission. (Did the writer already know the "divine anger" theory in oral form?). So he brings forward the suggestion: there is indeed a consequence of disobedience to be borne, but it is a consequence vicariously borne by the innocent on behalf of the guilty. This deep insight as regards the suffering implicit in the mediating role which Moses is called on to play is taken no further in Deuteronomy. It is, however, unfolded richly in the Servant Songs of 2 Isaiah (cf. Isa. 53:4-6) and achieves its full blossoming in the NT (cf. 1 Pet. 2:22-25; 3:18).

1:39-40 The phrase "your little ones, who you said would become a prey" is not in the LXX, and has probably been added here from Num. 14:31. It is not necessary to the sense, but certainly adds to the irony. "Your specious excuse for not obeying God's directives was concern for your children's welfare. Now in due time (after the lapse of a full generation; Deut. 2:14) they will enter, whereas you who made these protestations on their behalf will be excluded."

The children who "have no knowledge of good or evil" (1:39) are presumably two years old and under. What is in mind is probably not "moral discernment," but the ability to discern between edible and harmful substances (Isa. 7:15-16), which comes about the time the child begins to learn to talk (Isa. 8:4). "But as for you, turn . . . into the wilderness" (Deut. 1:40): so near and yet so far!

1:41-46 "We will go up and fight" (v. 41). Earlier they were unwilling to begin the occupation because of their lack of confidence in the help promised them (vv. 26, 28, 30). This new change of attitude is not a change of heart, but simply an ill-considered reaction to Moses' reprimand. The obedience which God requires is not formal compliance on the basis of "do this," "do that," but a sensitive aligning of the human will with the divine. This can only arise out of a sincere relationship with God and a consciousness of God's goodness. Where this is absent it cannot be supplied by instant and formal means. The pessimistic conclusion here is that it will take a full generation to re-prepare for the moment of entry. Yet — may we call this "gospel"? — the entry does eventually take place! God's covenant purpose is delayed but not thwarted by human insensitivity and fractiousness. A realization of this could certainly be "gospel" to the exile generation that the Deuteronomist is addressing.

The tautology of v. 46 marks it out as a link between two originally independent units.

Israel Traverses Edomite Territory (2:1-7)

The parallel material from the JE tradition is Num. 20:14-21.

The striking difference between the two versions is that according to Numbers it is Moses who takes the initiative and requests passage through Edomite territory — a request which is roughly refused, though it had been couched in the most conciliatory terms. In view of this refusal there is nothing for Israel but to make a long detour.

According to Deuteronomy, however, it is Yahweh who orders Moses to lead the people through Edomite territory. There is no hint of opposition, and no conciliatory pleading. The primary emphasis in the Deuteronomy version is on the wisdom and appropriateness of God's leading (through Yahweh's servant Moses) when the time has arrived for the covenant people to inherit the promised land. (See E. John Hamlin, *Inheriting the Land.*)

2:1-3   At last the period of re-preparation is over and the signal is given to move forward. The phrase "You have been going about this mountain country long enough" (Deut. 2:3) repeats 1:6, and resumes the gracious purpose which had been aborted through disobedience. Compare this with the new opportunity God gives Jonah (Jonah 1:1; 3:1), Peter (John 21:16), and others.

2:4-5   According to the patriarchal narratives the Edomites are descendants of Esau, and therefore blood brothers and sisters with the descendants of Jacob-Israel (Gen. 25:21-26).

Throughout the centuries Israel and Edom were in contact. Edom was subjugated by Israel in the 10th cent., reasserted its independence in the mid-9th, and was reconquered at the beginning of the 8th (2 Sam. 8:13-14; 2 Kgs. 8:20-21; 14:7, 22). A number of OT texts condemn Edom for its vindictiveness in "kicking Israel when they were down" at the time of the Babylonian conquests (e.g., Obad. 10-12; Lam. 4:21-22; Isa. 34:5-6; Jer. 49:7-8). It is interesting by contrast to note that Deuteronomy, which was approximating its definitive form about the same time, reflects a tradition sympathetic to Edom (cf. Deut. 23:7).

This sympathy for Edom is set in a wider theological frame. Yahweh is not narrowly "God of Israel." Rather, Yahweh is God of the nations. Both Esau and Jacob are Abraham's "grandchildren," so the God of Abraham is the God of their descendants. Yahweh, who gives the land of Canaan as Israel's heritage, also gives the hill country of Seir as Edom's (2:4). Faith and gratitude for Yahweh's goodness to "us" require respect for Yahweh's dealing with others who do not directly share the privileges of the covenant people.

This is true not only for Edom. The territory of Moab (v. 9), Ammon (v. 19), and even (by implication) of the Philistines (v. 23) is also allotted to them by God (cf. Amos 9:7).

The twentieth-century Church needs to take this Deuteronomic insight seriously and rework its theological implications vis-à-vis the multicultural dimensions of contemporary global society.

The fear that Edom will display in the face of Israel (Deut. 2:4) is a natural apprehensiveness, not the numinous panic which is part of the weaponry of "Yahweh's war" (v. 25; Josh. 2:9; 10:2). Israel is therefore not to read it as signifying Yahweh's permission for them to attack.

2:6-7 Israel has the wherewithal to purchase food and drink from the Edomites because God has "blessed them in all the work of their hands" (Deut. 2:7). The phrase opens a window on the possible activities that occupied Israel during the "waiting" period. Did they raise and sell cattle, wool, grain? Did they develop handicrafts (cf. 14:29)? This product of their own industry and ingenuity is regarded as part of God's blessing, equally with the more spectacular "manna" (8:3, 16) — which in the developing tradition increasingly assumed miraculous proportions (cf. Exod. 16 P). Both in the humdrum and the dramatic, God is provider. Yahweh "knows" the road that Israel has been traveling and the experiences along the road, throughout the whole forty-year period — "knowing" (*yada'*), here in the deep biblical sense of experiencing and empathizing. For a similar usage, compare Ps. 1:6, where God's "knowing the way" implies companionship, provision, overarching protection, in contrast to the way that "perishes."

Israel Traverses Moabite Territory (2:8-15)

The corresponding JE material (Num. 21:12-15 and the large block of the Balaam story, Num. 22:1–25:5) is only remotely connected with the Deuteronomic tradition. A comparison of the two would take us too far afield. Suffice it to note that the Balaam story, like the Deuteronomic tradition, bears witness, albeit obliquely, to the universality of God's self-revelation and of God's design for humanity.

2:8-9   Like Esau, Lot is also a member of the family of Abraham (Gen. 12–13), so that he and his descendants in some sense share the special blessing of the covenant God (Deut. 2:9).

2:10-12   Here we have two erudite notes which some scholar could not resist slipping into the finished text. Like so many of their kind they embroider rather than illuminate. (Is that in itself a "message" — that erudition for its own sake may detract from rather than enhance the hearing of God's word?). The conclusion of v. 12, however, serves positively to underline the universality of God's action; as Israel settled Canaan, so Edom settled Seir — both (implicitly) by the will of God.

2:13-15   These sentences form a further suture, linking this section to the following and at the same time harking back to what precedes (1:34) and declaring that "the time is now fulfilled and the realization of God's gracious purpose is at hand."

The "retaliatory" understanding of God's judgment expressed here ("the hand of Yahweh was against them, to destroy them") and through much of the OT, cries out for rethinking in the light of the NT, and of Jesus' death in particular. "Destruction" is certainly an undeniable facet of human experience. Are we closer to the reality when we reinterpret the "destructiveness of God" in terms of "self-destruction"? When we turn away from the good to which our highest "inspired" ideals challenge us, do we not deface or "destroy" the emerging or re-emerging image of God in us, and so "destroy" our God-planned destiny?

Confrontation with the Ammonites Is Forbidden (2:16-25)

The JE reference here is hardly a parallel, consisting only of the brief aside in Num. 21:24. If we follow the Hebrew text (RSV mg) of Num. 21:24 we gain the impression that the Israelites would indeed have penetrated Ammonite territory, had not "the boundary of the Ammonites" been "strong." It was only the difficulty of the terrain that deflected them. According to Deut. 2, however, it is Yahweh's explicit command that deters them — based on the fact that Ammon too is a branch of Abraham's family.

2:16-19 "I will not give you any of the land of the sons of Ammon as a possession" (Deut. 2:19). In a later age, the Ammonites were to claim that their ancient boundaries had in fact run to the banks of the Dead Sea, and that the western part of the territory had indeed been expropriated by Israel (Judg. 11:12ff.). The Deuteronomists are at pains to deny this, maintaining that Heshbon, the district in question, was a separate entity from Ammon.

"Do not contend with Ammon" (Deut. 2:19) is the last in a series of directives: do not contend with Edom (v. 5), Moab (v. 9), Ammon (v. 19)." Step by step God is guiding their road, till they reach the boundaries Yahweh has appointed for them — a training in sensitivity and obedience. We are reminded of the step-by-step process by which the NT apostles were guided (Acts 16:6-10) in their mission.

42

2:20-23   These verses constitute a further erudite note, evincing the same scholarly and theological interests as Deut. 2:10-12.

Like the Anakim (see above on 1:26ff.), the Rephaim ("sunken ones," "shades," "ghosts") and the Zamzummim ("whisperers," "mutterers") came to have mythical and preternatural associations. Just as the supernatural power of Yahweh was more than a match for the larger-than-human adversaries of Israel, so it is for the wider family of Abraham and for the human family in general. That Ammon was presumably unaware of their Champion is beside the point: known or unknown, acknowledged or unacknowledged, God is all-powerful.

With the mention of the Caphtorim (Philistines, who entered Palestine = Philistia, originally from Caphtor = Crete), the divine overruling is given even wider perspective. Edomites, Moabites, and Ammonites all belong to the wider family of Abraham, so that could be assumed as the reason for God's attention to them. But the Philistines are of a different racial stock, so that the overruling in their experience is evidence of God's universal love. Compare the reference with Amos 9:7, which has probably influenced the Deuteronomic thought at this point.

2:24-25   These verses form a bridge leading into Deut. 2:26-37, the conquest of Heshbon. Theologically, they serve to mark the fact that Yahweh's moment has arrived. After the threefold "do not contend" (vv. 5, 9, 19) the command now is "contend." The language is that of "Yahweh's war." It is Yahweh who hands Heshbon over, and the primary weapon used is the numinous dread already referred to (vv. 4-5). "Dread" *(pahad)* is one of the ancient proper names of "Israel's" God (Gen. 31:53), so the panic that engulfs Heshbon is engendered by Yahweh's presence contending in and through Israel. The word "take possession" *(yarash)* literally means "inherit," implying that the land is at Yahweh's right of disposal, and is now gifted to Israel.

That the "fear" falls on "the peoples that are under the whole heaven" is somewhat of an exaggeration in this context (cf. its use in Deut. 4:19; Job 37:3; 41:11), but its intent is clear. The fame of what Yahweh has done will reach the ends of the earth, for Israel is an instrument in God's universal design (Gen. 12:1-3).

Sihon King of Heshbon Is Defeated (2:26-37)

There is a close parallel here between the Deuteronomic account and the JE version, Num. 21:21-30. The difference of emphasis is that Numbers stresses the heroism of Israel, whereas the Deuteronomic presentation is more theological, acknowledging that Yahweh's role in the victory is decisive.

2:26-29 Israel is poised midway along the eastern border of Sihon's territory. The path to the north lies through Ammonite land and is forbidden to them. The only way forward into the promised land proper "over the Jordan" (Deut. 2:29), is west through Sihon's territory. Deuteronomy is at pains to stress that "words of peace" were addressed to Sihon — an offer to purchase all supplies and make a disciplined, peaceful crossing of his land. We are not meant to assume that these words are merely tongue-in-cheek. We need to remember that the whole passage is theological reflection from centuries later, on the divine overruling whereby the promised land concretely became Israel's possession. How was it that the conciliatory approach which was successful in the case of Edom (vv. 5-6) met with such implacable resistance from Sihon? Surely Yahweh brought about this "unforeseeable" reaction in order to hand over the land to Israel? From the human side the rejection of this peaceful request makes Sihon the aggressor, and therefore responsible for his own defeat.

2:30 "God hardened Sihon's spirit and made his heart obstinate." Taken in isolation, this phrase makes Sihon seem a mere pawn on the divine chessboard. It is helpful therefore to break open the isolation and trace the roots of the "hardening" concept in the JE tradition. The clearest example is in the Exodus narrative, specifically the reluctance of Pharaoh to release Israel from servitude in Egypt. In that account the "hardening" is described at three levels or phases:

- Pharaoh hardened his heart (Exod. 8:15, 32).
- Pharaoh's heart became hard (Exod. 8:19).
- God hardened Pharaoh's heart (Exod. 4:21; 10:1; 14:8).

In the light of this threefold description, it is obviously inappropriate to interpret "hardening" in purely fatalistic terms, as if God implants attitudes which automatically bring human beings to disaster, quite apart from their own choice or involvement. The Exodus texts seem to imply that the "hardening" phenomenon includes two factors of equal importance, like the two sides of one coin: the free decision of the person concerned, and the decision of God. God, as it were, pays humanity the respect of accepting and ratifying the human decision, so that the person is responsible for his or her own "hardness" (cf. 1 Sam. 6:6; Ps. 95:8).

These considerations may alleviate the difficulty, if they do not overcome it entirely. There remains the mystery of the divine overruling in all human history, and the conviction that the last word is with God. The topic obviously fascinated the Deuteronomic historian; he refers to it again in such passages as Josh. 11:20; 2 Sam. 17:14b; 1 Kgs. 22:19-23.

2:31-35 We have already noted several direct and oblique references to the "Yahweh war" tradition. The "utter destruction" *(herem)* mentioned in Deut. 2:34 belongs in the same circle of ideas.

The equivalent verb *(haram)* in Hebrew and other Semitic languages has the root meaning "forbid, or make taboo," hence "set apart to become the property of a deity." In practice the "devoted" person or object is often "handed over" to the deity by destruction or burning as an offering (Lev. 27:28). This was so especially when those defeated in battle and their possessions were regarded as belonging to an alien god. The "devoting" of the vanquished in sacrifice then became proof of the superior might of the victor's god over the god of the vanquished, and a thanksgiving for divine aid (cf. Josh. 6:16-19).

The *herem* concept was not peculiar to Israel, but common to the ancient Near East. Witness the Moabite Stone inscription: "I Mesha . . . King of Moab . . . took Nebo . . . and devoted (the inhabitants) to destruction for (the god) Ashtar–Chemosh." The earliest strata of the OT seemingly experienced no difficulty in assuming that the *herem* custom was sanctioned and indeed required by God (Josh. 7:10-13; 1 Sam. 15:1-3, 20-22, 32-33).

It is noteworthy, however, that the writer of Deuteronomy does not stress the sacrificial aspect of *herem* but characterizes it as a drastic but necessary step to ensure that Israel is not lured into paganism by the indigenous population of Canaan (Deut. 7:1-6; 20:16-18). This is the beginning of rationalization, a sign that the Deuteronomic writer is beginning to doubt whether Yahweh really does desire such "proofs" of Yahweh's superior might.

To us who know Yahweh as the God and Father of Jesus, the notion that God sanctioned the *herem* is unacceptable. We need to acknowledge frankly that there are aspects of OT Israel's understanding of God which fall short of that brought to us by Jesus. Yet there are points of continuing value, buried in the *herem* concept:

1. The successes we achieve as individuals and as Church are ultimately God's doing, for which we do well to offer thanks.
2. The struggles of life are fundamentally spiritual: in the struggle it is deadening and dangerous to arrogate to ourselves the honors and rights that belong to God.
3. The culture that surrounds us today can lure us into contemporary paganism. We need to combat it, not by a negative, destructive *herem,* but by committing ourselves completely to the alternative culture (John 17:15-18). There is a further element of rationalization in Deut. 2:35. The older practice called for total *herem* of property as well as people (Josh. 7) on the grounds that human personality impregnates and "contaminates" the property belonging to the person.

The Deuteronomist says in effect: "animals and goods cannot in themselves become lure to paganism: it is people that make them so."

2:36-37 These two verses serve to round off the section and smooth the transition to what follows. The promise of divine aid referred to in Deut. 2:25, 31 has been abundantly fulfilled. Also, the stipulation laid down in v. 19 has been faithfully honored.

The exilic generation addressed by the Deuteronomic historian would get the message: implicit obedience is rewarded with success, just as disobedience brings disaster.

Og King of Bashan Is Defeated (3:1-11)

There is almost word-for-word correspondence between Deut. 3:1-3 and Num. 21:33-35. Not only so, but the vocabulary and phraseology have typical Deuteronomic features. Scholars therefore conclude that the Og tradition is original to Deuteronomy and has been added to the Numbers narrative for the sake of completeness.

It is interesting then to note the parts of the Deuteronomic material that are not taken up into Numbers, namely, the strength of the fortifications as evidence of Yahweh's enabling (Deut. 3:5), and the rigorous application of the *herem* principle (v. 6).

In other words, it is the overt references to "Yahweh war" that are omitted. This stress, of prime importance to the Deuteronomic school in the crisis that climaxed in the Exile, had obviously lost its urgency in the postexilic period.

3:1-7 The command not to fear Og king of Bashan (v. 2) would sound salutary to later generations. For he too, like several enemies already mentioned (1:28; 2:10-11, 20-21), had assumed super-human proportions in the popular accounts, as the last remnant of a giant race (2:11). His "bedstead" (literally, "frame") probably refers to his last resting place (i.e., sarcophagus), and the "iron" from which it was made was basalt or "iron rock." Its measurements, 5.5 m. by 3 m. (18 ft. by 10 ft.), would certainly provide data for the fertile imagination! (Was it an above-ground tomb in the shape of a coffin?)

Picking up this popular story, the Deuteronomist uses it to reinforce the point already made, that Yahweh is more than adequate armament against whatever enemy may threaten.

Bashan, a fertile plateau stretching from Mt. Hermon in the north to the southernmost tributary of the river Yarmuk in the south, was well known for its lush pastures and fat cattle (cf. Ps. 22:12; Amos 4:1). Its acquisition was a rich prize of war, and firstfruits of Yahweh's intent to grant an inheritance.

3:8-11 These verses summarize the conquest of Transjordan. Into the summary two further erudite notes have been inserted (cf., e.g., 2:10, 20). For the rest, vv. 1-11 as a whole repeat and emphasize the theological points made in the previous section.

Heshbon and Bashan Allocated to the Transjordanian Tribes (3:12-22)

The whole of Num. 32:1-42 provides a parallel to Deut. 3:12-22. Numbers 32 is basically JE material (with subsequent editing and additions from the exilic Priestly source). This JE material itself, however, is not all of a piece; Num. 32:34-42 appear to be from a later stratum.

It is striking that in the JE source it is the Reuben and Gad tribes who take the initiative in requesting that Moses permit them to settle in Transjordan, in the territory just taken from Sihon and Og. This suggestion arouses misgiving on Moses' part in case Gad and Reuben should seem to be opting out of the ongoing struggle — a turn of events that would sap the enthusiasm of the remaining tribes. After due assurances are given, however, the request is finally granted.

The Deuteronomic version (Deut. 3:12-22) seems to be a corrective summary of the older account:

- The initiative is not from Reuben and Gad but from Moses himself.
- There is no hesitation or misgiving in Moses' attitude. He is portrayed as the all-capable leader, sustained and equipped by God.
- There is strong stress on the unity and family solidarity of all Israel: "your brothers" occurs twice in vv. 18-20.

From the later stratum of JE (Num. 32:34-42):

- Numbers 32:41 is taken into the Deuteronomic account as an erudite note (Deut. 3:14).
- The phrase "Moses gave to Gilead" (cf. also Num. 32:33 P) is picked up as a kind of refrain in Deuteronomy: "I gave . . ."

48

(Deut. 3:12, 13, 15, 16, 19, 20). That is, Moses (under God) and not Reuben or Gad, is the initiative taker.

3:12-17 Having sketched the campaign which had taken the conquest as far as the foothills of Mt. Hermon, the writer now summarizes the allocation of Transjordan, and as he does so brings the narrative full circle. Verse 17 brings us back to the slopes of Pisgah, the place from which Moses made his grand departure at the conclusion of his farewell speech (34:1).

The phrase "to this day" (3:14) occurs quite frequently in Deuteronomy, Joshua, and Judges, and certainly implies a rather lengthy time interval. Obviously a later generation is looking back on the circumstances of Moses' day.

3:18-20 The inheritors of Transjordan are specially privileged in that the firstfruits of the Conquest have been allotted to them. They are therefore urged to head the ongoing struggle, not in order to obtain a heritage but precisely because they have already obtained. The gift is from God; it behooves them to show practical gratitude.

These verses underline the principle that concern for the common welfare should outweigh personal or small group interests. The prosperity and blessings we receive turn sour unless they prompt us to ensure that our fellow human beings also receive their share. The principle applies equally to social justice issues and to the blessings of faith.

3:21-22 The message of these verses, based on 3:28, is "As the firstfruits, so the main harvest." Take courage from what has been achieved, seeing it as a pledge and foretaste of what will follow. The phrase "your eyes have . . ." (v. 21) occurs frequently in the exhortatory sections of Deuteronomy (4:3, 9; 7:19; 10:21; 11:7; 29:3). Its function there is to insist that each succeeding generation of the people of God is existentially involved in the great definitive and foundational events of their faith. Here the exhortation is addressed to the leader of the first succeeding generation. This existential involvement is a condition of genuine leadership.

49

Moses Debarred from Crossing the Jordan (3:23-29)

The theme of the mediator bearing the divine displeasure for the sake of his people has already been touched on in 1:37. Here it is expounded at greater length.

The Hebrew word *ethhannan,* translated "besought" (3:23), describes the needy throwing themselves on the compassion or "grace" *(hen)* of the strong (cf. Gen. 42:21; Job 9:15; Ps. 30:8). Here Moses appeals to Yahweh's compassion, that the verdict passed years previously (Deut. 1:37) may be revoked.

It is noteworthy that Moses, God's intimate (cf. Exod. 33:11), does not accept Yahweh's decision passively, as if "the will of God" is identical with "fate," but is bold enough to ask for a reconsideration. Such boldness is a constituent of biblical piety; cf. Abraham (Gen. 18:22-33), Amos (Amos 7:1-6), Paul (2 Cor. 12:7-9).

"LORD, you have only begun to show your servant your greatness." Although the greatness and power of God had shaped Moses' experience for many years (the burning bush, Exod. 3; the signs in Egypt, Exod. 7; the Red Sea crossing, Exod. 14; providence in the desert, Exod. 16), yet the special sign of God's greatness has been the conquest of Heshbon and of Bashan, marking as it does the beginning of the process whereby the land is given to God's people.

Moses is aware that everything he has experienced to date of God's greatness is a mere beginning. Vastly greater challenges await Israel on the west side of Jordan, requiring greater divine interventions than have yet been witnessed. But Moses is convinced that what God has begun, God will complete. Although he has reached old age, he still wants to be part of the ongoing action — to witness fulfillment. But it is not to be. He must be content to make his contribution within the limits of his capabilities and leave the finale to others, and to God.

The word for "anger" (Deut. 3:26) is a very strong one: "God's anger boiled over."

This renewed reference to God's anger (cf. 1:37) seems to imply that Moses' vicarious role is an ongoing one. Not only did he bear the weight of the former generation's rebellion, but on

Mt. Pisgah he is still bearing the divine displeasure on behalf of their descendants.

Perhaps there are two aspects. On the one hand, Moses is in solidarity with the rebellious generation of thirty-eight years ago. They have died (2:15), and he as their last survivor must die like them in the desert. This is filling up the cup of his identification with them.

On the other hand, and more widely, Moses' solidarity is not with one generation alone, but with Israel as a totality. The "you" addressed in 3:26 is the new generation of Israel, assembled in the plains of Moab. These too are rebels. Moses as Yahweh's servant is called to bear the shortfall of his people continuously, in a lifelong commitment.

Yet along with the judgment, there is also comfort: "You may not enter, but your eyes may see" (v. 27). The fact that Moses sees the promised land all around him — west, north, south, east — implies of course that he has already arrived! Let him accept this as sufficient, and be content to entrust the completion to his successor. The reference to the four points of the compass is probably a deliberate reminiscence of Abraham (Gen. 13:14-15), standing in the land promised as his and possessing it in faith though not yet in political terms.

Moses Offers Guidance to Israel (4:1-43)

In Deut. 3:28 (immediately before the suture, v. 29) we read that Yahweh has permitted Moses to climb Mt. Pisgah and see the promised land before he dies. The logical continuation of that scene is to be found in Deut. 31–34, where Moses completes the preparations for his departure:

- His successor is appointed (31:7-8, 14-15, 23).
- The Torah is written down and lodged for safekeeping (31:9-13, 24-29).
- Moses' final testimony is delivered (ch. 32).
- Moses' last blessing is pronounced (ch. 33).
- Moses climbs Pisgah, then dies (ch. 34).

The connection between 3:28 and 31:7ff. is so obvious that many scholars believe chs. 1–3 and 31–34 must originally have formed a unity, into which the massive block of chs. 4–30 has subsequently been inserted. However that may be, it is very apparent on even a casual reading that as we pass from ch. 3 to ch. 4 we are entering a very different atmosphere. Deuteronomy 4 seems to be compiled from various fragments of exhortatory sermons (or literary creations that copy the sermon style).

According to scholarly reconstruction of the setting, in the annual religious festivals celebrated down the centuries in ancient Israel, the core events of Yahweh's dealings with the people were rehearsed, and Yahweh's torah was read, explained, and urged upon the assembled crowd. Such exhortations would obviously show marked similarities from year to year. The basic themes regularly repeated would be:

- Yahweh's self-revelation on Horeb is definitive for the whole of Israel's faith.
- The content of that revelation is contained in Yahweh's torah ("signpost") relayed through Moses.
- At the heart of the torah lies the prohibition against worshipping other gods, and against the use of images (whether of other gods or of Yahweh's self).

If we accept this reconstruction of how material in Deut. 4 originated, then several things become clear:

- The repetition of certain basic themes
- The fluctuation between singular and plural (Some sermon fragments originally used the inclusive address "you," plural; others preferred the more intimate "thou," singular.)

It also becomes clear that we, the twentieth-century readers of the finished text, need to visualize several different "original audiences" to whom the material was "first" addressed.

First, we note the intention of the Deuteronomic historian, who invites us to receive the entire book as a transcript of Moses' farewell speech. In doing so he bids us envisage the crowd of "first hearers," gathered in the plains of Moab and attending to Moses' words.

On the other hand, we have just reconstructed the scene at Israel's yearly festivals; so we imagine the attentive crowds at the shrine in Shechem, Gilgal, or Shiloh.

Then again, the material obviously addresses the people of Israel in the 6th century B.C., when in the crisis of impending or actual overthrow and exile the Deuteronomic material is brought forward as a complete compilation.

All this means that in ch. 4 and what follows we are not being presented with a word of God spoken once for all time in the 13th cent. B.C. Rather, we have a word of God which was conveyed, urged, and applied constantly throughout seven hundred years of history. Indeed, it is a word that is urged directly upon us, God's people who seek to expose ourselves to the book of Deuteronomy here in the 20th century.

Yahweh's Torah, Source of Life and Wisdom (4:1-8)

In general, this section is in the plural form, except for one or two traditional phrases (4:1, "Israel, give heed"; v. 3, "Yahweh destroyed from among you"; v. 5, "Behold . . .").

4:1 "And now" *(we'attah)* is a cue word, indicating that a general summary or practical application is to follow. It occurs about one hundred times throughout the Deuteronomic history. Here in 4:1 it implies: "God has done all this for us: our fitting response is now to heed the expression of God's will and put it into practice."

The call "O Israel, give heed" (literally, "hear") is an ancient one used to assemble the people of God for consultation, battle, or worship. It presumably continued to be used in the religious festivals as a solemn claim on the worshippers' attention and to stress the importance of the sacred law about to be proclaimed (cf. 5:1; 6:4; 9:1).

"Statutes-and-ordinances" as a composite term is the common Deuteronomic description for the contents of the code or Torah. "Statute" *(hoq)* is literally something chiselled or written on stone, thus a symbolic expression for the firmness and permanency of Yahweh's law.

"Ordinance" *(mishpat)*, on the other hand, is the decision handed down by a judge *(shophet)*. In ancient times, before Israel's legal codes were compiled in systematic fashion, disputes were settled before a civic leader or priest, usually at a shrine or sacred place. The decision was remembered at the shrine and subsequently applied to similar cases. Thus a body of decisions slowly built up. Each new case for which there was no precedent was referred to God at the shrine, and the resultant decision was added to the common store. This collected mass of "decisions" was eventually systematized to become codes of law such as the Book of the Covenant (Exod. 21:1–23:22).

It was only after a rather long process that the *mishpat* code which had eventuated was connected with the Horeb event and attributed to Moses. Nevertheless, there is logic in the connection, for Israel was convinced that the Yahweh self-revealed at Horeb is the source of every sound law and regulation in Israel. Thus every subsequent development of law (including the developed *mishpat* codes, whose growth we have just described) was regarded as implicit in the "seed" laws given by Yahweh at Horeb.

From earliest time *hoq*-and-*mishpat* was used as a composite term meaning "directive from Yahweh" (Exod. 15:25b; Josh. 24:25; 1 Sam. 30:25). The Deuteronomic school adapted this ancient term by using it in the plural — perhaps to stress the rich variety and all-around completeness of Yahweh's directive. It is interesting to note that the total material of Deuteronomy is described as *huqqim*-and-*mishpatim*, both the code (chs. 12–26) and the exhortations (chs. 4–11, 27). Command and sermon alike contain the word of God.

The promise of "life" is typical of Deuteronomy (cf. 5:29, 33; 6:24; 30:19-20; 32:47). This is not "eternal life" as a sequel to physical death, but "length of days" (cf. 4:40; 5:33), which is more than mere longevity — a life possessing quality, because lived under the constant protection and guidance of God and in fellowship with God. As such it is the natural opposite both of "death" ("which will you choose: life or death?"; 30:6, 15, 19,

20) and of "mere existence" (5:33; 32:47) — life with verve and purpose, "abundant life" (John 10:10).

To "take possession" of the land is literally to "inherit" *(yarash)*. The "inheritance" idea carries subtle nuances. This land given to Israel is in fact "Yahweh's possession," "Yahweh's inheritance" *(nahalah,* Jer. 16:18). Israel too is "Yahweh's inheritance" (Deut. 4:20; 9:26, 29; 32:9). It is by Yahweh's gracious action that Yahweh's people inherit Yahweh's land. For it is Yahweh who makes the previous inhabitants "hand over the inheritance" (translated freely as "drives out," e.g., 9:3; 11:23).

In short, the gift of the land is both grace and responsibility.

4:2 The command "not to add . . . or take away" picks up an ancient Near Eastern formula which served as a kind of seal on important documents, to forbid their being corrupted (cf. 12:32). Later dogmatic theology, from the 2nd cent. A.D. onwards, used such verses as proof texts regarding the extent and authority of the scriptural canon. This goes far beyond the Deuteronomist's intent, which was simply to insist that Yahweh's word as conveyed in Deuteronomy be taken seriously. Let not the contents be manipulated or adapted to the taste of the times; rather, let the attitudes and conscience of the times be shaped by the contents.

The phrase "The commandments of Yahweh which I command you" is worth pondering. By virtue of his call experience and his intimate relationship with God, Moses becomes mediator and mouthpiece of God's word. The seeds of incarnation are in the intimacy so described.

4:3-4 The "Baal-peor" incident (Num. 25:1-5; cf. Ps. 106:28; Hos. 9:10; Num. 31:15-16) was so well-known that the writer of Deut. 4 saw no need to quote it in full. The passing reference is sufficient to underscore the crucial importance of the basic command: "No other gods before Yahweh." Baal of course simply meant "lord," "master" (even "husband"). But in the ancient Near East it became a title particularly of Hadad, the god-force inherent in wind, storm, and nature. Israel saw the choice as stark and clear: to worship the forces of nature or the Creator of nature.

The former leads to manipulation of the divine for human ends, the latter to grateful human submission to the divine ends.

To "hold fast" *(dabaq)* to Yahweh is typical Deuteronomic terminology (e.g., Deut. 4:4; 10:20; 11:22; Josh. 22:5; 2 Kgs. 18:6). In everyday language it means to "stick" (2 Sam. 23:10) or "stick close" (Ruth 2:8, 21). "Sticking" to Yahweh implies a bond of intimacy resulting in love, service, respect, and obedience.

4:5 The past tense "I have taught you" is interesting. Clearly in Deut. 4 we are still at the introduction stage of Moses' speech and the presentation of "statutes and ordinances" is still to follow. So how are we to account for the past tense? Two possibilities suggest themselves.

First, Moses may be here claiming that throughout the thirty-eight desert years since Horeb he has been constantly inculcating Yahweh's law so that Israel is now familiar with its requirements. Second, the passage may be a fragment, typical of the exhortations which once followed the reading of the law at the annual festival. If this is so, then the speaker is no longer directly Moses, but his priestly representative in some succeeding generation.

The second of these alternatives is the more persuasive. "Moses" continues to speak, as successive generations relive the Horeb event, and rehear the conditions of the covenant established then.

4:6-8 Through the eyes of faith the Deuteronomic writers see other nations as recognizing a "specialness" about Israel — a specialness stemming not from natural endowment or racial genius, but from the grace of God who has gifted them with comprehensive guidelines for their whole life.

Other nations in general believe that the gods are to be persuaded into graciousness by means of offerings. Such a faith provides imperfect ground for confidence: what if the offerings are judged insufficient? In Israel's case, however, it is God who takes the initiative and declares a purpose of constant goodwill. "God is near to us whenever we call"; this is certain because "our call" is in response to God's prior invitation. We have already (Introduction, 4-7) considered the strong probability that much of the present Deuteronomic code was originally taken over from

Canaanite sources. Also, we have noted the parallels with other
ancient Near Eastern legal codes. But there is this vital difference,
namely, that the other codes are regarded as being gifted and
inspired by the various ancient Near Eastern deities (e.g., Hammurabi's Code is promulgated as the gift of Shamash the sun-god)
whereas Israel's Torah is seen as Yahweh's gift.

The accent and interpretation of the code will certainly be
colored and determined by the character of the god who bestowed
it. Because Yahweh is merciful and gracious, this is the spirit that
predominates in the Deuteronomic Code, as a comparison with
other ancient Near Eastern codes makes clear. It is therefore
objectively correct that Israel's law is "righteous" (4:8) in comparison with others. Nevertheless, Israel's true wealth consists not
in a superior code as such, but in the presence of the living Yahweh
whose voice the code echoes.

The "statutes and ordinances" are described in v. 8 as comprising one comprehensive law (*hattorah*, "the law"), indicating that
the formulation here is from the latest strata in the development
of the Deuteronomic material.

The Meeting with God on Horeb (4:9-24)

Both grammar and content indicate that this passage is not a unity.
Grammatically, some verses (4:9, 10, 19, 21b, 23b, 24) are in the
singular, whereas others (vv. 11-18, 20-21a, 22-23a) are in the
second person plural. As for content, the verses written in the
singular constitute a general exhortation to faithfulness toward
the covenant God, whereas the plural sections are more specific.
The detail of the Horeb theophany narrative becomes the basis
for a theological argumentation: the fact that Yahweh did not
appear in visible form on Horeb proves that Yahweh does not
wish to be worshipped through visible forms (images).

From the point of view of content, it would seem that the
plural sections are a later development, built upon the original
(singular) stratum. In fact the plural section forms a kind of
literary-exegetical commentary on tradition. That the old traditions, which had come down since the 13th cent. in flexible form,
are now being treated as solid entities to be exegeted, shows that

the concept of "canon" or "scripture" is well on the way by this stage.

4:9-10   (second person singular)   Israel must not forget "the things which your eyes have seen" (v. 9). The Hebrew word *dabar* here translated "thing" can also mean "word," depending on context. This semantic usage is important theologically. The "things" Yahweh has done are alive with a "word" of revelation. Moreover, the "word" Yahweh speaks through prophet and mediator does not consist of mere syllables, but is a creative "thing," imbued with power to break down and re-create (cf. Jer. 1:9-10).

"Your eyes" have seen "these things." In fact, of course, the generation which actually participated in the Exodus events and witnessed the Horeb theophany are all dead (Deut. 1:35; 2:16). But succeeding generations (both the one that Joshua led into Canaan, and others attending the festivals down the centuries) are existentially involved in their turn. Through the recital and reenactment of the Exodus-Horeb events they are made to be "present" at Yahweh's action. The word-and-action is addressed to them as directly as to their ancestors. (We may compare the Christian congregation at the Lord's Supper; through the word and action of the liturgy they are "present" in the upper room "the night Jesus was betrayed," at the hill where Jesus died, and in the room where realization of Jesus' aliveness broke through).

The command to "make known to your children" presupposes a bridging process of family instruction and catechesis between annual festivals (cf. 6:7; 11:19; 31:13; 32:46). The heads of households who attended the festival (16:16) are urged to pass on to those at home the torah instruction and narrative tradition which they have received during the festival days. We may conclude that this family catechizing process was a second molding influence alongside the preaching at the festival itself, helping to shape the material which eventually became Deuteronomy.

Deuteronomy 4:10 reads as if Yahweh originally intended to speak directly to the people. Later we shall see (5:22-27) that this awesome prospect was too devastating for the people, so that they requested and were granted a mediator to bridge between God's holiness and their human weakness.

58

4:11-18 (second person plural) In this section 4:11-14 constitutes the text, while vv. 15-18 represent the "sermon" based on it. One specific point is picked out from the text ("no form was seen on Horeb"), and this becomes the ground for a sustained prohibition of using images ("forms") in worship.

Throughout its later history at least, Israel was extremely sensitive to the dangers inherent in the use of images representing God.

How does this concern "translate" into our contemporary context? At bottom it may be said that the use of images was an attempt to place God within reach and control of the worshippers. Throughout the OT, God comes through as sovereignly free, so that salvation consists in placing oneself within the space where God's self has chosen to act. The use of images seeks to reverse this. By setting up God's "picture" we claim to have "got God's measure." We have "fixed God's location" at the site of the image, so that henceforth God is to be available at the spot we have selected, as and when we feel the need.

This temptation to "domesticate" and "utilize" God is always with us. The prohibition of images is a salutary reminder that God is always available, but never at our disposal. Our salvation consists not in God's conforming to our will, but in our conforming to God's.

4:19 (second person singular) "The sun and the moon and the stars . . . God has allotted to all the peoples under the whole heaven." On this surprising statement, cf. 17:3 and especially 32:8-9. We may assume that 4:19 originally linked with v. 9: "Having experienced the greatness of the Creator Covenant God, beware then of deflecting your worship to created things."

That God has "allotted" the worship of nature to other nations implies that God may indeed be known generally, through creation. However, the contrast highlights the privilege of the covenant people, who are singled out for direct meeting with the Author of nature. The privilege is not, of course, a basis for pride. One people is chosen historically because all people are chosen intentionally (cf. Gen. 12:1-3). The one is chosen to be mediator for the many.

4:20-23 (basically second person plural) The "iron furnace (smelter)" (Deut. 4:20; cf. 1 Kgs. 8:51; Jer. 11:4) is a symbol of intense suffering. Let Israel remember the contrast between their suffering and their inheritance and be eternally grateful.

On the vicarious suffering of God's servant (Deut. 4:21-22) see 1:37; 3:26.

4:24 (singular) "The LORD your God is a devouring fire, a jealous God." The volcanic mountain belching fire (4:11-12) is regarded as an apt symbol for the awesomeness of God's presence. Verse 24 underlines that the symbol is close to the reality, while at the same time refining the symbol. The Hebrew word for "jealous" comes from the root *qana'*, meaning "fiery red" — like the face of a jealous lover. The deep emotion evidenced by the red face is the product of both anger and love. Thus the awesome fire of God is a perspective on God's "spouse-heart"! God has chosen Israel, and refuses to let the covenant partner fall under the fascination of any other lover. Hence the holy fire is a fire of jealous love.

God, Holy and Merciful (4:25-31)

The presence of singular (vv. 29b-31) and plural (vv. 25-29a) elements in this section suggests that the material has undergone revision. The concrete description of the Exile (vv. 27-28) supports the impression that the writer may be speaking from bitter experience, after 586 B.C. If so, the hope he holds out for repentance and acceptance based on God's mercy is moving testimony to the author's resilient faith.

The "growing old" referred to in v. 25 is not physical advance in years but a "growing old" in attitude — a lethargic taking for granted of privileges that once excited, inspired, and moved to gratitude. The great "aging" (corruption, ingratitude, evil) is to place a substitute god in place of the real God, or to attempt to manipulate and "use" the real God instead of serving and obeying (see above on vv. 11-18). Such behavior is a rejection of the covenant of grace and a bringing down on oneself of the inevitable consequences: to refuse grace is to go it alone and forfeit divine protection.

In the ancient Near East the treaties between overlord and vassal were witnessed by the gods of either side. But since Yahweh is the totality of all that is divine, there are no uncreated witnesses to attest the covenant with Israel. Accordingly, Yahweh's own creation is called on to witness the covenant and therefore attest Israel's rejection of grace — and reception of the consequences.

The language of v. 29 is reminiscent of Jer. 29:12-14. Both passages seem to reflect the exilic experience, and both affirm that Yahweh's last word is not "anger" but "loving faithfulness." The Hebrew word translated "merciful" (*rahum*, Deut. 4:31) is related to the word for "womb." Together they evoke the thought of "spacious and elemental maternal longing." Promises made five hundred years previous to Moses and twelve hundred years previous to the Exile still stand unimpaired by human waywardness, because they are grounded in God's faithfulness. It is impressive to see faith rising within the Exile to invoke this divine faithfulness. The phrase "obey God's voice" (v. 30; cf. vv. 24-26) is a significant reminder that "law" in Israel is never bare written regulation but essentially a communication of the mind of the living God. To obey the commandment is not to obey a rule, but to obey God.

God, Unique and Awesome (4:32-40)

This section (basically in the singular) is a preached application of the insights set out in the preceding part of the chapter.

"Human beings may not see the face of God and live" (Exod. 33:20), yet by grace and privilege the impossible happens (Deut. 4:33)! For "voice" and "face" of God are equally intimate disclosures. To see is to hear and to hear is to see. Hearing of course is hearing with intent, so vision and obedience go together.

The phrase "there is no other besides God" (v. 35; cf. v. 39) is new. It sounds a note of monotheism which comes to full expression in 2 Isaiah (Isa. 43:11; 44:6; 45:5, 22). The monotheism here in Deut. 4 is dynamic rather than philosophical: Yahweh fills the whole horizon of Israel's experience and gratitude, so that no other presentation of the divine has meaning or claim on imagination and obedience.

God speaks in order to "discipline" Israel (v. 36). The word occurs frequently in Proverbs to indicate the moral guidance offered by a parent to lead the children to maturity. This is the role and intention of Yahweh, in Yahweh's dealings with the covenant people — "that it may go well with you in Yahweh's land" (v. 40).

Moses Establishes Cities of Refuge (4:41-43)

This section is an addendum to the speech proper, describing not what Moses said, but what he did. Parallels are to be found in Num. 35:9-13; Deut. 19:1-3 (see the exegesis there), and Josh. 20:1-9 (where it is Joshua who actually establishes the refuges — acting in obedience to the dynamic of the word which Moses had heard).

In earliest times any altar dedicated to Yahweh could be a refuge to the fugitive accused of manslaughter (cf. Exod. 21:13-14). This ancient custom obviously persisted well into the kingship (1 Kgs. 1:50-53; 2:28-34). For this reason, some scholars suggest that the provision of cities of refuge (here attributed to Moses) is in fact much later — perhaps from Josiah's time. This presupposes that they resulted from the abolition of local altars and the centralization of worship at Jerusalem.

Others would trace the institution back through the 8th cent. (cf. Hos. 6:8; were Gilead and Shechem refuges in Hosea's day?) and further, to the reign of David.

The institution of such cities of refuge is unique to Israel. The theological principles undergirding it are that human life is sacred, that Yahweh is the source of justice, and that members of the covenant people may not take the law into their own hands.

THE SECOND
SPEECH OF MOSES

Deuteronomy 4:44–28:68

We have already seen (Introduction, 2-9) that the "book" of Deuteronomy in its basic substance had already been drafted as a legal code, then as a treaty document, before being cast in the format of a Mosaic speech (or speech-series). This complicated development of structure becomes especially apparent in the broad section we are about to discuss. Deuteronomy 4:44–28:68 includes such varied materials as:

- Narrative account of the Horeb theophany (Deut. 5) into which the Decalogue (5:6-22) is inserted
- Exhortations to remain faithful to the one God whose revealed will is recorded in the Torah (chs. 6–11)
- The Deuteronomic Code (12:1–26:15)
- Provision for covenant ratification, with blessings on the obedient and curses on the disobedient (26:16–28:68)

THE THEOPHANY ON HOREB
Deuteronomy 4:44–5:33

PREFACE TO MOSES' SECOND SPEECH (4:44-49)

As with the First Speech, the opening (cf. 1:1-5) sets the geographical location of the speech-making (see the discussion on 1:1-5). The conquest of Heshbon and Bashan (2:26–3:11) is then summarized. Further we are told to expect a presentation of the Mosaic laws and teachings (4:44-45). This signal, alerting us to an impending presentation of law, is in fact repeated several times in the ensuing chapters: 5:1; 6:1; 12:1 (and cf., e.g., 5:31; 6:17; 7:11; 11:1). Why the repetition? We may assume that in the recurring festival such formulas prefaced the recital of the law and punctuated the exhortations to faithfulness. Thus as the corpus of Deuteronomic material progressively expanded from bare code to code-plus-exhortation, each successive addition was introduced with the formula.

The terminology used to describe the laws and teachings is interesting. In 4:44 the whole body of material from here to the end of ch. 28 (30) is described as "the law" (Heb. *hattorah*), the definitive rule setting out the will of God for the covenant people. Thus Deuteronomy is viewed as a compact unitary whole. In 4:45, on the other hand, the variegated nature of the material is stressed; "testimonies" (literally, "witness": "I met Yahweh; I heard Yahweh say this"), "statutes" and "ordinances" (see on v. 1). Therefore, Deuteronomy is seen as the end product of a long process.

NARRATIVE ACCOUNT
OF THE HOREB THEOPHANY (5:1-33)

When we compare the structure of Deut. 5:1-33 with that of the corresponding account in Exodus (Exod. 19:16–20:21), two interesting factors emerge.

(1) First, in both cases the actual Decalogue (or Ten Commandments) sits rather awkwardly in the context, complicating the (Hebrew) grammar and breaking the narrative flow. It will be seen that Exod. 20:18 leads on naturally from Exod. 19:16a, so that the Decalogue with its bridging introduction appears as an insert. Similarly (though not quite so obviously) the Deuteronomic Decalogue (Deut. 5:6-22) appears to be an insert between 5:4 and 23.

This fact should alert us to the probability that the Decalogue has its own specific development-history. There can be little doubt that the definitive meeting with God on Horeb did include a core of "laws" around which the finished Decalogue crystallized. But the completed Decalogue itself may have taken some time to achieve its final form.

(2) In the second place, both the Exodus and the Deuteronomic versions of the Horeb narrative give the impression that originally the meeting was between Yahweh and the people. Subsequently the material has been reworked to highlight the role of the covenant mediator. Note for example the role of Deut. 5:5 in this regard (the awkwardness of the Hebrew grammar at this point shows that v. 5 is an addition). Interestingly, the Deuteronomic version adds emphasis to the role of the mediator by stressing that Yahweh's self approves the arrangement (vv. 28-31).

The covenant mediator has an important role as being the forerunner of the classical prophets — whose task it was to apply the historic Horeb revelation and its requirements to the concrete conditions of the people's ongoing life. Here Moses is pictured in a dual role: both receiver of the definitive revelation and interpreter of that revelation to changing circumstances. This underlines the importance of Moses for biblical faith: his contribution is vital both at the "beginning" and also in the ongoing process of revelation. The modern people of God still require both: the historic givenness of the word and its contemporary application. The covenant mediator represents the prophetic word within the Church.

Contemporizing the Meeting with God (5:1-5)

We have already noted that the hearers envisaged by the writer (i.e., the congregation either in the plains of Moab or in some subsequent annual festival) had not been historically present at Horeb. Yet by faith, imagination, and existential involvement, they are and must be "present." This comes through very powerfully in vv. 2 and 3.

"Our God made a covenant with *us* . . . Not others, but *us!* All of us! Here! Alive! Today!" In the dynamic of biblical exegesis our "today" is caught up also. Like the Deuteronomic generation, we too are addressed and made responsible. Verses 4 and 5 set down side by side two seeming incompatibles. On the one hand (v. 4), each member of the covenant people meets God "face to face" (awesome, "impossible" possibility: Exod. 33:20). Yet on the other hand (v. 5), it is the prophetic mediating ministry which brings them into this relationship.

What did the Deuteronomic editor intend by this juxtaposition? Is he suggesting that both are essential to the well-being of the covenant community — the members' personal relationship with God and their response to communal guidance through the mediating ministry?

Interestingly, the "word of Yahweh" which is mediated (Deut. 5:5) is referred to in the grammatical singular. The normal OT usage is that "words" (plural) refer to legal material, whereas "word" (singular) refers to the prophetic message. This serves to confirm the impression we have gained above.

The Decalogue (5:6-22)

We have already noted that the Decalogue appears to be an insertion in its present context, both in Exodus and in Deuteronomy — an entirely appropriate insertion, since revelation dissolves in mysticism if the voice of God has no perceived content.

The question of the origin and development of the Decalogue is indeed beset by difficult problems:

(1) The finished form of Exodus as we have it in the canon contains not one Decalogue but two. After receiving the first Decalogue (Exod. 20:1-17), Moses reascends the mountain to receive the Book of the Covenant (Exod. 20:21–23:33) and again to receive the instructions for Israel's worship (Exod. 25:1–31:17). At this stage the Decalogue is inscribed in stone and entrusted to Moses (Exod. 31:18). On coming down from the mountain, however, Moses discovers that the people have apostatized during his absence. He reacts in grief and anger by breaking the stone tablets of the Decalogue, thus canceling the covenant (Exod. 32:19). On Israel's repentance, God calls Moses to prepare two new tablets (Exod. 34), which are again inscribed with a Decalogue (vv. 10, 27). But the content of this second Decalogue (Exod. 34:14, 17-26) is different from the first. Scholars distinguish the two by referring to Exod. 20:1-17 as the Ethical Decalogue and Exod. 34:14, 17-26 as the Ritual Decalogue.

As we have mentioned, the structure of Deuteronomy is influenced by that of Exodus. The two Decalogues, both of which Exodus traces to Moses (or God through Moses), are to be found in Deuteronomy: the Ethical Decalogue in Deut. 5:6-22 and the Ritual Decalogue scattered throughout the Code (chs. 12–26).

Perhaps the most satisfactory way of explaining the relation between these two Decalogues is to assume that both are expansions of a common "Mosaic" core: "No other gods" (Exod. 20:3; 34:14); "No images" (Exod. 20:4; 34:17); "Keep the sabbath" (Exod. 20:8; 34:21); and perhaps "No association of Yahwism with magic" (Exod. 20:7: Yahweh's name in spells; cf. Exod. 34:26b: magic rite to ensure fertility).

The compiler of the JE tradition subsequently found two "Decalogues," each purporting to be from Moses; being unwilling to discard one, he included them both. Deuteronomy has been built on that tradition, but giving pride of place to the Ethical Dialogue.

(2) The "decalogue" (ten-member series) tradition is firmly embedded in the OT legal material: "the ten words" (Exod. 34:28; Deut. 10:4). Indeed, scholars have identified other ten-member

series besides the Ethical and Ritual Dialogues: Deut. 27:15ff.; Lev. 18:6-17; Lev. 20:2ff.; Ps. 15:2-5; Ezek. 18:5-9, to name the clearest examples. Why this predilection for "ten"? The answer is probably — literally! — at our fingertips! The counting off of a series on the fingers during the catechizing process would be a powerful aid to memory. (Incidentally, some series seem to swing between "ten" and "twelve" — ten fingers or twelve tribes of Israel.)

(3) The sentences of the Ethical Dialogue are not of uniform length, either in the Exodus or the Deuteronomy version. Some are long (Commandments II, IV, X), others are very short (Commandments VI, VII, VIII), while others again are of intermediate length (Commandments I and IX).

Form critics would examine the Decalogue starting from several basic assumptions: (1) that the formulation of the individual commandments has been shaped principally in the cultus; (2) that the formulation of the commandments would become more and more uniform through liturgical repetition until in their classical form the sentences would be approximately the same length; subsequent reduction to writing then opened the way for expansions and contractions; and (3) that in its classic form, each sentence would have been cast in the negative and been of intermediate length.

These form-critical assumptions, and the Decalogue reconstruction produced by Eduard Nielsen (_The Ten Commandments in New Perspective,_ 84-85) on their basis, will be useful to us in our consideration of the individual commandments.

5:6 The verse is identical with Exod. 20:2. In the Jewish tradition it counts as Commandment I, but in the Christian as introductory to the Decalogue as a whole.

Two translation possibilities present themselves:

(1) I, Yahweh, am your God who . . .
(2) I am Yahweh your God, who . . .

The first alternative implies that the name Yahweh is already familiar to "Israel," as in the Yahwist theology (Gen. 4:26) knowledge of the sacred name has been available to humankind from the beginning.

On the other hand, the second alternative pictures Yahweh as being introduced by name at Mt. Horeb. Earlier, God had been known as "God of the ancestors" (Exod. 3:13). Then at the inauguration of a grand new act, which is at once a new disclosure of character, God reveals God's self to Moses as "I am," Yahweh. This name, known initially to the leader, is now shared with the people.

Of the two alternatives the second is to be preferred.

Deuteronomy 5:6 is important, emphasizing as it does that "grace precedes law." The tenor of the Decalogue is not "Keep these rules in order to attain Yahweh's favor and help," but "Keep them out of gratitude because Yahweh has already favored and helped you."

5:7-10 The Roman Catholic and Lutheran traditions regard these four verses as comprising Commandment I. For Judaism, they are Commandment II, and in the Reformed tradition, Commandments I (v. 7) and II (vv. 8-10). There are grammatical grounds for regarding vv. 7-10 as one unit. "Gods" (v. 7) is plural, and so makes a more natural reference point for "them" (v. 9) than does the singular "graven image" of (v. 8).

5:7 We have mentioned earlier that for Israel Yahweh's self embraces the totality of divine manifestations. Hebrew expresses this conviction by normally designating Yahweh not as *el* ("god," singular) but as *elohim* ("God," "sum total of gods," plural). Verses 6 and 7 taken in conjunction then read: "I am Yahweh your 'elohim': you shall have no other 'elohim' before me." Two shades of interpretation are possible: "No other God"; "no other gods" — neither one supreme rival nor a multiplicity of competing rivals (cf. 4:32-40).

The phrase "before me" is literally "over against my face." Parallel instances of its use show that it has overtones of confrontation and deliberate provocation (e.g., Job 1:11; 2:5, "to your face"; Nah. 2:1, "against you"; Gen. 16:12, "over against"). We are reminded of the term "jealous God" (Deut. 4:24): to "flirt"

with another god "before Yahweh's face" is ingratitude for blessings received and a belittling of covenanted love.

5:8-10 We have seen that grammatically the prohibition of
images is a spelling out of the major injunction "no other gods."
The "images," then, are representations of foreign deities.

Though this is the meaning of the current text, it is by no
means certain that it was always so. Nielsen posits an original pair
of prohibitions:

Thou shalt not bow down before any other god.

Thou shalt not make to thyself any idol.

This reconstruction carries with it two consequences:

(1) The forbidden image may be of Yahweh's self, that is, may
constitute an attempt to "domesticate" Yahweh and "cut God
down to manageable proportions" (see above, on 4:11-18). This
is no less detestable than flaunting a direct rival in Yahweh's face.

(2) In contrast to Nielsen's two sentences of intermediate length
(arrived at by the application of form-critical principles), the
current text obviously constitutes "preached law."

(a) The types of forbidden representation are spelled out to
include not only human and animal forms ("on earth"), but
heavenly beings ("heaven above"), mythological monsters, and
dark powers ("under the earth") — and all their modern counterparts.

(b) A reason is adduced for the prohibition, namely, that "God
is jealous" (cf. 5:7) — a jealousy that is expressed in retribution
(v. 9), but above all in God's faithful love (v. 10). The retribution
reaches to grandchildren (third generation) and great-grand-
children (fourth generation), that is, all who live under the same
roof as the offender, in the context of the extended family. Here
is a solemn reminder that the consequences of our actions spread
out to influence everyone within our total living environment.
God's faithful love *(hesed)*, however, vastly outplays the effects of
"retribution." In parallel with the "third and fourth" of v. 9, the
"thousands" of v. 10 may in fact refer to "a thousand generations."

"Showing" (v. 10) is literally "doing" steadfast love; the concrete gift of land, overcoming of enemies, fertility of flocks and fields, creation of just and stable communities — all these are the deeds of God's "hesed."

5:11 According to Nielsen's reconstruction, the Third Commandment originally stated: "Thou shalt not take the name of Yahweh in vain" (the remaining clause is a "preaching" addition). "In vain" signifies "emptiness," "futility," "falsehood," "lies," and so forth. A similarly wide range of meaning is implicit in the commandment:

- Do not swear "by the name of Yahweh" to confirm a false statement (cf. Isa. 48:1).
- Do not use the name "Yahweh" in spells and incantations.
- Do not take Yahweh's name on the lips, while at the same time offering allegiance or worship to other gods (cf. Jer. 18:15).
- Do not worship Yahweh with empty hands, that is, with words only, unaccompanied by offerings which symbolize self-giving (cf. Exod. 34:20).

In ancient thought (Gen. 2:19-20) and still today in many cultures, the name symbolizes the personality or being. As a result knowledge of the name confers power over the person. In Gen. 32:22ff., for instance, Jacob conquers physically but is himself conquered "spiritually" in that he is forced to reveal his name, whereas the name of his Assailant remains undisclosed.

God indeed entrusts the knowledge of God's name to humankind in self-revelation, yet not in such a way that humanity can "use" or "control" God. A key passage here is Exod. 3:14, where God reveals the sacred name "I am who I am" (Heb. *ehyeh asher ehyeh; ehyeh,* "I am," is the first person equivalent of Yahweh, "He is").

The name sets forth both the constancy and the mystery of God. The name is given as assurance that God is utterly to be relied on. Nevertheless, God remains sovereign Freedom and Mystery, beyond reach of human manipulation.

5:12-15   Following the form-critical principles outlined above (70), Nielsen posits an original Commandment IV:

Thou shalt not do any work on the sabbath day.

The "preaching" additions which have crystallized around the original show marked variations when those of Deuteronomy are compared with Exodus:

Deut. 5:12-15	Exod. 20:8-11
Observe the sabbath	Remember the sabbath
As Yahweh your God commanded you	———
Or your ox, or your ass, or any of your cattle.	or your cattle.
That your manservant and your maidservant may rest . . . (vv. 14b-15).	———
———	For in six days Yahweh made heaven and earth (v. 11).

The origins of the Israelite sabbath are obscure.
Suggestions include:

- Development from the monthly *sappatu,* that is, (probably) "inauspicious" days of ancient Babylonia, when important work was proscribed as dangerous.
- Origins from the Kenites, a southern subtribe who became incorporated into Israel. Etymologically "Kenite" means "smelter," and the prohibition of kindling fire on the sabbath (Exod. 35:3) may have had an original connection with smelting.
- Connections with an original weekly market day, for which work ceased and within which religious observances came to have a part.

Whatever the origin, impressions are that in earlier times the sabbath was for respite and recreation. No specific sabbath cultus or liturgy was prescribed. In later, postexilic times, however, the observance became hedged round with burdensome regulations, so as to become more obligation than privilege.

The theological basis for the observance, as set out by the Deuteronomic writer, is interesting.

(1) "Remember . . . Egypt" (Deut. 5:15). During that period of slavery rest was forbidden. The sabbath rest is now a reminder of God's goodness in setting them free, and of the new status they now enjoy.

(2) Their own experience of servitude and gratitude for release should instill in them compassion for the servant class in their own society. Employees should enjoy weekly rest along with their employers.

This "humane" interpretation of the sabbath makes an interesting contrast with the more "doctrinal" perspective of the Exodus version (from the Priestly source): Rest, because Yahweh rested on the seventh day from the work of creation (Exod. 20:11). The keynote is celebration. God rests because God's action is complete. God's people may now imitate the divine rest, confident in the assurance that everything necessary for their well-being has been achieved. It is sufficient, then, to acknowledge the fact and rest in their God.

We may note that Jesus' attitude to the sabbath (Mark 2:27-28) builds on the "humane" Deuteronomic foundation referred to above.

5:16   Nielsen's reconstruction of Commandment V reads:

Thou shalt not despise thy father or thy mother.

With the concrete and negative-flavored "despise," compare Exod. 21:15 ("strike"), 17 ("curse"); Deut. 27:16 ("dishonor").

The Hebrew word *kabbed*, which here in 5:16 is translated "honor," originally had the concrete meaning "place a high value on." One is reminded of the note in Lev. 27:1-6 which sets the market price for male and female servants. It is noteworthy that with the onset of old age the value of a servant falls sharply (from fifty shekels to fifteen for males, and from thirty shekels to ten for females).

The commandment, then, may originally have meant "don't be tempted to evict your aged parents when they become an economic liability" (cf. Prov. 19:26).

The concrete economic/physical aspects of "honoring" one's parents still deserve consideration. We note, too, the complete parity with which father and mother are treated here. However "patriarchal" Hebrew society may have been in general, in the matter of rearing and educating children father and mother are accorded equal status and honor. The "parent" referred to would originally have been head of the extended family, which consisted of second, third, and fourth generations (Deut. 5:9). The compactness and therefore survival of the family depends in large measure on the authority of the head, hence the prudential "that it may go well with you. . . ." In the long term, enlightened self-interest favors honoring the head of the clan-family.

Commandment V has been named the "bridge commandment," linking as it does the duties to God (Commandments I-IV) and humanity (Commandments VI-X). We have indeed noted the parents' role in the catechetical process, passing on the sacred traditions and inculcating the love of God and neighbor in the oncoming generation.

5:17   Commandment VI is numbered V by Roman Catholic and Lutheran reckoning, VII according to Philo. Here Nielsen posits an original:

> Thou shalt not pour out the blood of thy neighbour (cf. Gen. 9:6; Jer. 7:6; 22:3).

This is longer and more general than the Deuteronomic version.

The Hebrew word translated "kill" *(ratsah)* has a quite limited and specific reference. According to J. J. Stamm (*The Ten Commandments in Recent Research,* 99) it means: "illegal killing inimical to the community." Examples of the usage are Job 24:14; 1 Kgs. 21:19.

The term is indeed applied also to unintentional killings, cases for which the cities of refuge (Deut. 4:41-43) were established.

When an unintentional killing incites individual revenge and leads to ongoing vendetta, this becomes *ratsah* in the specific sense. This would imply that Commandment VI does not refer either to killing in the context of war or to imposition of the death penalty in the dispensation of justice. Both of these are urgent moral issues, but the biblical input for their discussion should be drawn not from Commandment VI but from more directly relevant NT texts. Nevertheless, it may be added that the insights which become explicit in the NT are as it were "latent" in OT texts, including this one.

The matter concretely at issue in Commandment VI, then, is the rule of law. Indeed, it is likely that the more generalized statement (such as Nielsen posits) was shortened and particularized into its Deuteronomic form precisely in order to curb the operation of jungle law/vendetta. (The NT takes the matter further by stressing that the "rule of law" should be motivated by love; Rom. 13:9-10.)

5:18   For Commandment VII Nielsen suggests:

Thou shalt not commit adultery with thy neighbour's wife.

A study of the OT word usage makes it clear that "committing adultery" (Heb. *na'ap*) has to do with violation of the marriage relationship (e.g., Prov. 6:27-29, 32-35; Lev. 20:10; Jer. 29:23). It is necessary to underline this, because there have been periods and strands in the Christian tradition where virtually every type of sexual misdemeanor was categorized as "sin against the Seventh Commandment." This is unfortunate for two reasons. First, it tends to support the unbiblical prejudice that sexuality is intrinsically suspect. Second, it blurs the essential focus of Commandment VII, namely, the importance and centrality of the marriage relationship for the structure of church and society.

The positive aim of the commandment, then, is to safeguard the integrity of the husband-wife relationship. That being so, the implications are very wide-ranging: the well-being and security of the oncoming generation, the stability and cohesion of society, the ability of the community to resist external attack, and so on.

The links with Commandment V are thus apparent. To ensure its continuity and stability, society needs a strong line along which its faith norms are responsibly transmitted. It is supremely the family that fulfils this role; the marriage relationship which provides the family sinew is correspondingly vital.

We should note also that "adultery" is used throughout the OT as a metaphor for apostasy. The Yahweh-Israel covenant is pictured as a marriage relationship, so that to defect to other objects of worship is described as "playing the harlot," "leaving one's true husband," and so forth. See especially Hos. 1–3; Ezek. 16.

5:19-21 In order to delimit the meaning of "steal" in Commandment VIII it is necessary to compare it with the word "covet" in Commandment X (Deut. 5:21). The word translated "covet" (Heb. *hamad*) invariably includes the idea of physical appropriation: "want and take" (e.g., Exod. 34:24; Deut. 7:25; Josh. 7:21; Mic. 2:2).

We may safely assume, therefore, that originally Commandment X prohibited not the emotion of "desiring" the neighbor's property but the act of taking it — in other words, "stealing." But in that case Commandment X would be duplicating Commandment VIII. In the light of form-critical principles, however, such duplication is unlikely: the "polishing" which took place in the liturgical process would produce an economy of expression from which redundancies were eliminated.

Following this lead, Nielsen (with others) has suggested that Commandment VIII originally referred to a specific form of stealing, namely, "kidnapping." Thus he proposes:

Thou shalt not steal any man from thy neighbour.

5:19 Kidnapping was regarded in Israel as a serious crime deserving the death penalty (Exod. 21:16; Deut. 24:7). The "stealing" of a man's wife or servant as in Commandment X (5:21) is considered an infringement of his property rights. As such it does not come under Commandment VIII, which seemingly relates specifically to the personal freedom of the free-born citizen. Stated in modern terms, Commandment VIII then seeks to safeguard the legitimate personal freedom of the individual within society. Its application is still circumscribed, in that it is limited to one class within society. But by appeal to the principle of "latency" (v. 17), we may regard the commandment as containing the seeds of acknowledgment of a universal human right.

A possible reason why the longer form of Commandment VIII (suggested by Nielsen) was shortened to that of the Deuteronomic text is that gradually the meaning of "covet" (v. 21) became "spiritualized" to focus on "desire" — leaving room for a more clear-cut condemnation of physical theft (see further on v. 21 below).

5:20 Form-critical considerations would suggest that Commandment IX is still in the classical decalogic form, compared with which other commandments have been expanded or shortened.

The word "false" translates Heb. *shaw'*, which literally means "empty." The identical term occurs in v. 11 (see above). The parallel version of Commandment IX in Exod. 20:16 uses the more concrete term "lying witness" (Heb. *sheqer*). In practice the two terms are virtually equivalents. The phrase "bearing false witness" has its setting in the judicial process. "Bear" becomes a technical term meaning either "accuse" (e.g., 1 Sam. 12:3; 2 Sam. 1:16) or "defend" (e.g., Job 9:14, 15; Mal. 2:12).

In Israel, where ordinary citizens could be called to give testimony (e.g., Ruth 4:2, 11) and where the life of the defendant could well be at stake (e.g., Num. 35:30), it was important that witnesses were aware of their heavy responsibility.

The shift in emphasis from "lying witness" (Exodus) to "idle witness" (Deuteronomy) may indicate the beginnings of a broadening process whereby the application of Commandment IX is extended to cover all speech that disadvantages our fellows. One can endanger life by sarcasm, innuendo, and character assassination, as well as by false testimony in a court of law.

5:21 We have seen that the various modern traditions have different ways of subdividing the Decalogue into its ten component commandments. Some achieve the round number ten by counting Deut. 5:21a as Commandment IX and v. 21b as Commandment X. Others count the whole of v. 21 as Commandment X.

A comparison of Deut. 5:21 and Exod. 20:17 reveals several differences. First, the order of clauses one and two is reversed: according to Deuteronomy, "wife" precedes "house," whereas in Exodus "house" is mentioned first, then "wife." Second, "covet" (Heb. *hamad*) is used throughout Exod. 20:17, whereas Deuteronomy uses *hamad* in 5:21a but *hit'awweh* ("desire") in v. 21b. Third, coveting of fields is listed in Deuteronomy but not in Exodus.

Nielsen concludes that the Exodus form of the commandment is earlier than the Deuteronomic, and posits an original:

Thou shalt not covet thy neighbour's house.

"House" here is interpreted as "household," an inclusive term encompassing wife, servants, cattle, land, buildings. The subsuming of "wife" under "household" in this way is offensive to modern sensibilities, but objectively is in keeping with the sociology of early Israel. It may very well be that the Deuteronomic writer has reversed the first two clauses precisely because of the growing sensitivity to women's position (cf. Deut. 21:10-14; 22:13-19; 24:1-5).

We have already seen that the term "hamad" includes both desire and aggressive act (5:19-21). Indeed, the accent is on the latter, so that the motive for "coveting" the wife and servants would not be adultery (Commandment VII) but greed — to sell them into slavery.

It is also unlikely that in the classic form of the Decalogue, where "polishing" has produced uniformity (see above, 70), Commandments V-IX are directed against antisocial acts and that X alone should be concerned with interior motives. So we may agree that originally Commandment X also condemned aggressive behavior. The change of vocabulary in v. 21b from "want and take" to "desire" does, however, indicate that the process of "interiorization" (which comes to full flowering in the NT, Matt. 5:21-30) had already begun in the Deuteronomic school.

Summary (5:6-21)

We may sum up the contents of the Decalogue:

- Table I (Commandments I-IV) urges honor and loyalty to Yahweh.
- Table II (Commandments V-X) urges respect of parents (V); and of one's neighbor's life (VI), marriage (VII), freedom (VIII), reputation (IX), and property (X).

It should be added that objectively speaking "neighbor" in the text means "fellow Israelite" (fellow countryman, fellow believer). Yet here, too, the principle of "latency" (cf. Deut. 5:17) may be invoked. The seeds of universal "humane-ness" (cf. Luke 10:29, 36-37) are implicit in the decalogic concern for "neighbor."

5:22 That Yahweh "added no more" means two things. First, the people who have heard this decalogic kernel of revelation directly from Yahweh will henceforth hear through the mediator. Second, the material sealed by this formula (cf. Deut. 4:2; 12:32) is in principle definitive and complete. The Decalogue is indeed the core of the Deuteronomic code, of "revealed law."

"Yahweh wrote . . . ," either directly (Exod. 32:16) or through Moses (34:28). In any case, the language is anthropomorphic. God "speaks" through humanity, and the resultant word is permanent, "inscribed on stone."

The Office of Mediator Is Established (5:23-33)

We saw above (67) that 5:23 is a continuation of 5:4.

The purpose of the passage is to highlight the office of covenant mediator by tracing it back to Moses. The same purpose is already apparent in the Exodus version (Exod. 19:16-19; 20:18-21), but gains additional emphasis in Deuteronomy. The theological motivation behind this is that the Deuteronomic school of the 7th cent. B.C. wish to stress their authority as contemporary mediators of covenant law. Let the people be assured that their teachers

81

stand in Moses' shoes, teaching and applying the authentic word given by God on Horeb.

The Moses generation's request for a mediator is couched in terms reminiscent of Exod. 33:17-23. Like Moses the people have stood with God and, indeed, to all intents and purposes, have "seen God's face and lived" (Deut. 5:24). They are overwhelmed by the realization of their awesome privilege, and God commends their reverent reticence (vv. 28-29) while granting their request. In recounting these beginnings of the mediating office the Deuteronomic law teachers wish to stress that distance does not involve loss. The conscientious hearers of the law in the 7th cent. B.C. (and the 20th cent. A.D.!) are just as truly in the presence of God on historic Horeb as were their forebears.

Having heard the basic torah (Decalogue), Moses will now receive and transmit the explanatory code (v. 31), which will be expounded for subsequent generations in the main body of Deuteronomy (chs. 12–26). The phrase "to your tents" (v. 30) was obviously a technical term used in Israel to dismiss civil or military assemblies, including the congregation at the annual festivals (16:7; Josh. 22:7; 1 Sam. 13:2; 2 Sam. 20:22). Its use here implies that the historic assembly at Horeb is regarded as the first in a long line of torah assemblies, stretching down to the Deuteronomic writer's own day.

BODY OF THE
SECOND SPEECH (PART I)
Deuteronomy 6:1–11:32

TITLE ANNOUNCING PROCLAMATION
OF THE TORAH (6:1-3)

This paragraph is virtually a paraphrase of Deut. 5:31-33. The repetition underlines the importance of the teaching about to be presented.

In ch. 4 we have already met the term *hattorah*, signifying the totality of teaching viewed as a unitary whole (see above on 4:8, 44). Here (and in 5:31) "the commandment" (Heb. *hammitswah*) is used in a parallel sense. The two terms indicate an advanced stage in the development of legal teachings into canonical torah.

The land "flowing with milk and honey" is for the Deuteronomic school a favorite picture of prosperity and divine blessing (11:9; 26:9, 15; 27:3; 31:20). Compare the similar "wheat and honey" of Ps. 81:16. The richest resources of nature are Yahweh's to dispose. The gift of them is a reminder of God's goodness and an incentive to gratitude and obedience.

BASIC INTRODUCTION TO THE CODE (6:4–7:21)

One Yahweh and One Response (6:4-9)

"Hear, O Israel"; on this solemn call to assembly, see 4:1. The sentence which follows is highly condensed, consisting of only four Hebrew words: "Yahweh our-God Yahweh one." It is susceptible of various interpretations (see RSV footnote), the most convincing of which is "Yahweh is our God, Yahweh alone." Thus the primary reference is not to the metaphysical Oneness of the deity (as, e.g., Muslim theologians would contend), but to Yahweh's claim to total and undivided loyalty. Implicit also in the formula is the declaration that Yahweh is the reality toward whom all human religious aspiration is feeling — whether nature worship (Baalism), astrology, occultism, or "self-realization."

In Judaistic tradition Deut. 6:4 became the core of the daily credal confession known as the Shema ("hear . . .").

It is important that love can be commanded (v. 5; cf. 11:1, 13, 22). It is not therefore an emotion only, but is closely bound up with obedience. To love God means full commitment to follow God's intentions. For example, because God is concerned for the stranger, loving God means sharing that concern (10:18-19).

6:5 The Hebrew terms for "heart," "soul," and "might" require a little unpacking.

"Heart" *(lebab)* in Hebrew signifies not only the physical organ but also the inner core of personality (the physical and spiritual being regarded as indivisible aspects of the one total person). *Lebab* hosts the emotions of joy (Prov. 27:11), sorrow (Neh. 2:2), courage (2 Sam. 17:10), trust (Prov. 31:10), and hate (Lev. 19:17). It is also the source of reason (questioning, Judg. 5:16; planning, 1 Chr. 29:18; scheming, Gen. 27:41; discernment, Ps. 90:12) and the breeding ground of moral attitudes (pride, Deut. 8:14; stubbornness, Jer. 3:17; cynicism, Job 36:13).

So, to love Yahweh with the whole heart means to open to God all the processes of thinking, feeling, and deciding, to be shaped and honed as instruments aligned to God's purposes.

"Soul" (Heb. *nephesh*) does not mean the "immortal part of personality that survives death," but rather the principle of life shared by humans and animals (Gen. 2:7, 19, "living nephesh"!). By stages the word meant neck, breath, principle of human life, human being — and strangely, even a corpse can on occasion be described as a *nephesh* (Num. 6:6).

Compared with *lebab, nephesh* is related more closely to emotion, feelings, and desires: appetite (Job 6:7), thirst (Isa. 29:8), greed (Ps. 10:3), hope (Deut. 24:15), sadness (Isa. 38:15), and so forth. Hence to love with the "nephesh" means to place our feelings and desires at God's service and conform them to God's will.

"Might" (Heb. *me'od*) literally means "muchness," "exceeding-ness," "intensity." In 2 Kgs. 23:25 Josiah's "turning . . . with all his might" is described, in the context of 2 Kgs. 23, as a single-minded endeavor to establish everything required by God's torah and to eliminate everything forbidden by it. *Me'od* then is a single-minded, love-inspired zeal and determination to realize the whole will of God.

6:6-9 The "words" (Deut. 6:6) are the bridge between love and obedience. Therefore they are to be made fresh (literally, "sharpened") for each new generation by their elders. "Sitting . . . walking . . . lying . . . rising" are together representative of the total daily activity, from morning to night, work and leisure (v. 7). The command to bind them on hands and forehead (v. 8), door-post and gate (v. 9), extended this symbolic representative impact. Let the words of God guide every movement of the hand and eye, every domestic and community activity. But then subsequent generations began to take the "binding" literally. Little leather boxes *(tephillim)* containing Torah verses were strapped to the left wrist and forehead at prayer times. Similar boxes *(mezuzah)* were fixed to the right door- and gateposts.

Such "visualizing" of symbolic language is valid providing it does not detract from the all-embracing nature of the Torah's demand by limiting it to the specific chosen texts (Exod. 13:1-10, 11-16; Deut. 6:4-9; 11:13-21).

God's Goodness and the Fear of God (6:10-15)

The "previous history" section of the ancient Near Eastern vassal treaties (see Introduction, 8) normally included an inventory of the land and effects possessed by the vassal. Deuteronomy 6:10-11 includes such a list: "cities . . . houses . . . cisterns . . . vineyards . . . olive trees." All these are Yahweh's gifts, and their continuance is dependent on Israel's covenant-faithfulness (cf. Amos 5; Deut. 28:30-31; cf. also 7:12-13; 8:7-8; 11:10-11).

Interestingly, thirty times in Deuteronomy God is said to "swear" faithfulness, whereas only twice are God's people exhorted to "swear by God's name" (6:13; 10:20). The contrast underlines the constancy of God's dealings founded in the constancy of the divine nature.

The "fear of God" (6:13; cf. 4:10) is a difficult concept for twentieth-century people, especially when allied, as here, with anger and destruction (6:15).

The term is to be understood here in the light of its context. God's people are not to forget their experience of God's liberating grace (v. 12) nor God's jealousy (which we have seen to be the expression of consuming love; 4:24). Thus the "fear" is not a paralyzing recoil, but a reverential awareness of the responsibilities entailed in being so loved. "Fear" finds expression in "serving" ("worshipping") and in undivided loyalty. One "swears by" one's ultimate point of reference; so swearing by Yahweh is implicitly an acknowledgment that Yahweh is the focus of our personal and community life.

Do Not Put God to the Test (6:16-19)

These verses are in mixed form: 6:16-17 in the plural, vv. 18-19 in the singular. This suggests that an originally general exhortation (vv. 18-19) has been strengthened by the addition of a concrete example (vv. 16-17).

The name Massah indeed means "testing." The way the reference is introduced here is reminiscent of 4:3-4 (the Baal-peor incident). The tradition is so well known that the hearers need no more than a mere reminder to see its relevance for their situation (for the full text, see Exod. 17:1-7). The core of this is Exod. 17:7: the "test" consisted in asking, "Is Yahweh among us or not?" There are two motives in posing such a question: a panic-stricken doubting that there is in fact any Protection or Guidance amid the exigencies that pressure us; and an arrogant assumption that "God is too remote to see or care about me and my actions."

Such a stance effectively repudiates God's self-revelation, and is tantamount to carving out for oneself another god with other characteristics. This is to "try" God and arouse God's lover-jealousy (Deut. 6:15).

To "test" (v. 16) is to assay, or to determine the genuineness of an article over against possible counterfeits. Thus the older sources speak of God's "testing" the people (Exod. 15:25; 16:4; 20:20; and the locus classicus, Gen. 22). But to seek to "test" God is to impugn the integrity of God's self-revelation, to call God's constancy into question, and to express one's trustlessness by refusing to obey God's clear directives. Obedience, on the other hand, is a tacit declaration that God does not need to be "proved." The loyal carrying out of what is "right" (i.e., upright when measured against the true vertical standard of God's words) is the certain way to true well-being.

Tell It to Your Children (6:20-25)

The constantly recurring "we," "us," and "our" throughout these verses are reminiscent of Deut. 5:1-5. Generations long after the era of Moses can still say, "*we* were there when God met our people at Horeb." It is of the essence of faith that the historic saving encounter become present experience for each succeeding generation.

Gerhard von Rad has suggested that Deut. 6:21-23 forms an ancient credo, originally independent of its present covenant renewal context in vv. 20-25. He would trace its origins to a cultic celebration at Gilgal, commemorating the Conquest and apportioning of the land. It need not be doubted that vv. 21-22 are credal; but the attempt to divorce them from their present context is unconvincing. See further on 26:1-11.

The fiction of the Mosaic farewell speech requires the material to be given a future location: "in time to come" (literally, "tomorrow"; 6:20). In actual fact, the question "What does it mean?" envisages the catechetical process that continued as a present experience between festivals, down the generations. In Exod. 12:26 the question runs, "What do you mean by this Passover liturgy?" Here in Deut. 6:20 it is "What do you mean by these testimonies, statutes, ordinances. . . ?" The comparison is instructive. For the Deuteronomic school, the torah is the heart of all

God-awareness, eclipsing every other liturgical element. Yet once
again (cf. 5:6) the evangelical basis of law is firmly underlined.
The answer to the young person's question is a story, recounting
the saving acts of God which provide the basis and rationale for
the obedience required in 6:24. In fact the law is both grace-based
and grace-oriented: obedience is "for our good to preserve us
alive" — or more literally, "to quicken us into life."

The section ends with the summary, "It will be righteousness
for us, if we obey." It is interesting to compare this with Gen.
15:6 (paraphrased): "It was righteousness for Abraham that he
believed. . . ." The two statements are not in tension. Indeed,
they are two sides of one coin. The openness of faith which
constitutes right relation with God is characterized precisely by
obedience.

No Compromise with Paganism (7:1-6)

Modern sensibilities are strained by the seeming chauvinism of
such passages as this. Seven "great and mighty nations" are
"cleared away" (Deut. 7:1) to make room for the people whom
God has "chosen" (v. 6). The impression is that "choosing," for
Israel, means "disaster" for the nations Israel displaced.

Having noted this emphasis, we need to place it in context.

The concept of Yahweh's adopting Israel or Israel's ancestors
as a special possession is an ancient one: Abraham was called
(Gen. 12:1-3), Moses entrusted with a task, Israel brought into
a covenant relation, Israel "known" by Yahweh (Amos 3:2).
Nevertheless, it is the Deuteronomic school that introduce and
stress the "choosing" terminology. In the Deuteronomic history,
Eli (1 Sam. 2:28), Saul (1 Sam. 10:24), and David (e.g., 1 Sam.
16:8, 12) are "chosen" (Heb. *bahar*) for office. Moreover,
throughout Deuteronomy the people as a whole are said to be
"chosen" (Deut. 4:37; 7:6-7; 10:15; 14:2; cf. 1 Kgs. 3:8).

In the older tradition at its best, God's grace to Israel is set in
a universal context. Abraham is called so that through him all
nations of the earth should be blessed (Gen. 12:3). The predom-
inant note is not exclusiveness but wonder. The broadness (see
Deut. 4:19) and wonder persist in Deuteronomy; but it cannot

be denied that in passages like 7:1-6 there is a certain narrowing. Why so? Two related factors should be noted:

(1) The Deuteronomic school are writing in the shadow of the Exile (impending or actualized). The very existence of Israel seems threatened, and morale is in crisis. At such a time it was inevitable that all theological energy should be focused on survival: "God has chosen us over against other nations." The circle of concern and of vision narrows in the crisis.

(2) Second, this account of the occupation of Canaan is highly theologized. The older traditions suggest that the indigenous peoples of Canaan were *not* simply "cleared away" like dust before the broom. On the whole, they stayed and became integrated into Israel. (See E. John Hamlin, *Inheriting the Land*, xxi.) In this theological retrospect, the Deuteronomic writer is tacitly acknowledging that fact and tracing Israel's apostasy to these indigenous influences. The "clearing away" is an idealized "might have been," the crux of which is not disregard for the fate of those fellow human beings but a yearning for the purity of faith which would have preserved Israel from its current disaster.

That the Canaanites are said to comprise "seven nations" (v. 1) is probably a way of saying that "the totality of indigenous peoples" must give way before the purposes of Yahweh. Other lists include ten (Gen. 15:19-21), eleven (Gen. 10:15-18), 6 (Exod. 3:8, 17; Deut. 20:17), and seven (Josh. 3:10) nations.

The "pillars" and "Asherim" (Deut. 7:5) belonged to the apparatus of Canaanite Baal worship (see above on 4:3). The pillar was basically a marker identifying a particular locale as a sacred place where deity could be contacted. It served either to "pin down" the deity by ensuring the deity's presence, or to symbolize the male worshipper's desire and intention to be present. The pillar (Heb. *massebah*) had male associations and on occasion seemed to have been a phallic symbol.

The *Asherim* were corresponding female symbols of indeterminate form. (Being constructed of wood, they have left no hard evidence for archaeological research.) Asherah was the fertility-goddess in the Canaanite pantheon. So we may surmise that *massebot* and *Asherim* together were part of the setting for fertility rites possibly involving cultic prostitution. This cultic act was thought by a "sympathetic" process to stimulate fertility in nature — flocks, fields, orchards. Such practices are inimical to Yahwism, for in principle fertility religion seeks to bend to human ends the divine energies latent in nature. Israel, however, acknowledges Yahweh as Creator-Liberator, who is the source both of nature and of grace. Appropriate worship therefore consists not in seeking to manipulate Yahweh for human ends, but in offering oneself to Yahweh for Yahweh's purposes.

The passage also raises the question about the interrelation of biblical faith and indigenous culture. Here the pattern is total rejection.

On the other hand, Canaanite laws (Introduction, 4-7) and architecture (the layout of Solomon's temple) did profoundly influence the shape and content of Israel's faith. To distinguish the compatible from the inimical requires great sensitivity — now as well as then. No overall rule of procedure can be applied, but each instance must be weighed in its concrete setting. The basic criterion must be that the essentials of biblical faith are enhanced by the new dress, whatever subtle change of coloring or idiom they may incur in the process.

Couched in rather different terms, 7:1-6 poses for us the wide question of the relation between religious conviction and tolerance.

Election Based on God's Goodness Alone (7:7-11)

Verses 7-8a are in the plural, whereas the surrounding material is in the singular — another case of a fortifying addition, designed to firm up the general exhortation. The effect of vv. 7-8a, in fact, is to rule out possible misunderstanding. The "choosing" referred to in the previous passage is no excuse for pride, because it is not based on any perceived merit or strength in the chosen party, but solely on divine goodness.

The language is warm and emotional. Verse 6 has described Israel as God's "treasured possession"; verse 7 continues, "God set God's own love on you." The Hebrew root *hashaq* ("to bind," "attach") is used of a young man drawn and captivated by a young woman (Gen. 34:8; Deut. 21:11). In Israel's case there is no beauty to account for the attraction ("a small and insignificant people"). Paradoxically, the captivation has its source in the heart of the captivated: "It is because Yahweh loves (Heb. *aheb*) you" (7:8; cf. v. 13; 10:15; 23:5). This is a wonderful tautology: "God loves because God loves"!

The term *aheb* is used to describe loving relationship over a wide range: man-woman, friend-friend, parent-child, master-servant, neighbor-neighbor. But it was Hosea who applied it most movingly to the husband-wife relationship between God and the chosen people. It is likely that Hosea's thought has influenced Deuteronomy here — with the difference that the strongly erotic background which colors Hosea's presentation is absent in Deuteronomy.

The divine love is characterized by faithfulness. Here as frequently throughout Deuteronomy, succeeding generations are assured that the historic love attested by their forebears is unchangeably theirs also. Unchangeably? Yes. Yet this entirely undeserved and uncaused love requires the response of obedience. Even when God is the prime partner, it takes two to sustain a loving relationship. It is foreign to the genius of love that it could simply be imposed. So close is the correlation between love and obedience that the opposite of obedience is said to be "hate" (7:10). Yet even obedience rests on grace: the love persists to a thousand generations (cf. 5:10), eliciting ongoing obedience as it flows.

Once again (cf. 6:1) the total body of God's torah is described in the all-inclusive singular: "the commandment" (7:11).

The Blessings of the Faithful God (7:12-16)

These verses describing the blessings that follow obedience are reminiscent of the covenant sanctions (Introduction, 8) which were part of the annual covenant renewal liturgy (cf. 28:2-6). Perhaps the fragment once formed the conclusion to the piece of festival preaching-exhortation which now stands at 7:1-11. For similar inventories of the land's wealth, cf. 6:10-11; 8:7-8; 11:10-11. "Grain . . . wine . . . oil" are the three important products of the land in Palestine (11:14; 12:17; 14:23; 18:4; 28:51). With these are linked the fertility of flocks and herds, also regarded as

Yahweh's blessing. "The young" of the flock are literally the *'ash-tarot* — gifts of Ashtarte, goddess of fertility. The pagan terminology, however, has become dead metaphor in Hebrew (cf. "by Jove!" in English): it is Yahweh who is the acknowledged giver of fertility and increase.

That there is a general connection between health and obedience to God cannot be disputed. But to link health as directly with reward and "the diseases of Egypt" (dysentery, elephantiasis, trachoma) with punishment as 7:15 does is problematic. Compare John 9:1-3: disease is not God's punishment but God's opportunity.

Deuteronomy 7:15, then, needs to be read in its context: the urgent and almost frantic call to repentance, from within the shadow of the Exile.

The same would apply to v. 16: "Your eye shall not pity them." In reading the phrase, we need to keep firmly in mind that this is Deuteronomic retrospect (see above on 7:1). The writer is surveying the course of Israel's history from the brink of the Exile, with a shake of the head: "If only our ancestors had wiped out all traces of paganism when they first occupied the land, we would have been able to maintain a pure devotion to Yahweh. That so-called 'human sympathy' for the relics of paganism has proved to be a mask to cover up our compromises."

We can respect the religious zeal that motivates the Deuteronomists. Yet at the same time, we need to acknowledge that their recipe for attaining pure religion is wrong. The "enemy" is not to be "eliminated" but transformed by goodwill (Matt. 5:43-45).

At this point, then, the OT does not address us directly. We should not imitate the attitude to opposition advocated here. Yet the Deuteronomists' zeal for the honor of God's name is something that should inspire us.

This passage also reads as though prosperity, health, and victory are guaranteed, provided God's people obey all God's commands. This contention does not stand up against human experience. Good people do suffer (Job; Ps. 73; Isa. 53; Deut. 1:37; 3:26; 4:21). Yet it remains true that there are connections between prosperity and obedience to God. God has unveiled principles for appropriate agricultural method and social guidelines to check poverty and exploitation. Conscientious attention to these would undoubtedly improve the quality of our common life. Attention to the laws of hygiene would contribute to the control of infectious diseases. And so on.

In the last resort, misconceptions as to the content of God's requirements can be forgiven — though they have wrought untold havoc throughout the course of human history. The self and the community genuinely desiring to be totally obedient — this is the core of the Deuteronomic intention, and the kernel of the ongoing message.

God Will Grant Success, Provided
Israel Remains Loyal (7:17-26)

It is implicit in this section that the Israelite occupation of Canaan was not all plain sailing. There were setbacks and opposition (7:17-18, 22). This is in keeping with the older tradition (Judg. 1) but rather at odds with the highly theologized and idealized account presented by the Deuteronomic historian (Josh. 11:16-20; 21:43-45).

7:18-21 The exhortation follows a universal preaching method. The constancy of God's character and intention is underlined; and clear examples of God's action in the past are summoned up, to illustrate the kind of help that may be expected in the difficulties that the congregation are currently facing.

"Remember" (Heb. *zakar*) does not imply a mere printout of facts from the past but a vivid "reliving" of the past situation, with a deliberate recourse to the divine help that was evident then. This concept plays an important role throughout Deuteronomy. The people are called upon to remember: God (Deut. 8:18), God's action (11:3), the desert journey (8:2), the past (32:7), oppression in Egypt (e.g., 15:15), the hostility of the Amalekites (25:17, 19). Every such "remembrance" has power to alter current attitudes and conditions (cf. the "remembering of Jesus" at the Lord's Supper; 1 Cor. 11:24).

If the "hornets" (Deut. 7:20) are to be taken literally, the thought would be that nature itself opposes those who oppose

93

God's purposes — and implicitly supports those who are in the line of God's intention (cf. Judg. 5:20). If the reference is symbolic, it may point to the military might of Egypt (Pharaoh Thutmose III and his successors took the hornet as their emblem). Deuteronomy 7:20 would then constitute a promise that the resistance of the indigenous population would have been already broken by the Egyptians, before Israel entered Canaan.

On the whole, the literal interpretation is the more likely. "Do not fear them" (v. 18) . . . "for Yahweh your God is fearsome" (v. 21). If "perfect love casts out fear" (1 John 4:18), then it may also be said that "perfect fear casts out fear." Yahweh is awesome to opponents, awesome also to God's people. Wholesome awe of Yahweh is an energy urging believers to overcome lesser fears and pursue with courage their God-appointed course. (On "fearsome" [Heb. *nora'*] see further Deut. 10:17.)

There is a touch of rationalization about 7:22 — an accommodation of the theological ideal to the everyday reality. The ideal says that "Yahweh swept the land clean." The reality is intransigent opponents and dangerous wild animals to contend with. The accommodation is that God has a positive purpose in making us face these difficulties: it is for our good.

The "wild beasts" remind us of conditions in northern Israel during the 7th century. Possibly the Deuteronomic writer has actually experienced those seventh-century conditions and used them to color his "thirteenth-century" narrative.

Images (v. 25) were frequently carved from wood, then sheathed in precious metal. The wooden core was burned and the metal became *herem* (see above on 2:31-35). Anyone who steals what is *herem* becomes infected as it were with its mystic quality (which stems from the foreign deity it once represented). Such a person becomes *herem* in turn and must be destroyed.

Such ways of thinking are still powerful in many cultures, though not in the "First" World. Perhaps one can express the thought by saying that in the realm of spiritual reality it remains true: "Those who play with fire are sure to be burned."

Tampering with what is "taboo" in this deeply compromising way is said to be "revolting" ("abomination") to God. For other examples of "revolting" behavior, cf. 17:1; 18:12; 24:4; 25:14-16.

This is a very powerful anthropomorphic image. It makes God
sick!

REMEMBER THE WILDERNESS (8:1-20)

Chapter 8 as a whole sets out to forearm the people against two
possible threats to their faith allegiance, namely, the experiences
of hardship and of prosperity.

(1) In face of hardship, the congregation is invited to recall
the difficulties that once confronted the Exodus generation —
heat, sand, snakes, scorpions, hunger, thirst. In such conditions
they were often tempted to ask, "If God really loves us, why is
all this happening to us?" By way of response they were offered
a threefold encouragement:

* Remember the trough from which Yahweh lifted you (v. 14).
  Things are hard at present, but think what they were before!
* Remember the goal of your journey (vv. 7-10): fulfillment of
  your highest desires.
* Remember the current tokens of providential care that you are
  meeting along the way: your food (v. 3), drink (v. 15), clothing
  (v. 4), and health (v. 4) have been provided, sometimes in quite
  extraordinary ways.

These factors which framed the perspective of the Exodus generations have their ongoing counterparts. So let succeeding generations also take them into consideration and draw strength from
them in facing hardship.

(2) Prosperity also can pose a threat to faith allegiance. The
faith pattern presented in ch. 8 is a dynamic one, oriented toward
achievement. "Digging" (v. 9) and "getting" (v. 18) are accepted
as normal positive behavior. Achievement, however, brings with
it the danger of arrogance: "I did it myself; I am self-made."
Individuals, churches, and whole societies are prone to fall into
this trap. The antidote is to recall that our physique, energy,
astuteness, and resourcefulness are sheer gift (v. 18a), coming
down to us (through a long process of inheriting; v. 18b) from
the Creator.

On both accounts, then, the nub of the matter turns out to be obedience. Follow the guidelines faithfully (vv. 1, 11), and the final outcome is assured.

God's Providential Care in the Desert (8:1-6)

"Forty years" (vv. 2, 4) represents the interval between generations. Here the meaning widens to the equivalent of "a lifetime." Life experience provides the evidence of God's faithfulness. The "humbling" (vv. 2, 3) intended in the hardships that are experienced is not calculated to humiliate or demean. The Hebrew word used here (*'anah*) has connotations of "poor," "afflicted." Compare the "poverty of spirit" which Jesus cites as a hallmark of true happiness (Matt. 5:3). To be "humbled," then, is to be led to an awareness of our own meager resources and hence into trustful dependence on the resources of God. The "manna" reference (Deut. 8:3, 16) is yet another of Deuteronomy's passing allusions to well-known tradition (cf. 4:3; 6:16). For a full account of the incident, see Exod. 16. According to the popular etymology recorded in Exod. 16:15, "manna" means "what is this?" (Heb. *man hu'*) — recording the people's puzzlement at the strange foodstuff.

Scholarly research suggests that the "manna" (still found on the Sinai peninsula) is the excretion of certain insects which feed on the sap of the tamarisk shrub. It is thus a natural product. Israelite tradition, however, regarded its availability as a sign of God's providential care and heightened the sense of the miraculous in the telling. What must have been available in rather minor quantities was "expanded" in the tradition to become sufficient for hundreds of thousands of people continuously for nearly four decades.

The lesson drawn by the Deuteronomic writer is that God pushes back the boundaries of natural possibility in response to trustful dependence. Bread is God's normal gift, but when need arises God speaks (Ps. 78:23-24) and "unimaginable" things become "bread" at God's word. God's range of options is infinite.

The provision of clothing too was not originally regarded as "miraculous" in the dramatic sense. Yet it was God who helped the people to the wherewithal (Deut. 2:6-7) or provided what was necessary. So it becomes true to say that all is "miracle" in the wider sense for those committed in trustful dependence to Yahweh's way.

The Bias Towards Forgetting God (8:7-20)

8:7-10 Deuteronomy 8:7-10 constitutes another of the "inventories of wealth and property" already referred to (6:10-11; cf. 11:10-12). These verses also have a poetic quality (as do 8:12b-13), perhaps from the Deuteronomic preacher himself, or perhaps his quotation from popular poetic sources.

The "springs" (v. 7) are literally "great deeps," a welling up of the primeval ocean — chaos turned by God into grace and blessing. What a contrast between the lush land of promise (vv. 7-9) and the bleak wilderness of current experience. The preacher-writer may well wax lyrical! The "iron" and "copper" (v. 9) are possibly part of the poetic license, as no deposit of these metals has been found in western Palestine in modern times. That God should "bless" humanity (e.g., Gen. 1:22; 9:1; 12:2; Deut. 1:11) has a clear (if astounding) meaning. But should humanity "bless" God (8:10)? To bless is to bestow gifts and well-being. Our blessing God means that we acknowledge the wealth of gifts God has lavished on us and that we then symbolically "return" them. That is, we gratefully dedicate our total selves, with all these gifts, to the service of God, who is their source.

8:11-16 Verses 11-16 are a recapitulation of vv. 1-10, with an overall loose chiastic structure. Verse 11 picks up vv. 1-2 and 6; v. 12 picks up v. 10; vv. 13-15 correspond to vv. 7-9; and v. 16 picks up vv. 3-5.

For the spiritual dangers implicit in prosperity, cf. the preaching of Amos (Amos 4:1-4; 5:10-15; 6:1-6; 8:4-8). Could the message of the eighth-century prophet have influenced the Deuteronomic school at this point?

The "water out of the flinty rock" is yet another case of a familiar old tradition (cf. Num. 20:1-11) which does not need repetition here. The bare allusion will suffice to alert the hearers/readers to its import. (We have met similar examples in Deut. 4:3; 6:16; 8:3.)

On God's "testing" of people, see 6:16. Here (8:16) the motive is explicitly stated: not the negative "humbling" which is demeaning and life-diminishing, but the positive attainment of God's "good," which is life-enhancing. Because God is the source of life and good, obedience to the torah which embodies God's mind and intention is the path to life and good, that is, the enjoyment of God's self. "Life" and "good" are constant themes throughout the whole body of Deuteronomic exhortation.

8:17-20 The "wealth" (Heb. *hayil*) referred to in vv. 17-18 includes not only goods and land, but strength (political and economic), status, capability, energy. The phrase "get wealth" (v. 18) is elsewhere translated "do valiantly" (1 Sam. 14:48, and frequently in the Psalms). God's gifts are thus seen not as handouts to the passive but as enabling for the initiative-takers. God's people should exert their full personal and community initiative, being gratefully aware throughout that the total wherewithal for the effort — material resources, imagination, planning, skills, energy — is in the last resort given by God.

This principle of "human initiative blossoming on the stock of divine grace" is recapitulated in the solemn warning that the human partner in "the everlasting covenant" may in fact "perish" through disobedience (Deut. 8:18b-20). The awesome paradox is that human refusal to obey can cancel the "everlasting promises." God's "choosing" is the great reality of Israel's existence, but "choosing" does not spell favoritism. By implication the former inhabitants of Palestine were expelled for their rejection of God's natural law (v. 20a). In like manner, Israel will be expelled if they reject the so much clearer presentation of God's intention available to them in the torah.

The use of "voice of Yahweh" (Heb. *qol YHWH*) as a synonym for torah is a significant key to the later stages of Deuteronomic thought. The phrase occurs seventeen times throughout Deuteronomy, in a relatively late stratum of the text.

In chapters 4 and 5 the *qol* is both thunder and presence-in-speech of Yahweh's self. The natural phenomenon becomes the vehicle for Yahweh's personal address to the people. It is real meeting with God and real listening to God that is being experienced and described. So when *torah* and *qol* are equated, the effect is to stress the existential quality of the torah. Its commandments and statutes are not "law" in an impersonal sense, but the vibrant address of the present God to God's attending people. Subsequent generations who were not present at the theophanic meeting on Horeb lose none of the immediacy of the divine encounter when they allow God to address them through the torah.

No Ground for Pride (9:1-6)

We have already met with the Anakim (9:1-2; see above on 1:28). "Against us are ranged superhuman powers, but on our side is the 'devouring fire'" (9:3). As we noted at 4:24, there is a close connection between Yahweh's "devouring fire" and Yahweh's "jealousy." God's jealousy at Israel's turning aside to other gods is precisely a reflection of God's love. The corollary to this is that the same fire which burns against Israel's apostasy also burns against those who seek to hinder God's purposes for Israel the chosen.

The picture of the indigenous population "being destroyed . . . subdued . . . driven out . . . perishing" (v. 3) in order to make room for Israel is difficult.

We have attempted a brief discussion of the issues at 7:1-6 and 12-15. The present context (9:4-6) indicates that the Deuteronomic editor himself is not altogether at ease with the "chauvinist" interpretation to which the doctrine of divine election is prone, and feels that an apologetic is called for. The editor's approach is to stress that the Canaanites were driven out not simply to make room for Israel but "because of their own 'wickedness'" (vv. 4b-5). As we have suggested at 8:17-20, they are regarded as having infringed natural law and (we may add) the norms of universal God awareness. Their worship involved behavior that is classed as ethically and religiously "revolting" to God: soothsaying and all the associated practices (18:9-14), idolatry (e.g., 7:25-26), child sacrifice (12:31; 18:10), transvestism with its possible sacral-prostitution implications (22:5), and Baalistic nature worship with its abuse of human sexuality to stimulate the fertility of field and flock (12:31; 20:18). These practices are "revolting" because they run directly counter to the essence and mode of God's self-revelation. We have seen how this is so in the case of idolatry (see above on 4:15-18) and of Baalistic nature worship (see above on 7:1-6). The other points will be covered when we come to the appropriate passages.

"Righteousness" (Heb. *tsedaqah,* 9:4, 5, 6) has already been linked with "obedience" (see above on 6:25). The word has a wide semantic range. Here it is rather close to its root meaning of "straight," "upright." Israel is not "upright" when measured against the norms which reflect the mind of the Creator–covenant God — either the universal norms by which humanity in general is judged or the specific norms given at Horeb. Left to Israel's unaided initiative, the covenant would be in abeyance and indeed Israel's humanity compromised.

Is the apologetic successful? Philosophically, it is probably not. But practically, as an incentive to awareness and gratitude, awe and conscientious obedience, it has strength.

MOSES' TESTIMONY (9:7–10:11)

This section forms a distinct unity; as in chs. 1–3, Moses speaks throughout in the first person. It is "testimony" in that it has Moses giving a firsthand account of his mediatorship. As such it could not be regarded as originating in the Deuteronomic preaching-exhortation, as is the case with most of the material in ch. 4 and 6:1–9:6. It is more likely to be the composition of a Deuteronomic literary artist at a comparatively late stage in the development of the Deuteronomic material.

Stylistic similarities between chs. 1–3 and 9:7–10:11 give rise to speculation as to whether the two originally formed a unity. Both sections draw heavily on the older tradition, to the point where some literary dependence on a written version of JE seems feasible.

The overriding theme is the stubbornness of the wilderness generation (and subsequent generations). One gets the impression of two strands in the material: either a short account of Israel's stubbornness (9:7b, 8, 22-24) with a vast expansion of the "Horeb" example, or a "Horeb" account with insert (9:22-24) offering parallel examples. The Horeb account in particular poses a striking contrast with ch. 5. There (ch. 5) the focus is on the awesome self-revelation of God and the people's reverent obedience. Here (chs. 9–10) it is the awesome wrath of God and the people's blatant apostasy.

The Apostasy at Horeb (9:7-29)

The story of the golden calf obviously draws on the tradition of Exodus, notably Exod. 32 (E). There is also probable influence from Num. 14:1-25 (J). There are, too, obvious and detailed parallels between Exod. 32 and 1 Kgs. 12:25-33. The latter tells how Jeroboam set up "calves" (cf. Exod. 32:4: "These [calves] are your gods") at Bethel and Dan to neutralize the influence of the Jerusalem temple on the citizens of his breakaway northern kingdom. These parallels have invited much scholarly research and reflection, the results of which are as follows:

(1) There seems to have indeed been a genuinely ancient tradition concerning the making of a bull image (derisively called "calf") in the wilderness period. Archaeology suggests that this may have represented a visible pedestal or mount for the unseen God (cf. Borobudur in Central Java, where Nandi the ox is represented as the mount of the Hindu god Shiva). From ancient times God bore the title *Abir* ("mighty one," or "bull") of Jacob (cf. Gen. 49:24).

(2) Jeroboam may have sought to "cash in" on this ancient tradition by fixing on the bull as an alternative and powerful symbol for the real presence of Yahweh in the north, over against the Jerusalem symbolism of temple and ark.

(3) In the setting of the Canaanite culture the bull symbol turned out to be dangerously compromising, through its proximity to the symbols used by the fertility cult. Hence it was judged idolatrous.

(4) Exodus 32 (E, the northern Israelite source) in its present form represents a polemic against the compromising Bethel cult

101

— a polemic in which the ancient tradition is used as a kind of incitement pamphlet.

This being its background, the use of the "golden calf" incident in Deut. 9 as an illustration of Israel's stubbornness is very telling. This is no mere excerpt from ancient history, but (before 722 B.C.) a bold indictment of the religious corruption that was provoking the wrath of Yahweh or (after 722) a solemn reminder of how apostasy had already provoked retribution, that is, in the fall of the northern kingdom.

Successive generations of rabbis regarded the golden calf apostasy as *the* sin par excellence, somehow symbolizing the essence of all human sin.

9:7-8   "Yahweh . . . was ready to destroy you" (v. 8). For the fuller tradition, cf. Exod. 32:9-14. The Deuteronomic author assumes that his audience is familiar with the details.

"Even at Horeb you provoked Yahweh." That apostasy penetrated and defiled the inner sanctum of the faith, the foundational theophany experience in which the covenant was born, is surely a shocking thing. How great the grace that persists against such odds!

The "wrath of God" (Deut. 9:7, 8) plays a prominent role throughout Deuteronomy and is expressed with a range of terminology: incensed (e.g., 1:37), heated (e.g., 6:15), "poisonous" (e.g., 9:19), boiling (3:26), at breaking point (1:34), annoyed (4:25). See the comments at 1:37; 4:21; 6:15.

In seeking to understand what for most people is a difficult concept, we should begin by reminding ourselves that this is anthropomorphic language. There is a quality in the divine nature which reminds of human anger but is nevertheless something else. Normal biblical usage categorizes human anger as "sinful," whereas divine wrath is "holy." What are the bases for this differentiation?

(1) Human anger is normally allied to hate (either momentary or sustained). But God is love, which implies complete absence of hatred toward any part of God's creation. God's anger, then, is aroused by the self-hate of the creature who embarks on a course inimical to the divine intention and therefore inimical to the creature's own true well-being.

(2) Human anger is also normally allied to frustration, a sense of being thwarted in our intentions by insuperable barriers of stubbornness and obtuseness. God's all-sufficiency is not exposed to such frustration.

(3) Human anger frequently arises when our false estimate of self-worth is impugned. But the love of God is genuinely "altruistic" or outflowing. There is nothing corresponding to human "egoism" in God's nature. Therefore the divine anger does not flow from such a source.

(4) Human anger is frequently linked with intimidation — a display of pyrotechnics aimed at achieving some negative end by blustering and force. But the wrath of God is always directed to positive ends, to the establishment of truth, right, holiness — that is, to the defense of God's own character.

In short, then, God's wrath is not in conflict with love and right. Indeed, "wrath" means God's fixed purpose to eliminate everything that is opposed to love and right.

9:9-11   On these verses, cf. Exod. 24:12a, 18b. "Forty days" (Deut. 9:9, 11) is frequently cited in the OT as the duration of a period of crisis, testing, waiting, and so forth (e.g., Gen. 7:4ff.; Exod. 24:18; Num. 13:25; 1 Sam. 17:16; 1 Kgs. 19:8; Jonah 3:4; cf. also Matt. 4:2; Acts 1:3).

Its origin may be sought in the old understanding that forty years is the span of a human being's vigor — from the beginning of adulthood at thirty years till death at seventy years. So "forty days" becomes a symbol of a "a complete and rounded block of time," "a person's total vigor" — "a period of decisive importance for the life-and-death issues of existence."

The fast which Moses observed (Deut. 9:9) is to concentrate his potential for the spiritual task (cf. Matt. 4:2: Jesus as the new Moses?). That the commandments were "written with the finger of God" (Deut. 9:10; cf. Exod. 31:18b) is not incompatible with the stones' having been prepared and inscribed by Moses. The term "finger of God" is clearly anthropomorphic language; its purpose is to insist that both the covenant and its official text are truly from God. The people may be confident of their standing, in that the covenant is grounded in Yahweh's own faithful decision.

103

But they must also be aware that the fence posts around the field of covenant grace are also immovable, having been put in place by God's self. Those therefore who place themselves outside the fence of God's commands have withdrawn from the covenant. "The words which Yahweh had spoken with you" (Deut. 9:10) implies that the Decalogue was addressed directly to the people, whereas the explication of it (the code) was mediated through Moses (cf. 5:25-27).

"The day of assembly" (9:10; cf. 10:4) would normally refer to the annual gathering of "all Israel" for celebration of festival. Its use here implies that the Horeb meeting was the definitive fountainhead and paradigm for all subsequent worship gatherings in Israel.

9:12-21   Deuteronomy 9:12 ("your people whom you have brought . . .") stresses both Moses' solidarity with his people and the people's imminent danger of losing their covenant status ("your people, not mine").

It is clear that besides the influence of Exod. 32 the text of Num. 14:22-23 has also helped to shape the Deuteronomic account at this point — even though Num. 14 deals not with the golden calf incident but with the people's rebelliousness at Kadesh. That material from other contexts is adapted to reinforce the "golden calf" narrative confirms our earlier impression that this is, for the Deuteronomic school, *the* sin par excellence.

"Let me alone!" (Deut. 9:14) implies that God is anticipating Moses' intercession for the people. God knows the heart of the servant; and (paradox!) it was for this heart that the servant was chosen. In the present text of Deut. 9, the detailed intercession is delayed till vv. 25ff.; in the earlier versions (Exod. 32:11-12; Num. 14:13ff.) it followed directly.

It is strange (Deut. 9:25; cf. v. 14) that Moses is more compassionate than the "compassionate God" (4:31). Yet the compassion and intercession of Moses are God-inspired. We are here once more in the love-wrath nexus (see above).

That the stone tablets were "broken before the people's eyes" (9:17) makes them witnesses that with the destruction of the text the covenant itself is cancelled. (There are ancient Near Eastern parallels for such covenant annulment). In the Exodus version the tablets are broken "at the foot of the mountain" (Exod. 32:19), the mountain therefore being invoked as witness.

"Prostrate . . . as before" (Deut. 9:18): the first meditation/waiting time (vv. 9, 11) was a gestation period out of which the text of the torah was born. Now with this dramatization of covenant annulment the period is recapitulated in intercession and vicarious repentance. The repetition highlights two things: the completeness of the annulment, so that the process as it were moves back to square one; and the complementarity of insight and repentance — forty days for the reception of revelation and forty days to "atone for" its rejection. The phrase "that time also" (v. 19) may refer back to vv. 9-11 (where God heeded Moses' longing for insight and granted the torah to him and his people). More likely the reference is to the rebelliousness at Kadesh (1:34-39; cf. Num. 14), where the intercessory role of Moses may be taken as implied, though not specifically stated in the text (see below on Deut. 9:23).

Moses' intercession for Aaron (v. 20) is unique to Deuteronomy. The corresponding Exodus reference (Exod. 32:21-24) is more forthright about Aaron's culpability and prevarication but offers no prayer. The Deuteronomic version has Moses (regarded perhaps as the fount and origin of prophecy) interceding for Aaron (representative of priesthood). Does this imply a call to the charismatic-prophetic element within Israel's later leadership to help renew the institutional?

9:22-24 The incidents at Taberah, Massah, and Kibroth-hattaavah are all well known from the older tradition (Num. 11:1-3; Exod. 17:1-7; Num. 11:4-13). Massah has already been referred to at Deut. 6:16, and Kadesh-barnea at 1:19-33. Concerning the latter, we have noted above (9:12ff.) that the material which in the older tradition applied to Kadesh has been taken over and incorporated into the Deuteronomic account of the "golden calf" apostasy.

"Rebellious from the day that I [first] knew you" (v. 24) may refer to the incident related in Exod. 2:13ff., or perhaps that of Exod. 5:21. The LXX and Samaritan texts, however, read: "since the day Yahweh first knew you." This would then refer to Yahweh's first intervention (through Moses and Aaron) to begin bringing about "Israel's" release from Egypt (Exod. 5:21-22).

9:25-29 Throughout the OT intercession is stressed as a principal prophetic task: Abraham (Gen. 18:23-32), Moses (e.g., Exod. 32:11-14), Samuel (1 Sam. 8:6-9, 21, 22), Elijah (1 Kgs. 18:36-39), Daniel (Dan. 6:10-11). Its essential core is to "remind" God of God's own nature and promises. Hence we have the opening gambit (Deut. 9:26), *"Your* people, LORD!" — in response to v. 12, "Your people, Moses." "Mine, LORD, in my capacity as your servant. But in the last resort, yours."

Previously (see above on 7:18-21) the people have been called to "remember." Now, boldly, Yahweh is asked to "remember." Again, remembering is not bare recall: when God "remembers," God acts — decisively and savingly on behalf of those to whom God has made promises (Gen. 8:1; 9:15-16; 19:29; Lev. 26:42; Ps. 105:8-9).

The prayer reminds God (Deut. 9:26, 29) of the great evangelical introduction to the Decalogue: "I am the LORD your God, who brought you out of the land of Egypt" (5:6). God has set the divine name at stake in the eyes of surrounding nations: God the all-powerful, God the all-loving. Both names are discredited if rebelliousness succeeds in turning love into hate (9:28). God surely needs no "reminding." But the prayer is powerful, as a pledge of the servant's bold intimacy and utter involvement in the divine purpose. Mysteriously, the intimacy and involvement of human beings do constitute resources by means of which the divine purpose comes to fruition.

Moses' historic intercession undoubtedly spoke powerfully to the Exile generation which the later Deuteronomists were addressing. God's evident rejection of the covenant people was undoubtedly the occasion for deep heart-searching among the exiles: Are the promises cancelled? Has Yahweh's power waned? Does Yahweh not care that the pagan nations draw blasphemous conclusions from Jerusalem's overthrow? This boldness in "reminding" God of God's own nature is an enduring characteristic of biblical faith and intercession (Gen. 18:25b; cf. also Ezek. 36:22-23; Isa. 43:25; Ps. 25:11).

A Fresh Text of the Decalogue (10:1-5)

The rather abrupt and awkward transition from Deut. 9:29 to 10:1 is evidence for a redaction process behind the finished text as we have it. Did 10:1 originally link with 9:21? Or do 10:1-5 and 6-9 constitute two interpolations between the intercession and the final summary?

Scholars have long noted that no JE account survives in the finished text regarding the construction of the covenant box (or ark). Some have speculated that such an account did once stand between Exod. 33:6 and 7 but was eliminated by the Priestly redactors in favor of their own more elaborate version (Exod. 25:10-22; 37:1-9). It could well be that Deut. 10:1-5 reflects the lost JE narrative at this point. The traditions surrounding the origins of the ark (Heb. *aron*) are extremely complicated. The *aron* was undoubtedly ancient. Did it even, in fact, pre-date Moses? That is, was it part of the inheritance of one of the ancient tribes which eventually came together as "Israel"; and did it crystallize on to the Mosaic core as tradition unified and developed?

According to the old pre-Deuteronomic sources, the important functions of the ark were to:

- Guide Israel's journey (Num. 10:33-34);
- Galvanize and empower for battle (Num. 10:35-36; Josh. 3:14-17, etc.; 2 Sam. 11:11);
- Serve as a focus for worship (1 Sam. 3:3);
- Symbolize and guarantee Israel's political unity (1 Sam. 6:1– 7:1; 2 Sam. 6:1-23);
- Serve as Yahweh's throne (Jer. 3:16).

In summary, the ark represented and expressed the presence of Yahweh among the people, to guide, protect, and receive their loyal worship.

The outstanding feature of the Deuteronomic ark tradition is that the undoubted "mystical" aspects of the earlier ark concept are subjected to thoroughgoing "demythologizing." For the Deuteronomic school, the ark is purely and simply a receptacle for the text of the torah — that and nothing more. The primary guarantee of God's presence and help is not some ancient symbol but the torah itself, summarized in the Decalogue and continuingly vibrant with the echo of God's voice. This deliberate highlighting of "torah" makes it clear that torah is not to be regarded as bare text, but as ever-effective vehicle for the living word. A comparison of Deut. 9:9-10 (giving of the original copy of the Decalogue) and 10:1-5 (giving of the fresh copy) shows that the two accounts are closely parallel. This is to stress that Israel's condition and status are completely restored after their apostasy. The reissue of the Decalogue is proof of God's grace and forgiveness.

"*He* wrote on the tablets" (v. 4) means that God wrote exactly as before (9:10). Likewise as regards content, the fresh text is (implicitly) the same Decalogue as 5:6-21. Contrast here the Exodus version, where the fresh tablets are inscribed, not with the Ethical Decalogue, but with the Ritual Decalogue (see the discussion on 5:6-22, 68-70).

"And there they are" (10:5). Is the phrase addressed to the Mosaic/wilderness generation or to subsequent generations worshipping at the festival? Cf. the similar phrase at 1 Kgs. 8:8, which more naturally refers to the preacher's generation than to Solomon's. The voice of Moses reverberates in the contemporary scene.

Fragment of Israel's Wilderness Itinerary (10:6-7)

This itinerary fragment breaks the continuity of Moses' speech. It has obvious connections with the itinerary in Num. 33:30-33, but the relationship is difficult to determine. The place names can be matched, but the order is different. Some scholars seek to harmonize the lists by equating Moserah (Deut. 10:6) with Mt. Hor (Num. 33:37-39) as the place where Aaron died and then regarding Deut. 10:7 as the second leg of the journey, continuing on from Num. 33:33-38. Others attempt to solve the discrepancy by rearranging the order of verses in Num. 33.

Theologically the Deuteronomic writer seems to be making two points:

(1) Deut. 10:6-7 balances 9:22-24. There is nothing in the tradition to suggest that Israel was rebellious at Bene-jaakan, Moserah, Gudgodah, or Jotbathah. The impression we are meant

to receive is that grace and intercession have prevailed. Previous rebelliousness is left behind. Yahweh forgives and leads Israel forward from Kadesh to Jotbathah and (implicitly) to Canaan (cf. 10:11).

(2) More specifically, Moses' intercession for Aaron (9:20) is also successful, for Aaron did not die at the time of the apostasy, but only later. That his son became his successor (10:6) is the seal on God's forgiveness of Aaron.

Appointment of the Levites (10:8-9)

Here the appointment of the Levites is a continuation from the making of the ark. Their task consists largely in caring for the ark (cf. 31:9), though they also "minister" (cf. 18:1-8) and "bless" (cf. 21:5).

In 33:8-10 the Levites' function is described somewhat differently: to handle the *Urim* and *Thummin* (sacred dice, perhaps connected with giving *mishpat* or legal decisions), teaching torah, and burning incense (cultic duties).

Putting the two prescriptions (Deut. 10 and 33) together, we can conclude that to "serve the ark" is in effect to serve/teach the torah, the summary of which rests in the ark.

To "bless in God's name" (cf. "put God's name upon the people," Num. 6:27) implies an intimate relation with Yahweh and with the power inherent in Yahweh's name — a position therefore of great honor and privilege, and great responsibility.

The material in the older source which parallels Deut. 10:8-9 is found in Exod. 32:25-29. This passage contains a strong criticism of Aaron and can be read as a northern Israelite assertion of the rights of the levitical priesthood over against the Aaronic. If this is so, it is noteworthy that in Deut. 9:20; 10:6b, 8-9, the tension between "Aaron" and "Levi" is played down — as part of the process of accommodating the Deuteronomic tradition to the Jerusalem setting. (Later strands, Ezekiel [Ezek. 40–48] and P [Exod. 28–29; Num. 3–4], draw sharp distinctions and demote the Levites to the status of assistants to the Aaronic priesthood.)

We have already noted (Introduction, 13-14) Deuteronomy's

special interest in the welfare of the Levites. Cf. also Deut. 12:12; 14:27, 29; 18:1. That "Yahweh is the Levite's inheritance" (10:9) refers to their right to a share in the sacrificial offerings, that is, to "eat from Yahweh's table."

Moses, Mediator and Pioneer (10:10-11)

These verses recapitulate the basic thrusts of Moses' testimony, namely, God's horror at apostasy and the reality of God's forgiveness.

Verse 10 links back to 9:29 (following the two insertions in 10:1-9), and virtually repeats the content of 9:9 and 25. Deuteronomy 10:11 reassures that God's ancient promises stand firm in spite of the people's apostasy.

LET ISRAEL BE GRATEFULLY OBEDIENT (10:12–11:1)

The section is built from fragments or reminiscences of covenant festival preaching around the theme of loyalty to the covenant's basic principle.

10:12-13 The summarizing "and now" (v. 12; cf. 4:1) leads on to a statement of the twin obligations: to be aware ("fear," "love") and to obey ("walk," "serve"). The formulation is reminiscent of Mic. 6:8. Its tone suggests that this obligation is not some high-flown idealism beyond human attainment, but a practical possibility (cf. Deut. 30:11-14, ". . . you *can* do it").

To "serve God" (Heb. *'abad;* cf. also "serve other gods," e.g., 5:9) is both to worship and to obey; the one cannot be separated from the other. The same combination is of course implicit in our English usage: "a service of worship."

10:14-15 There is no reference in 10:14 to the stages of heaven such as we find in later pseudepigrapha ("seven heavens") and 2 Cor. 12:2 ("third heaven"). Rather, the language is poetic: "all the contents of heaven and earth are God's creation and possession." Yet (wonder of wonders!) out of all this incalculable array of wealth, God's heart was "attracted" (see above on Deut. 7:7) to Israel — to us! This is a powerful statement of the uncaused electing grace of God!

10:16-19   These verses, expressed in the grammatical plural, are in a grammatically singular setting — which may mean that they are a concretizing and reinforcing addition to the overall passage: "Circumcise . . . your heart" (10:16).

Circumcision is an ancient custom, widely though not exclusively practiced among Semitic peoples. It seems originally to have had two basic references: as a sign of male readiness and preparation for marriage (cf. Exod. 4:24-26) and as a ceremonial act initiating adult males into full membership in their tribe — in Israel's case, membership in the people of God (Gen. 17:11).

On this basis, the term "circumcise" acquires a range of figurative meanings in the OT:

- "Uncircumcised lips" (Exod. 6:12, 29): a youth not yet mature and forcefully convincing in speech.
- "Uncircumcised trees" (Lev. 19:23 MT): for three years the young tree is like a callow youth, not yet mature for adult or "legitimate" fruiting.
- "Uncircumcised ears" (Jer. 6:10): ears not mature to "hear," because not attuned by awareness of God's goodness.
- "Uncircumcised heart": attitude which is hard like dry ground (Jer. 4:3-4), unbending (Lev. 26:41), stiff-necked and stubborn (Deut. 10:16).

In contrast, the "circumcised heart" is aware and receptive of God's grace, sensitive to the privilege of membership in God's people, and "fruitful" in the God-like qualities of compassion which that membership involves.

God is a great and fearsome warrior (v. 17). This is language from the vocabulary of the "Yahweh's war" tradition, adapted now to the concern for justice. Yahweh's adversary here is not the Canaanites, but greed, corruption, and manipulation. Verses 17b-19 recall the "mirror for judges" in 1:16-18 (see above, 34). Here as there, the judge's responsibilities are grounded in the

111

Judgehood and character of God (1:17: "the judgment is God's"), whom he is to imitate. (See further on 16:19.)

The fatherless, widows, and sojourners were the three groups typically at risk in ancient society. For that reason Yahweh becomes their personal protector. On the sojourner (Heb. *ger*), see Deut. 1:16ff.

The "justice" which Yahweh executes (10:18) is literally *mishpat* (see above on 4:1). God is not "partial" to the little people (1:17) — as if there were some romantic plus in being poor or threatened. But God is the firm defender of their rights and full human dignity. This is not favoritism but justice, right. On our part, practical love for the vulnerable (10:19) is simply a matter of passing on or reflecting what we ourselves have experienced at the hand of God (cf. 5:15). As God gives us our dignity, so we make ourselves available as instruments for giving them theirs.

10:20–11:1   On the "fear of God" (10:20), see 6:10-15. It is noteworthy that in the present context, fear of God is defined in terms of practical compassion for the vulnerable (10:16-19). Fearing, loving, cleaving (4:4), and pledging with loyalty and integrity (6:13) are interdependent aspects of one common response to God. "God is your praise" (10:21). God is known through deeds and interventions, which are undetachable from God's self. It is not merely God's deeds but God's self which becomes the focus for our gratitude and thankfulness. Each succeeding generation can say, "Our eyes have seen Yahweh in action" (v. 21; cf. 3:23), as the foundation events of the faith are re-presented in the liturgy. Thus the initial meeting with God becomes a mirror in which contemporary experience becomes clear.

On 10:22 see 1:10. Since the faithfulness of God spans past generations, it may be trusted to span the generations to come — provided God's people are faithful for their part (11:1). "Charge" is a new term for torah. It means literally "keeping": "Keep carefully what God has entrusted to your keeping" — by way of insight, God-awareness, guideline, example. We "keep" by practicing; we lose by neglecting.

MORE FRAGMENTS OF
FESTIVAL PREACHING (11:2-32)

If 10:12–11:1 comprises preaching fragments on the theme of loyalty to the covenant's basic stipulations, 11:2-32 picks up other aspects of the covenant treaty:

- The previous history of the Great King's dealings with his people (vv. 2-7);
- Inventory of the subject people's territory (vv. 10-11);
- Covenant sanctions, blessing and curse (vv. 16-17, 22-25, 26-31).

Seemingly it was customary that preachers at the festival should base their exhortation on some specific part of the covenant text. What we have here, then, are liturgical texts which have been used as texts for sermons.

The Greatness of Yahweh (11:2-7)

The re-presenting or contemporizing of God's action which we noted in 10:21 forms the setting of this section: "I am not speaking to your children (but to *you*)" (11:2); "*your* eyes have seen" (v. 7). The incidents which the congregation are invited to relive are not recounted in detail. Since they are well known, the bare allusion is sufficient for recall. The accent is to fall rather on the practical contemporary application of the relived experience.

In this passage we again (cf. 7:1-6, 12-16; 9:1-6) encounter the notion of God's directly wreaking disaster on Israel's opponents, while lavishing protection on "the faithful." How are we to respond to this imputing of calamity to God? We may say that, at base, the Creator God is in final control of the creation, so that no epidemic, plague, eclipse, tidal wave, or earthquake is in the last resort entirely fortuitous. We may go further and express the conviction that a moral order in creation works for the establishment of whatever harmonizes with the Creator's purpose and the undermining of whatever does not (cf. Judg. 5:20). But to go still further and presume to trace the detailed outworking of the principle in the lives and destinies of ourselves and others is extremely hazardous, leading almost inevitably to arrogance and judgmentalism. It has to be acknowledged that the Deuteronomist here has not entirely escaped the pitfall. Nevertheless, the positive emphases which the examples are made to serve are still very powerful. In a time of deep crisis, the renewed awareness of who God is (mediated through the recital of God's reputed deeds) is a source of strong encouragement. God's people may misread the significance of individual details encountered along the road. Still, there is a road that is being travelled. It had a recognizable starting point, and the people are now at a (more or less) recognizable point in relation to that beginning. The journey as such is witness to the undeniable reality of guidance and enablement: how else would they be where they now are? This awareness then becomes a powerful incentive to recommitment and reaffirmation of faith for the next leg of the journey.

A fuller account of the Dathan-and-Abiram rebellion is found in Num. 16:1b-2a, 12-15, 25-26, 27b-32a, 33-34. In Numbers the story is interwoven with two other "rebellion" strands to form a composite whole. In one of these, Korah is the leader of 250 rebels (Num. 16:2) who oppose Moses' and Aaron's "arrogant" claim to spiritual authority (v. 3). In the other strand, Korah leads the Levites (v. 8) in claiming priestly authority over against Aaron (vv. 10-11).

For the Deuteronomic writer, God's drastic dealings with Dathan and Abiram are an example of the divine "discipline" (Heb. *musar*) referred to in Deut. 11:2. The verbal form of the word occurs at 4:36 (see above). One could claim that there is an apologetic note in its use here: the fate of Dathan and Abiram is not vindictive but deterrent in intention.

Obedience Brings Blessing (11:8-9)

These bridging verses link the "previous history" (11:2-7) with the "inventory of the land" (vv. 10-15).

Is there in v. 9b a conscious contrasting reference to Num. 16:13, where Dathan and Abiram complain, "You have brought us up out of a land flowing with milk and honey (Egypt), to kill us in the wilderness"? Egypt was only seeming prosperity; in fact it was slavery. Canaan genuinely flows with milk and honey because it is space for the exercise of God-given freedom-in-obedience.

Inventory of the Land (11:10-15)

Grammatically this section is a mixture of singular and plural forms. The basic stratum in the singular has presumably been subjected to retouching in the plural.

The aim of this "inventory" is to arouse a sense of thankfulness and to underscore the connection between "blessing" and "obedience." The processes of both history and nature are in God's control and yield blessing or otherwise at God's behest.

The contrast between the measured fertility of Egypt and the abundant fertility of Palestine has a touch of theological exaggeration about it. An objective comparison of the Nile Valley with Ephraim (the area first occupied by Israel) would scarcely support the superiority of the latter. However, the purpose is not literal topographical comparison, but thanksgiving for nationhood, destiny under God, freedom and space to be. The contrast between mechanical irrigation (treading the waterwheel? manipulating small earthen dams with the feet?) and natural irrigation symbolizes the limitations of human effort over against the limitlessness of divine grace. Hills and valleys (Deut. 11:11) are not amenable to artificial irrigation, but neither need they be, for God's care provides rain (vv. 11, 14), brooks, fountains, and springs (8:7). The "care" of God for the land is expressed by the Hebrew term *darash* — the care of the scholar lovingly poring over the sacred text or the researcher examining a case conscientiously, the care that counts the hairs of the head and keeps an exact inventory of the sparrows (Luke 12:6-7). Harvest, which marks the end of the year and its beginning, is the supreme physical manifestation of God's loving care for land and people (Deut. 11:12).

The phrase "hear (RSV 'obey') my commandments" (v. 13; cf. 28:13) is relatively rare. There is an echo of Horeb in it: "Hear the voice of the God whom you met and know." Cf. also the echo of the Shema (6:4-5): "Love with all the heart." Hear, serve, and love are triple aspects of one attitude. "The early and later rains" (11:14), which are essential for the maturing of the harvest, become special symbols of God's providing grace (cf. Ezek. 34:26). The early rains fall in October-November, a few weeks after the New Year/harvest, softening for ploughing and sowing the land baked hard by the dry season (June-Sept.). In Palestine 15 percent of the annual rainfall occurs October-November. The later rains (about 5 percent of the annual total) come during April and early May, and fill out the maturing grain.

Thus the early and later rains mark the beginning and end of the rainy season proper, December-March.

Success to the Obedient (11:16-25)

This preaching fragment centers on the blessing-curse sections of the covenant formulation. In general it is in the grammatical plural. Deuteronomy 11:18-20 may constitute an insert; they repeat former (obviously well-known) material (cf. 6:6-9) and incorporate traditional phrases expressed in the singular.

The "silly," "simpleton" heart (11:16; cf. Hos. 7:11; Job 5:2) is like that of the gullible village lad who falls easy prey to the city slicker. The lie that baits the trap is that natural fertility and prosperity are the gifts of the Baals (Deut. 11:16) and not of Yahweh (v. 17), so that it is the Baals who deserve worship. In fact, the fertility-producing rains are part of the covenant blessing given by the Great King Yahweh to the covenant people. If the people turn aside from their loyalty, they break the covenant, forfeit its blessings, and incur disaster (v. 17). The giving and withholding of rain are also mentioned among the covenant sanctions at 28:12, 24.

"As long as the heavens are above the earth" (11:21) virtually means "forever." In general "the heavens" are symbolic of all that is enduring. With rare exceptions (e.g., Ps. 102:25-26), it is only with the rise of apocalyptic that heaven's passing away is seriously considered (cf. 2 Pet. 3:10, 12; Rev. 6:14).

Deuteronomy 11:23 rings the changes on the Hebrew root *yarash* (literally, "inherit"; see above on 2:24): "Yahweh will cause these nations to yield their inheritance to you and you will become the inheritors of nations. . . ." Implicit in the terminology is the conviction that the land is Yahweh's and that the rights of occupation and inheritance are Yahweh's to dispose.

Originally a literal treading of the boundaries was a way of claiming ownership over a specific parcel of land (11:24). Subsequently the literal treading gave way to a symbolic passing of the claimant's sandal around the boundaries (cf. Ruth 4:7-8; Ps. 60:8).

Theologically, the phrase speaks of the necessity for active participation in grace. The land is Yahweh's gift; nevertheless, it must be energetically claimed, tramped over hectare by hectare. Only so does the promised become actual possession.

The limits noted in Deut. 11:24b (cf. 1:7) are the ideal boundaries, approximating those achieved under King David and upheld as the ideal throughout subsequent generations.

The numinous fear (11:25), as we have noted on 2:25, is part of the weaponry of "Yahweh's war."

Blessing and Curse (11:26-32)

This further example of preaching on the covenant sanctions forms a kind of "provisional conclusion," rounding off the block of material in Deut. 5–11. The more definitive conclusion, Deut. 28, will round off the whole Deuteronomic exposition of Yahweh's torah.

The neat assumption (11:27-28) that "hearing the commandments" (cf. v. 13) brings blessing while failure to hear brings curse is rather simplistic, that is, if blessing and curse are to be interpreted in material terms.

The farmer is right in thankfully acknowledging rain and fruitful seasons as God's blessing. But is drought necessarily the sign of God's disapproval and rebuke (cf. Hab. 3:17-18)? The Bible, in fact, hints that sometimes it is precisely faithfulness to God that triggers off misfortune and suffering (Ps. 44:17, 22). Nor, on the other hand, does the fact of success infallibly indicate God's approval (Ps. 73:3-5).

This inherent unpredictability is an essential component of the situation where faith operates. If obedience guaranteed success, then "faith" would be degraded to a mere commercial contract.

Nevertheless, the primary thrust of Deut. 11:26-28 is also basic to faith: ultimately, Yahweh's torah is life, and obedience to the torah has the fragrance of life upon it. To have begun building up a repertoire of experience which confirms this is to "know" Yahweh (cf. v. 28).

Details of the covenant ritual of Mts. Gerizim and Ebal are discussed in ch. 27. Here it is the location of the two mountains that is in question. The well-known Gerizim and Ebal are situated about 10 km. (6 mi.) SE of Samaria in central Palestine. Ebal is on the north (left-hand side) of the town of Shechem, and Gerizim on the south (right).

According to the ancient tradition, Shechem was the first center of Yahwism in Palestine, and it is likely that from the beginning Gerizim and Ebal had important significance in the Shechem covenant renewal ceremonies. Deuteronomy 11:30a is accurate: the Syria-Egypt highway does pass through central Palestine, to the east of Shechem. So from the perspective of the speaker in the plains of Moab (1:5), Gerizim and Ebal are "behind" (i.e., west of) the highway.

The nearby oak of Moreh (11:30) can be traced even further back into the ancient past. It is associated with the patriarchs Abraham (Gen. 12:6-7) and Jacob (Gen. 35:4) and is probably referred to in Judg. 9:6 and Josh. 24:26. The name "Moreh" means "giver of *torah*" (*torah* is directive, guide, signpost). From Josh. 24:26, one gains the impression that in Canaanite (pre-Israelite) times the oak was a sacred place where oracles were sought and received, and that this Canaanite usage was then incorporated into the Yahwistic shrine.

Gilgal (Deut. 11:30) means "circle (of stones)" — the reference being to a Canaanite sacred enclosure — and was probably applied to several sites in Palestine. If the Gilgal intended here is the well-known Hebrew shrine of Josh. 5, and so forth, then we need to note that its location is in fact 45 km. (28 mi.) SE of Shechem, between Jericho and the Jordan River. The description which places it "in the Arabah" (Deut. 11:30) certainly fits this identification.

If this is so, then the question arises as to why Shechem and Gilgal are linked in this way. It would seem that the Deuteronomic redactor has deliberately juxtaposed the two in order to emphasize that in the formative period of the land settlement northern (Shechem) and southern (Gilgal) shrines each had an important role.

Furthermore, it may be that the facts of history justify his harmonizing intention. Aspects of the Gilgal tradition (e.g., circumcision) may very well have been incorporated into the Shechem cultus. Likewise there are indications that "Shechem" (i.e., aspects of the Shechem blessing-and-cursing ritual) may have traveled south and been incorporated into Gilgal or Bethel worship patterns (cf. Josh. 8:33-34). This would mean that "Gerizim" and "Ebal" were eventually not simply geographical locations but symbolic terms for "blessing" and "cursing" in the liturgical context, whether at Shechem, Gilgal, or elsewhere. To "set" the blessing and curse on the mountains (Deut. 11:29) may have meant calling upon them, as natural sentinels, to witness to God's covenant sanctions.

THE COVENANT CODE:
BODY OF THE SECOND
SPEECH (PART II)
Deuteronomy 12:1–26:15

We have already noted in the Introduction (4-7) that there is a close connection between the Deuteronomic code and the Book of the Covenant in Exodus (Exod. 20:23–23:33) — so much so indeed that the Deuteronomic code may fitly be described as an expansion of the Book of the Covenant.

We also noted that many sentences of both the Deuteronomic code and the Book of the Covenant are similar to provisions in ancient Near Eastern legal texts. This prompts us to ask how the material entered the Yahwistic tradition. Was it part of "Israel's" ancient Semitic heritage from Abrahamic and pre-Abrahamic times? Or was it in large measure borrowed from Canaanite neighbors after Israel entered Palestine? The number and closeness of the parallels suggest that the latter was the case.

Did the Deuteronomic school borrow directly from Semitic and Canaanite sources, or indirectly through the Book of the Covenant? If they did borrow from Canaanite-Semitic sources, was it by way of written or oral tradition?

Of theological interest, all the legal material which accrued to Israel through what must have been a long and complicated process was linked with the name of Moses and presented as part of the directives revealed by Yahweh to him on Mt. Horeb. In other words:

(1) Yahweh God of Israel is represented as revealing the divine will to the whole human race. Under Yahweh's inspiration each nation has formulated laws as individual and collective guidelines for its own society. Moreover, every groping after healthy life-ordering principles is to be seen as bestowed by Yahweh, as part of a universal and general revelation.

(2) This universal general revelation comes to its crystallization point at Horeb. In that definitive revealing of Yahweh's intention, all general revelation is implicit and takes its meaning from there. So, from this perspective the claim that all Israel's laws, borrowed or otherwise, were given at Horeb on the one definitive occasion is not a falsification or distortion of historical fact, but a formulation of deep theological insight (a telescoping of the historical process).

As a preliminary step in understanding the dynamics of the Deuteronomic code, it will be helpful to look in a little more detail at the structure of the Book of the Covenant.

STRUCTURE OF THE BOOK OF THE COVENANT

(1) In the introduction to the Decalogue (5:6-22) we mentioned that in the JE tradition there are two claimants to the position of the "ten sentences delivered to Moses": the so-called Ethical (Exod. 20:2-17) and Ritual (Exod. 34:14, 17-26) Decalogues. Further, the JE tradition states that apart from these two Decalogues, Yahweh also provided a small code to be the foundation text of the Yahweh-Israel covenant, the "Book of the Covenant." It is noteworthy that the Book of the Covenant itself also includes a version of the Ritual Decalogue (i.e., Exod. 20:23; 22:29b, 30a; 23:12-19). It is this Ritual Decalogue which in fact forms the framework of the Book of the Covenant.

(It must be acknowledged that in its present versions the Ritual Decalogue consists not of ten but of thirteen sentences. Various attempts have been made to explain how the presumed expansion took place, none of which is entirely satisfactory. Perhaps the most persuasive is that, in the outline below, V is an insert, X-XI were originally one, and XII-XIII likewise). The following comparative table shows the connections between Ritual Decalogue, the Book of the Covenant, and the Deuteronomic code.

	Sentence	Book of the Covenant	Ritual Decalogue	Deuteronomic Code
I.	Make no image	Exod. 20:23	Exod. 34:17	Deut. 5:8-10
II.	Firstborn	Exod. 22:29b-30	Exod. 34:19-20a,b	Deut. 15:19-23
III.	Sabbath	Exod. 23:12	Exod. 34:21	Deut. 5:12-15
IV.	No other gods	Exod. 23:13	Exod. 34:14	Deut. 5:7
V.	Be present three times a year	Exod. 23:14, 17	Exod. 34:23-24	Deut. 16:16a,b
VI.	Unleavened bread	Exod. 23:15 a,b	Exod. 34:18	Deut. 16:1-8
VII.	Don't come empty-handed	Exod. 23:15c	Exod. 34:20c	Deut. 16:16c
VIII.	Feast of Weeks	Exod. 23:16a	Exod. 34:22a	Deut. 16:9-12
IX.	Feast of In-gathering	Exod. 23:16b	Exod. 34:22b	Deut. 16:13-15
X.	Passover without leaven	Exod. 23:18a	Exod. 34:25a	Deut. 16:1-8
XI.	Passover meat not to be kept	Exod. 23:18b	Exod. 34:25b	Deut. 16:1-8
XII.	Firstfruits offering	Exod. 23:19a	Exod. 34:26a	Deut. 26:1-15
XIII.	Do not boil a kid in its mother's milk	Exod. 23:19b	Exod. 34:26b	Deut. 14:21b

It is interesting that this material has no real parallels in ancient Near Eastern codes.

(2) The second ingredient in the Book of the Covenant is a chain of ritual laws separate from the Ritual Decalogue. (Presumably they have crystallized around the Ritual Decalogue in the process of development.) They are as follows:

Sentence	Book of the Covenant	Deuteronomic Code
1. The altar where God's name is placed	Exod. 20:24	Deut. 12:5, 11, 21; 14:23; 16:2, 6, 11; 26:2
2. Soothsaying prohibited	Exod. 22:18	Deut. 18:9-14
3. Bestiality prohibited	Exod. 22:19	Deut. 27:21
4. Do not curse God	Exod. 22:28	(Not mentioned)

Of these, all but the first (1) have parallels in ancient Near Eastern codes.

(3) The Book of the Covenant includes civil law. The following provisions are paralleled in the Deuteronomic code:

Sentence	Book of the Covenant	Deuteronomic Code
1. Redemption of slaves	Exod. 21:1-11	Deut. 15:12-18
2. Person beaten to death	Exod. 21:12	Deut. 5:17
3. Cities of refuge	Exod. 21:13-14	Deut. 19:1-13
4. Violence against parents	Exod. 21:15, 17	Deut. 21:18-21
5. Kidnapping	Exod. 21:16	Deut. 5:19; 24:7
6. Seducing a virgin	Exod. 22:16-17	Deut. 22:28-29
7. Giving false testimony	Exod. 23:1-2, 7	Deut. 5:20; 19:15-21
8. Partiality in the legal process	Exod. 23:3, 6	Deut. 1:16-18
9. Mirror for judges	Exod. 23:6-8	Deut. 16:18-20
10. Taking bribes	Exod. 23:8	Deut. 16:19b

All but the third sentence are paralleled in the ancient Near Eastern codes.

The following passages of the Book of the Covenant are not found in the Deuteronomic code (they all have ancient Near Eastern parallels): Exod. 21:18-19, 22-32, 35-36; 22:1-9, 13.

(4) The Book of the Covenant contains exhortations to compassion:

123

Sentence	Book of the Covenant	Deuteronomic Code
1. Compassion for so- journers, orphans, widows	Exod. 22:21-24 (cf. 23:9)	Deut. 10:18
2. Usury	Exod. 22:25	Deut. 23:19-20
3. Taking in pawn	Exod. 22:26-27	Deut. 24:6, 10-13
4. Strayed ox	Exod. 23:4-5	Deut. 22:1-4

Of these, only the fourth has an ancient Near Eastern parallel.

(5) Finally, the Book of the Covenant closes with exhortation, urging the covenant people to be sensitive and obedient to God's leading (Exod. 23:2-33). It may be fairly claimed that the whole of Deut. 1–12 parallels this section.

In summary, we may say that the Ritual Decalogue forms the framework of the Book of the Covenant. Other ritual provisions then crystallized onto this core. By further development, blocks of civil law and exhortations to compassion were sandwiched in at certain points. Diagrammatically the structure looks like this:

Exod. 20:22	Prologue
Exod. 20:23	Ritual Decalogue
Exod. 20:24-26	Ritual laws
Exod. 21:18–22:15	Civil laws
Exod. 22:16-19	Civil laws
Exod. 22:20	Ritual law
Exod. 22:21-27	Exhortation to compassion
Exod. 22:28-31	Ritual law
Exod. 23:1-8	Civil laws
Exod. 23:9	Exhortation to compassion
Exod. 23:10-11	Ritual law
Exod. 23:12-19	Ritual Decalogue
Exod. 23:20-33	Epilogue

Apart from the large block of civil law (Exod. 21:18–22:15), which is probably a relatively late insertion into the Book of the Covenant, all but four short sentences of the Book of the Covenant (Exod. 20:24, 26; 22:28a, 28b) are paralleled in the Deuteronomic code.

PREFACE TO THE DEUTERONOMIC CODE (12:1-28)

It is repeatedly stressed throughout Deut. 12 that Israel's sacrifices are to be offered only "in the place where Yahweh has chosen to set his name" (vv. 5, 11, 14, 18, 21, 26). This terminology obviously springs from the "altar law" of Exod. 20:24: "An altar of earth you shall make for me. . . . In every place where I cause my name to be remembered I will come to you. . . ." Exodus 20:24 does not imply that there is to be only one legitimate shrine for the whole country. Rather, altars are to be built at places where God's self is revealed, in the hope that succeeding generations will continue to encounter God at these spots hallowed by association.

Deuteronomy 12 is not a uniform composition, but the end product of a long development process. During the process the thought of Exod. 20:24 has undergone a series of applications. The primary aim of Deut. 12 as a whole is to safeguard the purity of Yahwistic worship, that is, to avoid the contamination of pagan accretions which would obscure the understanding of Yahweh's nature. With that in mind, the people are forbidden to take over former Canaanite places of sacrifice and adapt them to the worship of Yahweh. Rather, they are to worship only in the place(s) where Yahweh has specifically revealed Yahweh's self.

At the end of the process, the "chosen place" is declared to be a single site alone, namely, the Jerusalem temple. (At a penultimate stage, however, the "single site" may have referred to some other [northern] shrine.)

We noted in the Introduction (18) that the insistence on one only central place of worship was a feature of Deuteronomy (cf. 12:1-28; 14:22-29; 15:19-23; 16:1-17; 17:8-13; 18:1-8; 19:1-13). It needs to be underlined, however, that centralization is not an end in itself but a means to an end. The primary concern is for the purity of Yahweh's worship.

It is noteworthy that substantial sections of the Deuteronomic code betray no knowledge of this stress on the sole validity of the Jerusalem temple (e.g., 27:5-6). This implies that the "centralization" emphasis in its finished form belongs to the later strata of the Deuteronomic code.

A Single Place of Worship (12:1-7)

Chapter 12 includes three distinct sections on the centralization of worship: vv. 2-7, 8-12, and 13-19. Of the three, vv. 2-7 is probably the latest addition.

Verse 1 provides a title, announcing that the long-promised presentation of law (cf. 4:1, 44, 45; 5:1; 6:1) is about to begin. Cf. the title at the beginning of the Book of the Covenant (Exod. 21:1). As God has been faithful to age-old promises (Deut. 12:1), it behooves the people to reciprocate by being faithful to God's revealed will.

Evergreen trees (v. 2) are rare in the Northern Hemisphere, in contrast to the deciduous trees which appear to die and revive annually. The evergreens seem to be imbued with an undying spirit, and so commended themselves to ancient peoples as an appropriate place for seeking omens. They were thus natural sanctuaries, prominent as symbols of fertility and suggestive of revelatory omens in the rustling of their leaves (2 Sam. 5:24; see above on Deut. 11:30).

On the pillars and *Asherim*, see 7:5. Altars and trees, pillars and *Asherim* are to be replaced by burnt offerings and sacrifices, tithes and offerings (12:6). The keynote of these is not manipulation and plea for blessing, as in Baalistic worship, but rejoicing and gratitude that God *has* blessed (v. 7).

That God places the divine "name" in the sanctuary is a concept which undergoes development in the course of the OT. Exod. 20:24 in some sense summarizes the pious experience of the patriarchal period. The early narratives frequently describe an encounter between the patriarch and the "angel of the LORD" (e.g., Gen. 19:1ff.; 22:11-12; 28:12ff.; 32:22ff.; Exod. 3:1ff.). The "angel" in this early period is not the somewhat ethereal intermediary of the later postexilic age, but the visibility of Yahweh in human form. Yahweh's "name" is in the angel (Exod. 23:20-21). According to tradition, the patriarchal altars stood precisely at places where the angel of the LORD had appeared to guide and bless — Mamre, Shechem, Bethel, and so forth. Succeeding generations sought the name of God at these shrines, in hopes that their forebears' experience would be repeated for them.

In the Deuteronomic school the "name" concept has undergone a more sophisticated theologizing. Almighty God cannot be limited to any earthly sanctuary, because God is enthroned in heaven and fills all things (Deut. 26:15). Nevertheless, God places the "name" as an extension of the divine self in the earthly shrine. Here believers may worship and enter into true meeting with the transcendent God, through the name extension located at the place of worship.

Yet there is also a certain institutionalizing evident in Deut. 12: the name is "set" at the shrine (v. 5), in comparison with the free "coming" of God to the "memorial" death altar of Exod. 20:24.

The general terms "burnt offerings" (Heb. *'olot*) and "sacrifices" (*zebahim*, v. 6) cover a number of specific animal sacrifices. The Hebrew term *'alah* (cf. *'olot*) means "to rise"; the reference is either to the rising of the sacrificial smoke or the raising of the whole victim onto the sacrificial altar. The *'olah* becomes a vehicle for petition (1 Sam. 13:12), thanksgiving (Lev. 22:17-19), and atonement (Num. 6:11).

The term *zebahim* includes several types of sacrificial offering where portions of the whole were burnt on the altar, other parts reserved for the priests, and the remainder eaten by the worshipper's family. *Zebahim* are also called *shelamim* ("creators of peace"). The atmosphere is one of joy (Deut. 27:7), in keeping with the function of the *zebahim*, for this offering expresses thanksgiving, freewill offering, or the grateful fulfillment of a vow.

"Tithing" (12:6) is an ancient form of offering in Israel, the Semitic world in general, and beyond. As far as Israel is concerned, it seems to originate in the northern tradition (Gen. 28:22; Amos 4:4). Perhaps originally collected by the ruler (1 Sam. 8:15, 17) for the upkeep of the official shrine, it was later handed by the worshippers directly to the priestly guardians at the shrine. In the early period it was perhaps identical with the offering of firstfruits (cf. Deut. 26:1-15). Deuteronomy provides the first clear presentation of regulations governing tithing (cf. 14:22-29). The offering of "firstlings" (12:6; cf. 15:19-23) in earliest times included firstborn human children. "All that opens the womb is mine" (Exod. 34:19).

In the biblical period the practice of sacrificing firstborn children had (officially! cf. Deut. 12:31) stopped. Genesis 22 witnesses to the change. Firstborn children were to be redeemed — first with a substitute animal (Gen. 22:9-13), later with money (Num. 18:16).

Indications are that in primitive times the sacrifice of the firstborn was a spring ritual, believed to stimulate the fertility of flocks, fields, and family. In the early biblical sources the offering is still made a week after birth (i.e., in the spring; Exod. 22:30). The animal described in Deut. 15:19-23, however, is apparently older.

Communion, fellowship, and joy (12:7) are to constitute the ethos of Israel's sacrificial practice. The slaying of animals as an act of worship no longer speaks to us. But the note of exuberant gratitude which marked this Israelite worship (in contrast to the presumably somewhat anxious seeking of Baalistic blessings in Canaanite worship) bears eloquent testimony to the deep and abiding genius of Yahwism.

Orderliness in Worship (12:8-12)

The phrase "everyone doing whatever is right in his own eyes" (v. 8) occurs also in Judg. 17:6; 21:25. There it is part of a pro-monarchy stance (from the tradition of the royal shrine at Bethel or Dan?) — appreciation for the role of monarchy as stabilizer of an otherwise chaotic society. It may well be, in fact, that the use of the phrase in Deut. 12:8 is intended as a corrective to Judg. 17:6; 21:25. Stability derives, not from the office of kingship as such, but from Yahweh and Yahweh's gift of the promised land. We have noted (Introduction, 17-18) the ambivalence of the Deuteronomic school to the institution of kingship. Was this unbridled individualism indeed typical of the Mosaic period? Presumably the reference is to the repeated rebelliousness already recorded (cf. Deut. 9:24 and context). Once again, however, we are reminded that the Deuteronomic material is "preached law." The author does not intend bare historical recall; rather, he is addressing the current situation that was being experienced by the succeeding festival congregations and drawing salutary lessons for their present situation from the facts of the past.

"What is good in one's own eyes" stands in contrast with "what is good in Yahweh's eyes" (e.g., 13:18; 21:9; 1 Kgs. 11:38). For the Deuteronomists, "good in Yahweh's eyes" means "revealed in Yahweh's torah."

The reference to "Yahweh's rest" (Deut. 12:9) is evocative. The older tradition relates that Yahweh repeatedly provided temporary resting places throughout Israel's journeying (Num. 10:33). This is perhaps contrasted here with the "permanent" rest, that is, the successful occupation of the promised land. This is the goal toward which Yahweh has been leading Israel. From the "speech of Moses" perspective, the rest still lies in the (near) future; for the festival congregation it should be present reality. What is envisaged is a rounded spiritual-physical whole — "rest from enemies" (Deut. 12:10; 25:19), fertile land (11:10-11), rich harvests (16:10), comprehensive guidance (4:8), and divine presence (4:7).

The "rest" was achieved under Joshua (Josh. 21:44-45). Yet it does not descend automatically down the generations. It is reestablished and reappropriated by David (2 Sam. 7:1, 11) and Solomon (1 Kgs. 5:4). For the Deuteronomic historian the dedication of Solomon's temple should be the completion of the process. But even there there is no ultimate permanency. From the downward slide which follows that climax (1 Kgs. 9 onwards), there eventually emerges the eschatological hope of rest.

See Ps. 95:11 and its application in Heb. 3–4.

Meat Supply and Tithe (12:13-19)

The phrase "place . . . in one of your tribes" (Deut. 12:14) is still rather open-ended, compared with v. 5. The demand for only one shrine for the whole country is not yet categorical. The wording of v. 11 is intermediate between v. 14 and v. 5. Thus, as we have noted, it is in the latest stratum of ch. 12 that strict centralization becomes an explicit requirement.

In ancient times, all slaughtering of animals for food was regarded as "sacred" activity. Verse 15 reflects the ancient understanding that this "routine" slaughter would be performed on an ad hoc altar of earth (Exod. 20:24) or rock (1 Sam. 6:14). But the strict limitation of sacrificial worship to one central shrine meant that henceforth there would be only one legitimate altar. Recognizing the impossibility of requiring that all animals be butchered at one central place, the Deuteronomic school sanctions the separation of routine and ritual slaughter. The only stipulation is that the blood as the vehicle of life — and therefore peculiarly God's — be returned to God by pouring it out on the ground.

From ancient times human beings have considered it appropriate to offer in sacrifice domestic rather than wild animals. Presumably this is because the domestic animal was the more valuable gift. Thus gazelles, harts (Deut. 12:15, 22), and other such "clean" (Arabic *halal*) animals traditionally had no association with the altar. They could be slaughtered and eaten without accompanying ritual, provided only the blood was poured out on the ground.

With the Deuteronomic centralization of worship, the slaughter of sheep and oxen for meat is to follow the method that formerly applied to wild game. Thus a separation has been made between sacral activity and routine butchering. Can this appropriately be described as "secularization"?

"The unclean and the clean may eat of it" (vv. 15, 22). From earliest times certain categories of people have been considered especially vulnerable to the threatening spiritual forces inherent in nature and existence. In Israelite thought such categories included:

1. Sufferers from skin diseases popularly labeled "leprosy." (Such disease was regarded as inimical to the orderliness inherent in nature, and so presumably demonic in origin.)
2. Those experiencing discharge of bodily fluids: blood, semen, and monthly period (associated with the mysterious sources of life and therefore in the realm of the sacred; contact with Baalistic practice of ritual prostitution would strengthen the sensitivity).
3. Those in contact with a corpse or dead body. (Death was seen as militating against the good order of creation and therefore sinister. This primitive feeling was accentuated for Yahwism with the rise of the cult of the dead; Lev. 19:28.)

4. Various birds and animals were regarded as unclean, either through their association with pagan religions or their feeding on carrion. Contact with them spread the uncleanness.

Such vulnerability not only exposed those concerned to danger in the presence of the holy, but also vitiated and endangered the worship of the entire congregation. If such an "unclean" person were to partake of sacrificial meat, the consequences could be drastic. Under the new separation of sacrificing from butchering, however, the danger no longer applies.

"When God Enlarges Your Territory" (12:20-28)

The hope expressed in Deut. 12:20 (cf. also 19:8) that God will enlarge Israel's territory probably picks up the phraseology of the old Ritual Decalogue in Exod. 34:24 (J). There the Yahwist is writing with knowledge of the actual boundaries of the Solomonic kingdom and sees that expansion as the fulfillment of promises made to Israel by God since the days of the patriarchs.

In the context of the Deuteronomic preaching, the phrase takes on a more retrospective and conditional coloring: "In the golden age of David-Solomon, God expanded our territory because we were still obedient; if our borders are now contracted, that is because we have been unfaithful." To place these sentiments on the lips of Moses is to add to their poignancy.

The fourfold repetition, "do not eat the blood" (Deut. 12:23-25), is a powerful underlining device, indicating that an important principle is at stake. The principle is (v. 23) that "the blood is the *nephesh,* and you shall not eat the *nephesh* with the flesh." We have seen (on 6:5) that the *nephesh* is the essential vital force within human beings and animals. In the case of human beings, the life force is directly "infused" by God (Gen. 2:7); although the contact is less direct, God's infusion of life is equally true in the case of animals (Gen. 2:19). Thus the *nephesh* in all creatures is in some sense an inflow of the vital force of God, who is the "living God" (Deut. 5:26).

Belief that the *nephesh* resides essentially in the blood arose no doubt from the observation that the ebbing of life coincides with the flow of blood from the body (in battle, sacrifice, slaughter). On the other hand, too, menstrual blood is connected with the process of conception and birth. The blood, then, as the vehicle of *nephesh* is regarded as peculiarly "close" to God and within the sphere of the holy. For human beings to appropriate it for their own use is sacrilegious arrogance, which bears its own penalty.

Deuteronomy 12:28 constitutes a chain of Deuteronomic "slogans." It rounds off 12:1-27, giving the impression that these verses are a unit-in-itself specifically on the theme "centralization for the sake of purity of worship."

THE DEUTERONOMIC CODE IN DETAIL (12:29–25:19)

Warning against Idolatry (12:29-32)

That Yahweh is said to "cut off" the previous inhabitants of Canaan (12:29; cf. 19:1; Josh. 23:4; 1 Sam. 20:15) in order to make room for Israel is part of the language of "Yahweh's war" (see above on Deut. 2:31-35; 7:1-6). The "snare" (12:30) is one that threatens in times of radical social and cultural upheaval. It consists in the uncritical assumption that religious convictions and worship patterns shaped in the past are to be discarded, precisely because they originate in the past. Conversely, convictions and patterns born out of the new ethos are to be accepted, precisely because they are new. What is required, rather, is a careful discernment of essentials — so that the essential good in past traditions can be courageously reclothed in contemporary forms which are genuinely and creatively compatible with the heart core of the old.

The "abominable" ("revolting"; Heb. *to'ebah,* "abomination") aspects of Canaanite worship have been discussed at 9:1-6. Prominent among these is the practice of "burning their sons and their daughters in the fire" (12:31).

The similar phrase in 18:10 is, literally, "makes his son or daughter pass through the fire" (in honor of Molech; 2 Kgs. 23:10). Some scholars link this latter phrase with the practice attested from archaeology of passing the children rapidly through fire in order to imbue them with heroic powers or long life.

However that may be, Jeremiah certainly seems to equate the two expressions, "burn" and "pass through" (Jer. 32:35), and to interpret "Molech" (a variant of the Hebrew for "king") as referring to Baal (Jer. 19:5). Was there a group in Israel who regarded Yahweh as the sadistic king who demanded such sacrifices? If so, the imputation is strenuously denied: "Such a thing never came into God's mind" (Jer. 19:5; 7:31).

Such savagery is inimical to Yahwism, in that it constitutes an extreme attempt to pressure the deity into compassion. But Yahweh *is* compassion, who needs no such pressuring!

On the so-called "canonical formula" (Deut. 12:32b), see 4:2.

In view of the obvious and lengthy redactional process which the material of Deuteronomy has undergone, it is clear that the writer's intention here is not to "set in concrete" a definitive and unalterable text. Rather, the stress is on the binding obligation to obedience: do not trim the commands to your tastes, but take them seriously in their entirety.

WARNING AGAINST APOSTASY (13:1-18)

Deuteronomy 13 consists of three parts, the general theme of which is "apostasy." Grammatically, the chapter is in the singular, except for vv. 3b-5a.

The Issue of "False Prophets" (13:1-5)

The question of "false prophecy" was an urgent one for the community that set out to live by the word of God. That word was given as a definitive revelation through Moses in the past, and is continually applied to the developing situation by a chain of prophets who function as Moses' successors (see below on 18:15-22). Israel's theologians were therefore compelled to wrestle with the question: How can we be certain that a particular prophet has indeed been sent by God and is the bearer of an authentic word? Out of the wrestling several guiding principles emerged:

1. Because the holy God is implacably opposed to falsehood and unrighteousness, whereas human nature is prone to falsehood and unrighteousness, it follows that in general the authentic message from God will sound strongly of warning, rebuke, and the call to repentance. The prophet who sounds these notes is likely to be genuine. But the prophet who concentrates on "peace and safety" is suspect: only if and when her or his prophecies actually come about, is this person to be taken seriously.
2. When the thing prophesied actually happens, that authenticates the prophet (18:22). There was indeed a tradition in Israel that a prophet would nominate certain "signs," the fulfillment of which would verify the message (1 Sam. 10:1-2; 1 Kgs. 13:3; 2 Kgs. 19:29).

This criterion is not 100 percent reliable, however. In some cases the "signs" happened, yet the content of the prophecy itself was subversive (Exod. 7:22; 8:7). Thus a further criterion was needed.

3. If the so-called prophet advocated worship of other gods, he or she was false — whatever the "signs" the prophet produced. Conversely, the genuine prophecy would be a consistent application of the historic faith revelation to the contemporary situation.
4. Jeremiah puts forward the ultimate criterion, namely, that the genuine prophet is the one who has "stood in the council of Yahweh" (Jer. 23:18, 22). This terminology is rooted in ancient mythology: at set times the gods met in council to determine the destinies of humankind for the ensuing period. The person who "eavesdropped" on the council became privy to the divine plans and could relate them to others. So, to "stand in Yahweh's council" meant to understand the divine will for the future, through having been co-opted as it were into God's thought processes. Such a prophet knows the purpose of God from the base of deep and intimate fellowship with Yahweh and is therefore able to proclaim that purpose to the people.

This criterion is not available, however, to the general public. In the last resort, it is only the prophet's self who knows whether she or he has "stood in the divine council."

At the end of the day, then, the only objective criterion available is: does the message genuinely contemporize the historic faith of the people of God, without falsifying addition, subtraction, or distortion?

13:1 Interestingly, "prophet" and "dreamer" are paralleled, with the implication that dreams are a legitimate channel of revelation. The Bible in general indicates that "dreams are from God" and can illuminate God's purpose (Gen. 20:3, 6; 37:5-11; 41:1-2; Num. 12:6; 1 Sam. 28:6; 1 Kgs. 3:5-6; Job 33:14-15).

It is noteworthy, indeed, that most of the examples are from the patriarchal period or early Monarchy, that is, before the rise of classical prophecy. This seems to indicate that the flowering of prophecy rather displaced dreams as a medium of revelation. Nevertheless, their validity was still acknowledged. The prophet most critical of dreams is Jeremiah (Jer. 23:23-32). However, Jeremiah's criticism apparently is not of dreams as such, but of their manipulation or fabrication (Jer. 23:25).

Dreams, of course, occupy an important place in modern psychology, being recognized as the symbolic language through which the subconscious seeks to alert the dreamer to the processes going on deep within the self. This modern understanding is not in contradiction to the biblical, for it is agreed that God's revelation does not come to us in detachment from the processes of life and everyday experience. Most believers would accept that on occasion God intervenes in human life by planting or injecting "inspiration" in our conscious thought processes (God "speaks"). If that is so, then it is equally comprehensible that God should intervene in our subconscious thought processes.

13:3b "God is testing you" (cf. Deut. 6:16). We noted above that 13:3b-5a is grammatically plural: probably these verses are an apologetic addition responding to the question, "Why does God allow the vital revelatory (prophetic) process to become muddied by such dangerous ambiguity?"

An alternative or supplementary explanation of the phenomenon of false prophecy is given in 1 Kgs. 22:19-23: a "lying spirit" is given divine permission to mislead the false prophets, so that their false counsel should lure a sinful people to the place of judgment. The suggestion may seem somewhat bizarre, but the issue is a profound one, and the earnestness with which it is tackled is impressive.

13:5 "Rebellion against Yahweh . . . who brought you out . . ." recalls the classic prologue to the Decalogue (Deut. 5:6). Its quotation here implies that rebellion cancels the covenant and therefore destroys the foundations of Israel's existence.

"To purge (Heb. *ba'ar*) the evil" is related to a verbal root which means to "burn out" or "cauterize." The phrase occurs ten times throughout the code in connection with apostasy, murder, rejection of divinely sanctioned authority, perjury, adultery, and kidnapping. Cf. the similar phrase "cut off" in Lev. 17:4, 9, 10, 14.

Such (obviously ancient) formulas imply that the sin of the individual poisons the group life, so that unless the offender is "excised" the covenant is threatened and the communal life placed in jeopardy (cf. Josh. 7).

The modern covenant community rejects such drastic ways of dealing with blatant transgression. Nevertheless the principle remains that individual sin infects the community — of both church and state. The Church in particular is faced with the challenge of discovering forms of corporate discipline that reflect gospel values.

Enticement to Evil (13:6-11)

The similarity in vocabulary and phraseology suggests that there is a close relation between this and the preceding section.

Deuteronomy 13:6-7 insists that loyalty to Yahweh takes precedence over the closest human relationships (cf. Matt. 10:37-39). Not only are the corrupting suggestions to be rejected, but the life of the suggester is to be sacrificed for the good of the faith community (Deut. 13:8-9; see above on v. 5).

Verse 7 obviously contains a Deuteronomic retrospect on the process of history. When Israel first occupied Canaan the foreign gods which "tempted" were close at hand. As the empire expanded and trade prospered, gods from further afield exerted their more subtle pressures: "It is to your political and economic advantage to pay me at least outward deference." From the threshold of the Exile, the issues are clear in retrospect: "Had we been more uncompromising in our loyalty to Yahweh, our current situation would have been different."

Intimate family are to be first witnesses against the apostate (v. 9) and thus initiate the execution and assume primary responsibility for it (cf. 17:7). Normally it is the immediate family who become the "avengers of blood" (cf. 19:1-13). In their corporate identity as family, the behavior of each member involves the whole, and the whole is responsible for the deviations of each. Here the family declare, "This blood will not be avenged on you who participate in today's execution: we ourselves bear witness that our brother deserves to die."

That "all Israel shall . . . fear and never again offend" (13:11) is an expression of pious confidence which is not born out by history. The punishment was not retributive but deterrent; even so, it does not seem to have worked.

This again is sad Deuteronomic retrospect: "If we had been more strict from the beginning, could the current disaster have been avoided?" Realism must answer, "Not necessarily so. But God would be with you — as indeed God is still!"

A City That Turns Away From Yahweh (13:12-18)

The previous two sections have discussed cases of individual apostasy. Here the subject is a group, a whole town.

Most Israelite towns, especially in the north, were not founded by Israelite settlers but taken over from the original population (6:10-11). Contrary to the "idealistic" retrospect of 7:2, these cities were not taken over in an empty and deserted condition but (in general) complete with their inhabitants. The subsequent reversion of these indigenous people to their pre-Yahwistic faith was a constant open possibility. The Deuteronomic preacher is thus not predicting a vague future possibility, but describing the situation of his own times.

The "base fellows" (13:13) are literally "sons of *beliya'al*." This latter term is probably rooted in ancient mythology (cf. Ps. 18:4, where the "torrents of *beliya'al*" are clearly a feature of the under-world, the world of death). Popular etymology, however, supplied the meaning "useless," "corrupting." In the current passage it is this popular meaning of *beliya'al* that is paramount, though echoes of the sinister linger in the background. To turn from Yahweh to other gods is behavior so horrendous as to have a touch of the "demonic" about it.

On the "abominable thing" (Deut. 13:14), see 9:1-6.

According to 13:15, the *herem* ("utter destruction"; see above on 2:31-35) is to be applied not only to people but also to their animals and inanimate possessions. This represents a more primitive and thoroughgoing application of the ancient rite, compared with 2:31-35. For there (with a rationalizing tendency, as we noted) the animals are exempted. The principle underlying the "total destruction" required by the primitive rite is that the personality *(nephesh)* of a human being impregnates the clothing worn, the implements used, and the entire store of property owned by the person. So to eliminate the malign influence of the person, one must destroy everything contaminated by that *nephesh* (cf. Josh. 7:24-25).

It is clear from its call for the rigorous application of the *herem* principle that this passage is steeped in the spirit of "Yahweh's war." The difference is that, whereas in Deut. 2 and elsewhere the contaminating threat which had to be eliminated was external, here it is internal. Furthermore, the internal threat is the more pernicious of the two, in that it can proceed undetected till the process is far advanced. It is also more harrowing in that it is directed not against strangers but against kin. It is, in fact, applied at the corporate level (13:6-7).

That everything is to be burned "as a whole burnt offering to Yahweh" (v. 16) is an acknowledgment that the battle prowess and the victory are Yahweh's.

Just as the apostasy of the individual compromises and poisons the group (v. 5), so the apostasy of the town (congregation) compromises the nation (Church). The covenant people stands in unitary solidarity; sickness in a part is the disease of the whole.

138

The apostate city and its spoil shall be "a heap for ever" (v. 16): God is even-handed, knowing no favorites. The fate of the apostate Israelite city is the same as that of Jericho (Josh. 6:26) and Ai (8:28).

The chapter then rounds off with a sharp reminder that those who transgress the conditions of the covenant do so at their extreme peril.

ISRAEL AS A HOLY PEOPLE (14:1-29)

Deuteronomy 14 consists of three distinct sections. The common thread is that all three are concerned with the consequences of Israel's status as a "holy people."

Forbidden Mourning Rites (14:1-2)

Though brief, this passage is not uniform. Verse 1 is grammatically plural. Verse 2 is singular.

"Sons (children) of Yahweh" (v. 1) and "people holy to Yahweh" (v. 2) are in parallel and therefore equivalents.

The phrase "Sons (children) of Yahweh" is relatively rare in the OT. Its basis is Exod. 4:22-23, where "first-born" implies "chosen for covenant relation with Yahweh." The thought is picked up by Hosea (Hos. 1:10; 11:1), whose influence on the Deuteronomic school is clear. Around the time of the Exile Jeremiah (Jer. 31:9), Ezekiel (Ezek. 16:21), and Isaiah (Isa. 43:6; 45:11) also use the "child of Yahweh" theme.

It is noteworthy that in the ancient Near Eastern vassal treaty texts the vassal may be described as "son" of the Great King, hence Israel becomes "son" in the covenant treaty context.

The practice of "cutting" the body (Deut. 14:1) as a mourning rite is also forbidden in Lev. 19:28 (cf. Jer. 16:6; 41:5; 47:5). The custom was ancient and widespread and was frequently copied in Israel in spite of the prohibition. In its origins it may have represented a deliberate changing of facial or bodily appearance to avoid recognition by the potentially harmful spirits of the dead. Perhaps it signified indelible marks of remembrance for the dead.

Possibly these original motives no longer consciously influenced the mourners in Israel. However, the practice is regarded as inimical to Yahweh's absolute claim on the people's obedience and dedication.

Another possible interpretation is that "the dead" refers not to the deceased family but to the dying fertility god. Thus the "cutting" is a Canaanite religious rite aimed at fertilizing nature.

"Making baldness on the forehead" (Deut. 14:1) was likewise a widespread ancient rite imitated in Israel (Isa. 3:24; Jer. 16:6; Ezek. 7:18; Amos 8:10; Mic. 1:16). Originally it may have been a disguising technique, as with the "cutting." Another possibility is that the hair, as containing life force, was offered to invigorate the dead (a usage attested among the ancient Arabs).

The temptation to look to the spirits of the dead for help was a frequent one in Israel (1 Sam. 28:7-8; Deut. 18:9-14; Isa. 8:19-20). On the other hand, Deut. 14:1-2 insists that Israel may not rely on two spiritual sources at once. The jealous God will not tolerate a partial loyalty or a divided commitment.

Not only is such dividedness impossible, it is also completely unnecessary. Yahweh's resources are all-sufficient (v. 2), and covenant relation with Yahweh is all the assurance any people can need.

Verse 2 is virtually identical with 7:6 — a popular piece of Deuteronomic exhortation which could be used repeatedly in a variety of contexts.

Clean and Unclean Animals (14:3-21)

The passage lists the animals that are unclean *(haram)* and clean *(halal)* as food. This and the similar list in Lev. 11 are probably alternative versions of a common original. Deut. 14:3-21 is in the grammatical plural, which is often an indication that the material is a subsequent addition to the basic draft of Deuteronomy.

This material is much more detailed than the samples of "preached law" which we have considered so far. Possibly it was originally compiled as a guideline for priests and then included here by a later Deuteronomic writer as suitable for lay folk also.

On the terminology "clean" and "unclean," see above on 12:15.

Deuteronomy 14:3-21 raises the question as to what criteria were used in declaring certain animals unclean. It is difficult to answer; at most we can mention several factors that contributed to the end result.

(1) A number of the unclean animals had associations with pagan worship. The pig (cf. Isa. 65:3-4; 66:3, 17) is attested from archaeology as having been used in Babylonian, Syrian, and Canaanite sacrifice. The serpent was a symbol of Egyptian and Canaanite deities.

(2) Some animals were forbidden as food on the basis of ancient, long-forgotten taboos.

(3) Some animals (in certain cultures) arouse spontaneous revulsion and so are deemed inappropriate as food. In some cases the revulsion is grounded in experience, namely, that those who ate certain meat fell sick.

(4) Most of the "unclean" birds are carrion eaters and are therefore doubly contaminated — from the dead flesh and from the blood.

(5) Some creatures seem to have been regarded as unclean because they were held to transgress the orderliness of nature. Four-footed animals are "normal" to the pattern of creation if they are cloven-hoofed and cud-chewing. Animals that do not conform to this dual condition seem somehow to threaten the orderliness of creation as appointed by God. In the same way, "normal" fish have fins and scales; those that do not seem to side with the chaos that presses against the regular order of things.

Whatever the original criteria may have been, we may assume that by the time these prohibitions were written into the Deuteronomic code they were perceived simply as commands of Yahweh, to be obeyed without inquiry into their rationale.

Although the prohibition on specific categories of food is abolished in the NT (Mark 7:18-19), still the OT regulations bear witness to certain yet valid theological principles:

(1) Yahweh's people must offer total commitment to Yahweh. Thus everything which has associations with life patterns incompatible with that one, overriding loyalty must come under critical scrutiny and all compromising practices be rejected.

(2) The life of the covenant people is under Yahweh's discipline.

The characteristic of faith is unquestioning obedience, based on the conviction that Yahweh's commands and prohibitions are signposts to true well-being.

(3) Choosing for Yahweh means choosing for order, over against the chaotic forces which are bent on undoing what Yahweh is putting together.

From the historical perspective, however, it should be acknowledged that the categorization into "clean" and "unclean" in ever more complicated detail is a dead-end road. The emphasis on the technical and ritual tends to obscure the moral, and to enclose religious sensitivity in a framework which impedes the spirit of renewal (cf. Acts 10:28).

"Unclean" food in moral (as contrasted to ritual) terms would be:

- Food whose price is subsidized by the sweat and hardships of the poor;
- Food enjoyed in disregard of the world's hungry;
- Food and drink in excess to the detriment of the bodies God gave us.

Some points offer specific interest:

14:6 Whatever the primitive origin of the categorization, there is now nothing particularly health-supporting about cloven hooves and cud-chewing. For the Deuteronomic school these characteristics form a convenient aid to memory: animals with these characteristics are (fortuitously) not on the "prohibited" list.

14:21 The prohibition against eating blood (i.e., in the unbled carcass) applies to Israelite citizens, but not to sojourners (cf. 1:16) or foreigners. This implies no slight on the non-Israelites or callousness toward them (the food is regarded as objectively wholesome). Concern for the welfare of sojourner and foreigner is a constant feature of Deuteronomy (e.g., 1:16; 5:14; 10:18ff.; 14:21, 29). The prohibition rather highlights the covenant people's sensitivity that all life (blood) belongs to Yahweh. So abstention is reverence for the covenant God — and obedience to Yahweh's express command.

Perhaps the thought may legitimately be extended as follows. Just as the priests refrain from what is permissible to the laity, for the sake of their priestly ministry (Lev. 21:1-4, 10-15), so the priestly people (Exod. 19:6) must subject themselves to a special discipline, for the sake of their priestly ministry to humankind.

In the later Priestly source the prohibition described here applies to sojourner as well as Israelite. Apparently the sojourner is progressively integrated into the body of Israel.

The "boiling of a kid in its mother's milk" (cf. Exod. 23:19b; 34:26b) is seemingly a reference to an ancient Near Eastern fertility rite which the Israelites were tempted to adopt. Both the newborn kid and the milk were powerful symbols of natural fertility. If combined by dissolving the one in the other, the resulting mixture became a potent stimulant for the fruitfulness of field and flock when sprinkled symbolically along borders or furrows. (A somewhat problematic Ugaritic text on "The birth of the gods" seems to attest the ceremony.)

Israel is forbidden to seek the fertility of fields and flocks through such means, for Yahweh alone is the source of fertility. The blessings of nature which Yahweh bestows cannot be "stimulated" into actuality, but only gratefully received.

The Offering of the Tithe (14:22-29)

The tithe has already been mentioned at Deut. 12:6 (see above, 127). It is striking that the Book of the Covenant makes no mention of the tithe, but does discuss the offering of firstfruits. It may be surmised, then, that in the course of historical development the "firstfruits" came to be interpreted and calculated as 10 percent of the total produce. In this concretizing process, it would seem that a local tradition came to apply generally to the whole people. We noted earlier that the tithe in all likelihood originated in northern Israel (Gen. 28:22).

There are difficulties in assuming that firstfruits and tithe are identical. For example, the tithe was consumed by the worshipping family (Deut. 14:23), whereas the firstfruits were handed to the

143

priest (18:4). It would seem, however, that this differentiation was not absolute.

(1) One family could scarcely consume one tenth of their annual produce at one sitting unless they shared with many guests. It has been calculated that a family of twenty would need to invite one thousand (including Levites perhaps). Possibly part of the tithe in practice went to the priests and part to the family.

(2) On the other hand, 26:1-11 gives the impression that part of the firstfruit offering was given to the priest (v. 4) and another part enjoyed by the worshipping family (v. 11). This convergence of (1) and (2) strengthens the impression that tithe and firstfruits were in fact identical.

As well as the relationship between these two types of offering, there is the further problem of a seeming internal tension within 14:22-29. Verses 22-27 require that the tithe be offered "year by year" (v. 22) at the "place which God will choose" (v. 23). Verse 28, however, stipulates an offering "every three years . . . within your towns."

It seems clear that it is one and the same tithe which is being discussed; only the deployment of it has undergone change. Did the change take place from year to year, from place to place, or from age to age? The most convincing answer is that the understanding and practice of the tithe was subject to development in the course of Israel's history. Possibly, too, the development in the north was different from that in the south. The completed Deuteronomic code then contains material from various stages of this development process, which is now sketched out "on the flat." At the last stage, the utilization of the tithe is wedded to the centralization of worship at a single shrine (see ch. 12).

"Year by year" (14:22) implies that the offering was made annually — probably during the Feast of Weeks (16:9-12). Cf. 14:28: "at the end of every three years." Verses 28-29 represent a modification or adaptation of the general regulation outlined in vv. 22-27. We may guess that at a certain period in Israel's history the general regulation ceased to operate smoothly, so that the poor and the Levites were deriving little benefit from the distribution of the tithe. Perhaps changing socioeconomic conditions caused an increase in the number of unsupported widows and orphans and unsponsored sojourners. To redress the imbalance, a rider was attached to the old regulation to the effect that the tithe in every third year should not be used in family celebration but distributed directly to the local poor. In the further development, the method of tithe distribution laid down for the third year assumed greater and greater importance, to the point where the third year came to be known simply as "the year of tithing" (26:12).

It seems likely that in the development of this pericope 14:23 and 27 were originally connected, and that vv. 24-25(26) were added later to bring tithing practice into line with the centralization of the cult. If that is so, then "the place which God will choose" (v. 23) is likely to have referred originally to a range of local shrines, not to the Jerusalem temple. It is scarcely conceivable that every family throughout the country could bring offerings in kind to Jerusalem, prepare meals, and serve them in such a way that every Levite countrywide received some share. With the concession that foodstuffs be commuted to cash offerings, however, some centralized system would become feasible.

In v. 26 the atmosphere is one of joy and celebration. Festivity and concern for the poor need not be mutually exclusive. The license to buy "whatever you desire" does not remove the occasion from the sphere of the sacred; the celebration is "before Yahweh." Wine and strong drink (Heb. *shekar,* originally a barley product — "beer"?) are God's gifts, and good when used as God intended. Both were offered as drink offerings to Yahweh (Lev. 23:13; Num. 28:7). "Balance" might be a suitable word to describe the tithe regulations in their finished form — balance between:

- Celebration and concern for the needy;
- Support for "clergy" (Levites!) and for the community poor;
- Concern for those far away (Jerusalem) and for those near at hand ("within your towns").

145

THE SABBATICAL YEAR (15:1-23)

The Year of Release (15:1-18)

The release is of two kinds: the cancellation of debts, and the freeing of persons who because of debt or hardship have bonded themselves to servitude.

Cancellation of Debts (15:1-11)

The Hebrew term for "release" (Deut. 15:1) is *shemittah*. The corresponding Hebrew verb (meaning "set free," "let fall," "let be") is used in Exod. 23:10-11 for letting the land rest fallow in the seventh year (the "sabbath year," according to Lev. 25:1-7 P). This verb *shamat* is rare in the OT and is likely a technical term, which in early times applied in the agricultural setting and in later times was adapted to an urban and commercial economy.

The practice of leaving land lie fallow periodically has been widespread since seminomadic times. It is rooted in the experience that land that is continuously planted declines in productivity. Accordingly, the farmer must either rest the land or shift to a fresh location.

In Israel the custom took on a special quality by being related to faith in Yahweh. (In Exod. 23:10-11 the "sabbath" year is linked to the sabbath day.) Both are symbolic reminders of Yahweh's right-of-control — over time and over land — and of human dependence on God as covenanter and provider. What is especially relevant in the present context is that both "sabbaths" have a strong built-in socioethical component. The harvest which grows of itself in the sabbath year is for the poor. (On the ethical aspects of the weekly sabbath, cf. Deut. 5:14b-15.) The fact that the Deuteronomic code makes no mention of the sabbath year suggests the possibility that Deut. 15:1-11 is a reapplication of that old agrarian provision to conditions in an increasingly "urbanized" and monetary economy. Economic pressures, including an increasingly heavy taxation burden, often forced the poor into borrowing. When the pile of debt accumulated, the last resort was to sell or forfeit oneself and one's family into servitude. It was a creative innovation that took over the old *shemittah* ("letting be") of the land and reinterpreted it as a "letting be" of the debt-ridden.

Implicit in this readaptation of the "shemitta" is the understanding that just as Yahweh has sovereign rights over the land and its use, so Yahweh is in control over the economic system and its operation.

According to the Deuteronomic school, the *shemittah* law implies that the people of God must order their economy with full regard for the needs and rights of the poor. Thus in the seventh year, when the land is symbolically returned to its true Creator-owner, the economy erected on that land base is also submitted again to Yahweh's jurisdiction. The creditors acknowledge that their right to their wealth is not absolute but always within the context of others' needs. Thus they are required to cooperate in restoring the economic balance by foregoing some of their wealth in favor of the disadvantaged.

15:2 It has been suggested that the *shemittah* is a breathing space, a postponement in recalling the loan rather than a cancellation. Just as the agricultural process is "frozen" in the seventh year, so (it is argued) is the economic process. Others suggest that the interest (not the capital) was waived in the *shemittah* — just as the fruit was left ungathered on the land.

These suggestions have a logical and practical ring. Nevertheless, the language of the text gives the firm impression that the Deuteronomists envisaged total cancellation of the debt.

15:3 The *shemittah* is concerned primarily for the "brother or sister," that is, members of the faith community. Foreigners (traders) in Israel were generally economically strong, and so did not require special protection. Nevertheless, it must be admitted that the Deuteronomic school did not envisage the compassion embodied in the *shemittah* provision as applying universally. We may, however, appeal to the principle of "latency" previously mentioned. The covenant community are a particular people chosen for a universal purpose (Gen. 12:3; Isa. 2:2-4; 49:6). The end result will be that there are no more "foreigners"; all alike will experience and practice the same compassion.

On the formal level, there is contradiction between Deut. 15:4 and vv. 7, 11: "There will be no poor among you," but "if there is . . ." and "there always will be. . . ."

15:4   Verse 4 states the theological ideal: conscientious obedience to Yahweh's torah with its wise humanitarian provisions would effectively eliminate poverty, or redress it before it became chronic. Indeed, the whole tendency of the torah is toward mutual caring and support, as the fitting response to Yahweh's experienced goodness. Nevertheless, the lesson of history is that the people of God constantly fail to live by the torah. Hence social imbalance occurs through obtuseness and proliferates through hardness of heart (vv. 7, 11). The task of the preacher (Deuteronomic or otherwise) is to recall God's people to the compassionate implications of the covenant. Where there is the human will, God will provide the wherewithal to be compassionate (vv. 6, 10). (The "international lending" envisaged is probably thought of as being on the personal and individual rather than the government level.)

15:9   The "base thought" is literally a *"beliya'al* factor" (see above on 13:13). It goes together with the hardened heart, the closed hand (15:7), the hostile (Heb. *ra'ah,* "evil," "cruel," "mean," "bad") eye (v. 9), and the grudging (*ra'*) heart (v. 10). There is indeed something sinister, not to say "demonic," in the (deliberate) insensitivity which accepts the wealth of God's goodness and then refuses to emulate the Giver and share the gift.

Freeing the Hebrew Slave (15:12-18)

This passage consists of a casuistic law sentence (v. 12), which is then expounded in a sermon exhortation (vv. 13-18). The Book of the Covenant (Exod. 21:1-11), Deuteronomic code (Deut. 15:12-18), and Holiness code (Lev. 25:35-46) all legislate for the case of servitude through debt. On its widespread and long-standing occurrence in the Semitic world, cf. Code of Hammurabi 117 (18th cent. B.C.). 2 Kgs. 4:1 cites a case in point from the 9th century.

Interestingly, the (later) Holiness code connects the release from servitude with the "year of jubilee," that is, the fiftieth year, whereas in Deut. 15 it is the "seventh year." Is this later alteration a tacit admission that the Deuteronomic requirement had proved difficult to implement?

15:12 The etymology of the name "Hebrew" is disputed. Most scholars derive it from the verb *'abar* ("to cross"), thus designating either those who have "crossed" the Jordan into western Palestine or those who are continually "crossing" from here to there (i.e., seminomadic). The once confident equating of Hebrew with *'Abiru/'Apiru* (a seminomadic serf caste mentioned in ancient Near Eastern documents of 2000 – 1400) is increasingly questioned by modern scholarship.

Nearly all the occurrences of the name Hebrew are from the early period of Israel's history: the patriarchal time, the sojourn in Egypt, the conflict with the Philistines. (Jonah also refers to himself as a Hebrew.) Normally the name is applied by outsiders, often in a derogatory tone.

In Deut. 15:12 (cf. Exod. 21:2) the name indicates a full Israelite citizen in contrast to the *ger* ("sojourner"). Jeremiah (Jer. 34:9), in quoting Deut. 15:12, equates "Hebrew" and "Jew" as if the word is ancient and almost needs translating.

The reference to "Hebrew woman" (Deut. 15:12; cf. Exod. 21:3-4) implies that the status of women has changed in the period between the compiling of the Book of the Covenant and the Deuteronomic code. The Deuteronomic code implies that women have the right to sell themselves in servitude for debt, and therefore the prior right to own property and incur debt (cf. 2 Kgs. 8:3). In the Book of the Covenant, however, the woman was part of the man's household property; she went automatically into servitude along with her husband, and if sold by her father she had no relief in the year of release. She did gain certain rights if she was taken as a concubine (Exod. 21:8-11), but otherwise she was regarded as property.

15:13-15 The compassionate stipulation that the released person be provided with the wherewithal to begin a new life is based on gratitude for Yahweh's compassion which the master (and all Israel) has experienced. Cf. the "remember" of Deut. 5:15.

We may surmise that in the intervening period between the Book of the Covenant and the Deuteronomic code there has grown up a reluctance to refer to a fellow Israelite as "slave" (*'ebed*; cf. Exod. 21:2). The "in"-term is now "brother" or "sister" (Deut. 15:12; cf. Lev. 25:39) — a further example of the inner dynamic of the covenant relationship working itself out.

15:16-17   The reasons cited for declining release also reflect a more humane situation compared with that envisaged in the Book of the Covenant (Exod. 21:3-4). There the basic reason is that the wife (if provided by the master) and children remain in servitude as the master's property. The released slave must therefore choose between freedom and family. In Deut. 15, however, the dilemma is not mentioned — an indication perhaps that this unfeeling practice has ceased. (The Holiness code is quite explicit that the children must be released along with the parents; Lev. 25:41, 54.)

"Love" (Deut. 15:16) implies not so much "warm affection" as sober recognition that personal conditions cannot be bettered by accepting the release: "He fares well with you." In that case the ear, standing for "hearing," "obedience," is pinned to the door, as a symbol for permanent attachment to the household. The phraseology in the Book of the Covenant differs somewhat; for "bring him to the door," it reads "bring him to God" (Exod. 21:6). This implies a religious ceremony, either at the local shrine or before the household gods (so Martin Noth, *Exodus*). Did the Deuteronomist drop the reference to "God" because the centralization of worship had made the cultic aspect of the ceremony impractical?

It is noteworthy that the Holiness code makes no provision for permanent servitude. There must be a release at the Jubilee (Lev. 25:40).

15:18   Deuteronomy 15:18 is a parenesis that links back to v. 15. The intervening verses have discussed an exceptional case.

Some suggest that Heb. *mishneh*, translated "half," actually means "the same as" (cf. Deut. 17:18, "copy," "the same as [the original]"). This is unlikely, however. To sell oneself into servitude was to contract one's labor for payment in advance. No employer would choose this option unless it was financially advantageous, that is, at a lower overall cost than for six years' labor hired by the day. Isaiah seems to support this: one is paid off after three years (Isa. 16:14), presumably with the same amount as is paid in advance for six years' work (Deut. 15:18). The positive principle being stressed is that the "servant" remains a "brother" (v. 12), and therefore his labor must be purchased for a fair price. He is not a tool, but a member of the faith community.

The Firstborn Cattle and Sheep (15:19-23)

This section also consists of an apodeictic law, or straightforward "thou shalt" statement of absolute principle (v. 19a), followed by a preached application of it (vv. 19b-23).

The "firstborn" offering has already been alluded to at 12:6 (see above). The regulations governing it at various stages of Israel's history make interesting comparison:

- Exod. 13:11-16; 22:29b-30; 34:19-20 (JE);
- Deut. 15:19-23 (D);
- Lev. 27:26-27; Num. 18:15-18 (P).

The following observations can be drawn from this comparison:

(1) JE and P link the offering of animal and of human firstborn; D does not.
(2) JE links the death of Egyptian firstborn with the redemption of God's "firstborn," Israel (Exod. 4:22-23).
(3) D stresses that the offering must be free from blemish (Deut. 15:21-22).
(4) The disposal of the sacrificial flesh varies:
     JE — a burnt offering for Yahweh;
     D — a meal for the worshipper's family;
     P — provision for the priests.

The differences no doubt reflect stages in the historical development of Israel's cult.

151

15:21-22 To offer maimed or diseased animals in sacrifice was deemed insulting to God. Cf. the scorching indictment leveled against the practice in Mal. 1:6-14. See also Deut. 17:1; Lev. 22:17-25.

As food the maimed animal is wholesome and licit. However, it is to be consumed in an everyday context "as though it were a hart or a gazelle" (see above on 12:15, 22), not as part of a sacred meal within the context of worship.

THE FESTIVAL CALENDAR (16:1–17:1)

This chapter is basically an exposition of the three great religious festivals (vv. 1-17), to which are appended two small groups of apodeictic law. The first of these (vv. 18-20) is a "guideline for judges," and the second (16:21–17:1) is a cultic ruling.

The Three Great Festivals (16:1-17)

Expositions of the three festivals are found at each major stage of the OT tradition:

- Exod. 23:14-17; 34:18-25 (JE);
- Deut. 16:1-17 (D);
- Lev. 23:4-44 (P).

The special emphases of the Deuteronomic code in this regard are: (1) a stress on the uniformity of procedure for the three festivals. Each is to be celebrated "in the place which Yahweh will choose" (Deut. 16:2, 6, 7, 11, 16); and (2) preeminence given to Passover, in contrast to the JE emphasis on Booths as the original and primary festival. Perhaps the preference for Passover is related to the fact that it was the festival most easily historicized (built into the salvation history). The concentration of all three festivals at the central shrine, and their consequent removal from the agrarian setting, may have helped this historicizing process.

Passover (16:1-8)

It is striking that the JE tradition (see above) does not mention Passover in its description of the Feast of Unleavened Bread, whereas Deut. 16:1-8 ties the two closely together.

We may conclude from JE that the two feasts had different origins. Hebrew *pesah* ("Passover") is derived from a verb meaning to "pass," "jump over."

The rite was almost certainly observed among the pre-Mosaic tribes (cf. Exod. 5:1-3). Preparatory to moving the flocks from their winter holdings to the upland pastures in the spring, they would slaughter a lamb and sprinkle its blood on flock and tent poles to ward off malign influences on the journey.

In the context of the Exodus, the ancient rite acquired new significance by being linked with the "deeds of God" which (according to tradition) persuaded Pharaoh to release the Hebrews. Prime among these "deeds" was the slaughter of the Egyptian firstborn (see above on Deut. 15:19-23). The blood sprinkled on the Hebrew houses, however, caused (the angel of) Yahweh to "pass over" (*pasah;* Exod. 12:23) them. Also, in each Israelite house the family feasted on the flesh of the Passover lamb, as a "sacrament of liberation" — escape from death, escape into freedom. (It can be safely assumed that this household feasting, as described in Exod. 12:21-22, reflects the actual mode of Passover celebration as it obtained during the formative period of the JE tradition, i.e., 10 8th cent. B.C.)

The celebration of Unleavened Bread (Heb. *matstsot*), on the other hand, obviously originated in an agricultural setting and seems to have been associated with the shrine at a relatively early period. The Hebrew term signified bread from which the yeast has been "drawn out" *(matsah)*. This "yeast" consisted of a lump of sour, fermented dough planted in the flour mix to induce leavening.

From earliest agricultural times, the supply of grain would be used up by the end of a long dry season, and the leavening chain thus would be broken. A fresh start would then be made with the new grain of harvest.

In Canaan this new start had become the occasion of a sacral

153

rite. The rite may have included the symbolic destruction of the old grain and/or the offering of unleavened loaves as a thanksgiving to the gods of fertility. The Israelites on occupying the land took over the old rites and gradually combined them with the Passover celebration. Opinions differ as to when this conflation took place. 2 Kings 23:21-23 states that Josiah's centralized Passover celebration in 621 was the first of its kind "since the days of the judges." Julius Wellhausen *(Prolegomena to the History of Ancient Israel)* interprets this to mean that the conflation happened at this time. Others (e.g., Hans-Joachim Kraus, *Worship in Israel)* argue that Josiah did not innovate but revived an ancient practice. This second possibility is the more likely.

Leviticus 23 adds two fresh details to the celebration: a sheaf of new grain as a wave offering (v. 10) and, fifty days later, two loaves of new grain bread (v. 17). These rites may have originated at local shrines and then at a later date been incorporated into the central shrine ceremonial.

Structurally, Deut. 16:1-8 consists of an apodeictic (absolute law) sentence (v. 1a), followed by detailed exposition and application (vv. 1b-8).

"Abib" (v. 1) means "shoots," hence Spring (Mar.-Apr.).

The liberating deed of Yahweh was at night (Exod. 12:6-7), hence Passover continued as a night celebration (Deut. 16:1).

The widening of the regulation to permit the use of oxen as well as lambs for the Passover (v. 2; cf. Exod. 12:21) reflects the historical development in the centuries between JE and D.

16:3 The people are instructed to eat "no unleavened bread." By being combined with Passover, the celebration of Massoth took on new significance — without altogether losing its old meaning.

From of old, the unleavened bread represented the joy of fresh food supply and new beginnings. This symbolism of leaving the old and embracing the new was incorporated into Yahwism — calling successive generations to abandon their old rebelliousness and renew their commitment to Yahweh.

Specifically in their connection with the Passover tradition, however, the *matstsot* stand for "bread of affliction," that is, a reminder of the affliction suffered in Egypt (Exod. 3:7) and of the hurried flight from there (Exod. 12:8, 11, 34).

The question arises as to how far the details of Exod. 12 reflect the actual conditions of the thirteenth-century flight from Egypt under Moses. If "the making of bread in haste" is based on historical reminiscence, this feature would of course facilitate the conflation of Passover and Massoth.

16:7 The command to "boil" the flesh of the Passover sacrifice is surprising in the light of Exod. 12:9 (P): "Do not eat any of it . . . boiled with water, but roasted." The difference probably reflects the change in practice over the centuries. Alternatively the Hebrew word translated "boil" *(bashal)* may be used here in the weakened sense of "cook" (cf. 2 Chr. 35:13, "they *bashal* the passover lamb with fire").

"Go to your tents" (Deut. 16:7), as we noted at 5:30, was the traditional formula used to dismiss the festival congregation. Its use here is probably a survival from the time before Passover and Massoth were combined: "Go home. Passover is concluded." In the present context, however, the narrative (16:8) stipulates a *matstsot* observance lasting an additional week. "To your tents" must therefore be reinterpreted, "Return for the night to the festival encampment."

16:8 Cessation of work is an acknowledgment that the time is Yahweh's and should be ceded to Yahweh. Specifically, the inactivity is a symbolic recognition that the release from Egypt was Yahweh's work. Cf. the significance of the weekly sabbath (5:12-15).

The Feast of Weeks (16:9-12)

The Feast of Weeks was originally called the "feast of harvest" *(hag haqqatsir,* Exod. 23:16), but over the years it came to be known as the Feast of Weeks from the method of calculating its beginnings — a "week" of weeks (Deut. 16:9) or fifty days (Lev. 23:16; *pentekoste* in Greek). The counting began from the first

Sunday after the celebration of Passover (Lev. 23:15), the day on which the sheaf of fresh grain was presented as a wave offering.

In view of the fact that the harvest obviously did not ripen on precisely the same day throughout the whole land, Martin Noth suggests that each farmer (or district) brought a few stalks of grain, which were then combined at the sanctuary into one sheaf. This would then be waved on the appointed day.

The whole fifty-day period was in fact harvest and therefore sacral, from the first-ripe barley sheaves till the wheat harvest (Exod. 34:22). The Feast of Weeks marked the opening of the period for handing over the firstfruit offerings and tithes (cf. Deut. 14:22ff.). The period came to a close with the Feast of Booths (see below).

As with Massoth, the Feast of Weeks originated in the agricultural world and was presumably taken over from the Canaanites after Israel occupied the land. Unlike Massoth, however, the harvest festival was not quickly integrated into Israel's salvation history or reinterpreted in the light of that history. Only in the postexilic period did the Feast of Weeks become a commemoration of the giving of the torah at Horeb. The basis for this eventual identification was that Israel arrived at Horeb fifty days after the lamb for the first Passover had been selected (Exod. 12:3; 19:1).

Following Noth's suggestion, Deut. 16:9 would be interpreted, "Seven weeks after the individual first stalks had been combined and waved in the sanctuary."

16:10 The Hebrew word for "festival" is *hag*. Like its Arabic cognate "hajj" (cf. the annual pilgrimage to Mecca), *hag* signifies a religious journey to visit a shrine. In earlier times the shrine would be local; with centralization the venue would shift to Jerusalem.

The offering is freewill, proportionate to the prosperity which Yahweh has granted and based on personal awareness and gratitude ("remember," v. 12).

16:12 This verse (virtually identical with 15:15) belongs to the Deuteronomic school's stock of exhortatory material. Its use of the plural, "these statutes," shows that it applied not just to this pericope but to the code as a whole.

The Feast of Booths (16:13-15)

"Booths" is the oldest of Israel's communal festivals and is generally regarded as *the* feast par excellence. The early sources imply that originally there was only one annual festival (Judg. 21:19; 1 Sam. 1:3, 21), namely, the autumn festival in the month of Ethanim (Sept.-Oct.) — the precursor of the Feast of Booths.

The JE tradition (Exod. 23:16b; 34:32b) uses the name "Ingathering" (Heb. *asiph;* cf. Deut. 16:13), but makes no mention of "booths."

The Deuteronomic picture of the festival reveals several developments.

(1) Deuteronomy's preferred name for the feast is "Booths" (Heb. *sukkot,* "woven," from branches of trees or vines). The booths were obviously prominent in the celebration, though their function is nowhere explicitly described.

(2) In the seventh year, the year of release, a public reading of the torah was part of the program (31:9-13).

The Priestly tradition describes further expansion.

(1) The previously seven-day festival is extended to include an eighth day, "a day of solemn rest" on 22 Tishri (the later, Babylonian name for Ethanim).

(2) Two weeks before the festival there is to be a preparatory "day of solemn rest" (Lev. 23:24).

(3) The tenth day of Tishri is instituted as a Day of Atonement (Lev. 23:26; 16:1-34).

As to the origins of the feast, Julius Wellhausen and his followers trace Booths back to a Canaanite vintage festival: dancing (Judg. 21:20-21), free-flowing wine (cf. Eli's suspicions, no doubt based on experience, of Hannah's being drunk, 1 Sam. 1:14-15), and booths erected in the vineyards. Israel adopted the Canaanite celebration and eventually historicized it, so that the booths came to represent the tents in which the Israelite ancestors lived during the desert wanderings (Lev. 23:42-43).

Hans-Joachim Kraus *(Worship in Israel),* on the other hand, suggests that on entry into Canaan Israel immediately created their own festival of remembrance, an annual dwelling-in-tents to commemorate the Horeb meeting with Yahweh and the desert wanderings. Only subsequently did this tent festival become embellished with details adapted from Canaanite celebrations. Prominent among these features was the substituting of booths for tents.

On the whole, Wellhausen's suggestion is the more persuasive. The theological significance of the feast centers on two points.

First, the festival is a statement of conviction that Yahweh is creator and controller of nature. By contrast, Canaanite religion deified the forces of nature, and provided rites by means of which those forces could be stimulated and channeled for the benefit of the land's inhabitants.

Second, at base Israel's faith is built on a chain of historical experiences which are definitive for their whole understanding of who God is:

- Their release from Egyptian servitude;
- Their meeting at Horeb with the divine Power whom they believed to be their liberator;
- Their successful conquest of Canaan through (they believed) the help of that liberator.

These experiences of sovereign help formed the framework of their religion, into which they fitted material borrowed from the religious traditions of their neighbors. Ancient Semitic laws, for example, were adopted into the historic theophany experience at Horeb. The Festival of Weeks, too, was (finally) pressed into service as a commemoration of the law-giving on Horeb. Also, the Feast of Booths became an annual reliving of the desert wanderings.

Thus the dynamic of Israel's faith, grounded in God-events whose significance they appreciated and appropriated, enabled them (theologically, if not always materially) to impregnate with meaning every aspect of their ongoing life and culture.

16:13 The grain from the threshing floor is presumably the last of the firstfruits and tithes. As we noted above (Deut. 16:9-12), these would be offered in the period between the two festivals of Weeks and Booths.

In actual fact, all three festivals represent aspects of harvest thanksgiving: Massoth, the barley harvest; Weeks, the wheat harvest; and Booths, the vintage.

Festival Summary (16:16-17)

It is somewhat surprising that after the stress laid on Passover rather than Massoth in 16:1-8, the text here in the summary should revert to the traditional name for the spring festival (cf. Exod. 23:15; 34:18). What is the reason for the reversion? Is it simply the spontaneous use of traditional language? Or are those scholars correct who conclude that Deut. 16:16 is a later insertion?

Technically, too, the "all-male" emphasis is at variance with the more inclusive tone of vv. 11, 14.

In many places throughout the OT, the Hebrew verb *r'h*, here translated "appear," is equivocal. It may also be translated "see," depending on which set of vowels are supplied to the original consonants: "to see Yahweh" or "to be seen by/appear before Yahweh," at the sanctuary. In most instances the preference is for the first possibility. In either case, the language is anthropomorphic and emphasizes that awareness of and response to the personal presence of Yahweh is the climax of worship.

In preexilic times the sacrifices in Israel were basically expressions of gratitude and thanksgiving for Yahweh's goodness and acknowledgment of dependence on Yahweh. Thus coming "empty-handed" (v. 16; cf. Exod. 23:15; 34:20) shows a proud, "self-sufficient" bearing, which is inimical to the spirit of true worship. Cf. also 1 Sam. 6:3: to return the ark "empty" would imply that there was no serious desire to make rapprochement or amends to Yahweh.

A Guideline for Judges (16:18-20)

The structure of this little "guideline" is interesting.

The three core sentences are:

(1) Do not pervert justice.
(2) Do not show partiality.
(3) Do not take a bribe.

Of these sentences, the first and third are virtually identical with Exod. 23:2-3, 8, whereas the second corresponds to Deut. 1:17a (see above on 1:13-18 regarding the similar "guideline" there).

The threefold core of 16:18-20 is set in a framework stressing the primary importance of *tsedeq* ("straightness," "uprightness"; see above on 9:1-6) in all judicial dealings.

The function of 16:18-20 within its wider context also corresponds to that of 1:16-17. The "guideline" in 1:16-17 stands within a description of the judicial structure reputedly set up by Moses (see 1:9-18). In a similar way, 16:18-20 is set in a wider context, introducing as it does an account of the various offices within Israel: judges (16:18–17:13), kingship (17:14-20), priest-hood (18:1-8), and prophecy (18:9-22).

As we noted at 1:9-18, the ascription of the judicial system to Moses is theological rather than historical. In fact, the development of the tradition began long before Moses and continued long after. The following are salient points:

(1) According to general ancient Semitic usage and in early Israel, the clan elders administered the customary law to their people (cf. "justice in the gate," Amos 5:10, 12, 15; Deut. 21:19; 22:15).

(2) Difficult cases were "brought to God," that is, to the priest at the local shrine (Exod. 21:6; Deut. 17:8-9). The priest would either adduce an existing *mishpat* (precedent decision) or seek a new one from God.

(3) Codes of law embodying, reframing, and updating ancient customary law were promulgated by ancient Near Eastern kings under their personal aegis and with the blessing of their god(s). Since Yahweh was known in Israel as God and also as King (possibly since pre-Mosaic times), traditional custom law and shrine decisions were promulgated in Israel as Yahweh's law. The Israelite official was not a creator of law, but custodian of Yahweh's law.

16:19   As we noted above, the sentence concerning bribery is almost identical with Exod. 23:8. The frequent references to the subject in both prophetic and wisdom literature (Isa. 1:23; 5:23;

Ezek. 22:12; Mic. 3:11; Prov. 17:23) indicate that bribery was a chronic sickness in Israelite society.

16:20 "Justice and only justice" *(tsedeq, tsedeq)* picks up Deut. 16:18: "They shall judge. . . with a *tsedeq*-decision." There is an urgent intensity about the words which marks them out as Deuteronomic exhortation. Yahweh is just and insists on justice as the hallmark of the covenant people. To conform to Yahweh's standard (i.e., Yahweh's nature) is to "live" (v. 20).

A Cultic Ruling (16:21–17:1)

The points included in this ruling have already been mentioned (see above on 7:5, 25; 15:21). Perhaps they are inserted here to round out the "guideline for judges" (16:18-20) and to underline the principle that social-judicial integrity and cultic integrity go together.

16:21 As far as we know, there was never an Asherah set up by the altar in the Jerusalem temple. The reference is therefore probably to the local altars, and belongs to a strand of material presumably unaware of the strong stress on centralization of the cult (ch. 12).

APOSTASY, JUSTICE, AND KINGSHIP (17:2-20)

The chapter consists of three disparate sections: 17:2-7, concerning apostasy; vv. 8-13, concerning referrals to the central judiciary; and vv. 14-20, guidelines for kingship.

The first two sections are linked by the use of the summarizing phrase, "You shall burn out (RSV 'purge') this evil from among you" (vv. 7, 12; see above on 13:5). Sections two and three are linked by "you shall not deviate . . . to right or left" (17:11, 20). The phrase is typical Deuteronomic vocabulary. It requires complete and sensitive obedience to all that God commands (5:32; 28:14; Josh. 1:7; 23:6; 2 Kgs. 22:2).

161

Dealing with Apostasy (17:2-7)

There is a close connection between this passage and Deut. 13:1-18 (see above). Indeed, it is possible that the two originally formed a unity.

17:2   On the evolving status of women, implicit in 17:2, cf. 15:12.

The "covenant" here is the bond of personal relation between Yahweh and the people; to worship other gods is to cause the withdrawal of the "Jealous One" (4:24) and thus break the relationship. On the increasing emphasis on systematized torah as the content of "covenant," see further at 29:1.

17:3   On the widespread worship of sun, moon, and stars and the Deuteronomic school's reaction to it, see 4:19.

This Semitic and generally ancient Near Eastern practice was officially established in Jerusalem under Manasseh (2 Kgs. 21:3, 5) and abolished by Josiah (2 Kgs. 23:5, 11), precisely at a period when the Deuteronomic school was intensely active. What is described here, then, is not a remote possibility but a current threat to the very existence of the covenant people.

"The host (army) of heaven" is of course the stars. Astrology deeply influenced Babylonian thought and religion. Their almanac was based on the movement of the stars, and a sense of their orderly progression gave rise to the picture of them as an army. The view that their movements controlled the seasons and the finer details of human destiny stimulated the impulse to worship the stars — an impulse enhanced by the belief that each star was indwelt and steered by an angelic being.

Yahwism countered the attraction of astral worship by proclaiming Yahweh as the Commander of hosts, whose will all the astral and angelic powers serve (1 Kgs. 22:19-20; Job 38:7; Ps. 82:1), and the Creator of sun, moon, and stars, which are therefore creaturely and owe their influence to Yahweh's empowering (Gen. 1:16; Ps. 8:3-4).

The "I" speaking at the end of Deut. 16:3 is obviously Yahweh. This is impressive testimony to the intimacy envisaged between

Yahweh and Yahweh's servant, so that by an unconscious shift the words of the mediator become the words of Yahweh.

17:5 The execution "outside the gates" (cf. Lev. 24:14; Num. 15:36; Acts 7:58) signifies that the condemned conduct is a pollutant which could infect and endanger the whole community. The use of stones could have originated in the desire to avoid physical contact (cf., however, Lev. 24:14).

17:6 Cf. Deut. 19:15. In the ancient Near East, including ancient Israel, the burden of proof tended to rest with the accused rather than the accuser. The integrity of witnesses was therefore of crucial importance (see 5:20). It was also essential that the charge laid by the accuser be corroborated by the testimony of at least one other person ("accuser plus one, or accuser plus two"). For the same reason, heavy penalties are invoked against falsification of evidence.

The principle at stake is the sanctity of life. Lack of integrity (specifically in the area of testifying) is life-endangering and is therefore hateful to the living God.

On the provision that the witnesses should initiate the execution process, see 13:9.

Referral to the Central Judiciary (17:8-13)

A comparison with 1:16-17 suggests that 17:8-13 is a continuation of the "guideline for judges" in 16:18-20. We saw there that 16:18-20 elaborates 1:17a, and now 17:8-13 continues the theme by elaborating 1:17b.

17:8 Deuteronomy 17:8 cites some examples of the type of case that is "too difficult" to be settled by elders "in the gate": degrees of homicide (cf. Exod. 21:12-14), complicated disputations (cf. Exod. 22:7-8: were the "stolen" goods in fact stolen?), and degrees of assault (cf. Exod. 21:18-19).

We may query once again whether "the chosen place" was Jerusalem from the beginning, or whether the original reference had been to the provincial or local shrines.

163

17:9   Scholars have questioned whether a single court would be presided over by both priests and judge. Some have concluded therefore that "and to the judge . . ." is a later (Deuteronomic) insertion, designed perhaps to show that the judiciary did not suffer eclipse as a result of the Deuteronomic centralization policy. Others take the opposite view, that the Deuteronomic school's special concern for the Levites in the context of the centralization has led them to insert the reference to levitical priesthood in a context that originally applied only to judges. Certainty on this point is virtually impossible to achieve. In either case, the addition is Deuteronomic and designed to show that all matters civil and cultic are included within Yahweh's all-embracing torah guidance for the covenant people.

17:10-11   "Direct," "instructions," "instruct" (RSV "give") in Deut. 17:10b-11 are variations (noun and verb) of Heb. *torah*. As we have seen, a *torah* is originally a signpost pointing the safe way to travel.

In the latest stratum of Deuteronomy, the total body of legal stipulation and exhortation is *hattorah* — the great all-inclusive guidance. The usage in these verses is from an earlier stratum. Here *torah* is equivalent to "mishpat" ("decision"; see above on 4:1), that is, a specific piece of guidance for a concrete situation currently addressed.

It is appropriate that the same term *torah* is used for both the particular and the global. Yahweh, who is concerned about the details of personal existence, is the same God who is concerned for the universal issues affecting the total faith community and the whole human race. *The* torah comprises many little torahs.

17:12-13   To "act presumptuously" (v. 12) is literally to "boil over" like a pot of soup on a hot stove, frothing up in arrogance with complete insensitivity to one's place in the overall pattern. To assert one's individualism in the secular setting is sedition; to pit oneself against the bearers of torah is to oppose God.

Modern thought would consider it draconian to impose the death penalty for failure to obey a supreme court ruling. We also have difficulty with the concept that the decisions of an ecclesiastical court are absolutely binding because they infallibly represent the mind of God. The strictures against arrogant individualism, however, continue to have relevance for both Church and society. Mature faith involves a sober assessment of ourselves and of our place within the life of the community as a whole.

On v. 13, see 13:11.

Guidelines for Kingship (17:14-20)

These guidelines do not set out to defend or expound the king's rights, but rather to limit them (see Introduction, 17-18). The overall tone is not one of enthusiasm for kingship but reluctant acceptance that it is a historical given, which can be neither denied nor avoided. In keeping with this reluctance, the author seeks to ensure that the de facto king will not frustrate or hamper the people's commitment to the will of Yahweh their Great King (cf. Hindi *maharaja*). Indeed, Norbert Lohfink *(Das Hauptgebot)* suggests that the whole of Deut. 16:18–18:22 is a unit setting out a national constitution. Several functions which in the ancient Near East are normally accorded to the king are here pruned off: the judiciary (17:8-13; 16:18-20), the military apparatus (ch. 20), and mediation of the divine word (the institution of prophecy; 18:16-17). The sole function that remains to the king, then, is that of "exemplary Israelite," chosen from among his peers to model a life pattern that all should copy.

There are obvious points of similarity between 17:14-20 and the "anti-kingship" tradition of northern Israel (e.g., 1 Sam. 8:12). ("Anti-" and "pro-kingship" strands are interwoven in 1 Samuel: anti-, 1 Sam. 7:2-17; ch. 8; 10:17-27a; ch. 12; pro-, 9:1–10:16; ch. 11) Scholars on the whole agree that the anti-kingship strand originates in northern Israel, and the pro-kingship strand in the south. The high status of kingship in the south can be gauged from such Psalms as 2, 20, 45, 110.

The Deuteronomic school, on moving south after the fall of Samaria, accommodated their somewhat anti-kingship tradition to the pro-kingship ethos of Jerusalem theology. One of the basic Deuteronomic convictions is that it was the sins of the royal house which caused Israel's exile.

17:14 "A king . . . like all the nations that are round about" is
a clear echo of 1 Sam. 8:5. 1 Samuel 8 is generally agreed to be
Elohistic. In the Deuteronomic history, however, the old sources
have been Deuteronomically edited; so it is not certain whether
1 Sam. 8:5 is Elohistic or Deuteronomic. In either case, its
deliberate repetition in Deut. 17:14 is meant as a reminder that
from the beginning there was a group in Israel who saw kingship
as a threat to the special relation which Yahweh had created
between Yahweh's self and the chosen people.

17:15 The appointment of a king is by God's permission, not
command. Unlike the first king, whom "you have chosen for
yourselves" (1 Sam. 8:18; 12:13), the approved king will be
chosen by God. Let Israel humbly seek the mind of God before
presuming to proceed to the appointment.

Furthermore, the approved king is to be a "peer," that is, a
fellow member of Israel. Cf. 1 Sam. 12:14, 15, 25: "both you
and your king." King and citizens stand on one level and together
form one people before God. Obedience to God by king-and-
citizens-together brings blessing; disobedience on the part of
either party brings disaster on the whole people.

The fact that the king is a peer also implies deep existential
involvement with the covenantal basis of the people's existence.
An "outsider" (Heb. *nokri;* RSV "foreigner") does not have this
empathy; indeed, such a person's faith allegiance lies elsewhere.
There was bitter historical experience to substantiate this; Kings
Omri and Ahab of northern Israel, who "did evil in the sight of
Yahweh" (1 Kgs. 16:25, 30), were of mixed blood, and Jezebel
the notorious foreign wife of Ahab is portrayed as the archenemy
of Yahwism (e.g., 1 Kgs. 19:1-2). Stated positively, the emphasis
of Deut. 17:14-20 is that the leader must foster the faith loyalty
of the people to their covenant God, based on the leader's own
personal loyalty.

17:16-17 Again, the caveats entered here are born out of historical experience. On the multiplying of horses by Solomon, cf.
1 Kgs. 4:26, 28; 10:26.

Horses in the OT are normally associated with militarism and signify the pride which relies on secular might rather than on Yahweh for national defense. Cf. Isa. 31:1-3 and also Zech. 9:9-10 (where the ideal king rides the trader's donkey, not the warlord's horse).

The "return to Egypt" may mean as horse traders or as slave traders selling Israelite citizens back into servitude. The latter is the more likely. It would be hateful as tantamount to undoing the freedom-from-Egyptian servitude which God granted at the Exodus. Deuteronomy 17:16b seems to be intended as a direct OT quotation (cf. also 28:68). In fact, no such prohibition is recorded. The sentence is, however, generally reminiscent of Exod. 10:29; 14:13. (We may note also the strand in the patriarchal narratives [Gen. 24:5-8] which frowns on return to former places, regarding such returning as a reversal of salvation history.)

The warning against the multiplying of wives (Deut. 17:17a) is again reminiscent of Solomon, whose foreign marriage partners drew him into apostasy (1 Kgs. 11:1-10).

There is a realism in the injunction against amassing "too much" gold (Deut. 17:17b) — a recognition (contrary to the Rechabites, e.g., Jer. 35:1-10) that one cannot hold the clock back and reject all wealth in the name of an ancient (desert) ideal. Wealth should not become an enticement to compromise one's commitment to Yahweh. Positively, one should let wealth enhance one's solidarity with the needy among the covenant people and so in fact strengthen one's covenant commitment.

17:18-19   The "law" which is to be the king's guidebook is the Deuteronomic code (Deut. 12–26). It is described as *hattorah* (see above on v. 11). There may be a reference here to a rite within the coronation ritual, that is, the ceremonial handing to the king of a copy of the torah (cf. 2 Kgs. 11:12, "the testimony"; Ps. 132:12, "my testimonies"), which is to be his compass throughout his reign. The symbolism indicates that the king is not the source of law, but the upholder and executor of Yahweh's law. Interestingly, this parallels the ancient Near Eastern vassal treaties, where the vassal king is handed a copy of the treaty and required to read it publicly at stated intervals, while the Great King stores the original in the central state shrine.

Israel's king, then, is not mandated to compose his own legal code (like Hammurabi) but is commanded to rule by Yahweh's law — to which he himself is subject along with his people. In other words, Yahweh is Israel's Ruler, and the king Yahweh's representative.

17:20   Gerhard von Rad suggests that Deut. 17:20 originally connected directly with v. 17 (vv. 18-19 being an insert). The logical progression would then be that wealth causes pride and lust for power, out of which inhuman hierarchies of authority are born, with the result that "brother-sisterhood" (human dignity) is forgotten.

In those pre-secular times, Israel was both "church" and state. It would be naive to imagine today that the prescription of 17:18-20 could be literally fulfilled and the Deuteronomic code made the direct basis for governing church or nation. (Even in the Deuteronomic era it would have required a great deal of adaptation and interpretation.) Nevertheless, there are abiding principles patent or latent in the code which, if applied with integrity and imagination, would vastly enrich contemporary church and society. Prominent among these is the one stressed here, that ruler and people are "brothers." Authority is not for power, but for enhancing the real humanity of all concerned.

PRIESTS AND PROPHECY (18:1-22)

Deuteronomy 18 divides into two sections. Verses 1-8 deal with the rights of the levitical priesthood, and vv. 9-22 with prophecy as the authentic means of hearing God's contemporary word.

The Rights of the Levitical Priesthood (18:1-8)

The origin and status of the Levites has been touched on at Deut. 10:8, and the Deuteronomic school's special concern for them in the Introduction (14-15). The aim of the present passage is to set out in detail their rights to material support.

The structure of 18:1-8 is not simple. Verse 3 is probably the original core, to which has been added in successive steps: v. 4

(providing additional material support); vv. 1, 2, 5 (stressing the Levites' priestly status); and vv. 6-8 (providing for the Levites' changed circumstances in the light of cultic centralization).

18:1-2 This verse seems overfull. The phrase "that is, all the tribe of Levi" was perhaps added along with vv. 6-8. The intention is to provide not only for the Levites ministering at the central shrine but also for unemployed Levites in the regions.

It is strange that the offerings *(ishsheh)* by fire *(esh)*, that is, sacrifices burned entire on the altar, should at the same time be said to be "eaten by the priest." Recent scholarship has suggested an alternative derivation for "ishsheh": not from "fire," but from a Sumerian root implying "fellowship," "giving."

On Israel's "inheritance" see 4:1. On Levi's "inheritance" see 10:9.

The "promise" referred to at the end of 18:2 is not recorded in the extant JE material, but a Priestly version of it occurs at Num. 18:20.

18:3 The priests' "due" is literally their "mishpat" (see above on Deut. 10:18). Interestingly, the "levitical priest" is in v. 3 simply "the priest," as in the old source on which the Deuteronomic writer is drawing. "Priest" means "Levite," according to this verse. In earlier sources (e.g., 1 Sam. 2:14), the priest-Levite's position is not yet specified. In the later postexilic times, the Priestly tradition demoted the Levites to the rank of priests' assistants. (On the apportionment of "dues" at that stage, cf. Num. 18:8-32.) Deut. 18:1-8 therefore probably marks the high point in the history of levitical status.

18:4 If our surmise (see above on 14:22-29) is correct, that firstfruits and tithes were originally identical, then 18:4 (assigning the firstfruits to Levi) is the basis on which Num. 18:21-32 later assigned "him" the tithes.

Though it is nowhere explicitly stated, the "fleece" of the firstling lamb is regarded as part of the "firstfruits" offering (see 15:19-20). Thus the Levites' clothing as well as food is from Yahweh's offerings.

169

18:5   In discussing the duties of the Levites (10:8-9), we have already alluded to the circumstances surrounding their being chosen for priesthood. Exod. 32:25-29 connects this with the "golden calf" apostasy, as does Deut. 10:8-9.

But 33:8-11 refers the Levites' choice to the "Massah" incident (see above on 9:22-23). Both versions highlight Levi's "fanatical" devotion to Yahweh, choosing Yahweh above the claims of clan loyalty.

18:6-8   These verses deal with the situation created by the centralization of the cult under Josiah's reform (see Introduction, 18).

In the context of 2 Kgs. 23, which recounts the reform, 2 Kgs. 23:9 reads like an apology that one provision of the torah was not implemented, namely, that the redundant "priests of the high places" were *not* reemployed at the Jerusalem shrine. If these priests were in fact Levites, then the non-implemented Deuteronomic provision is Deut. 18:6-8 (however, not all scholars accept this equation).

Verse 8 is puzzling. What "patrimony" could a Levite have if Levites have no "portion" among the tribes (v. 1)? Would it be proceeds from the sale of produce or assets from the "forty-eight levitical cities" (Num. 35:7) — assuming that the allocation of these cities is indeed historical fact? According to Deut. 18:6 the Levites are to come to Jerusalem, not from a home base but from wherever they have been living as "sojourner" (*ger;* in contrast to 1:16, in 18:6 the Hebrew term implies not "foreign" but "rootless and vulnerable").

When the OT references to Levi are viewed as whole, a certain duality of tribal and priestly aspects emerges. Did all members of the ancient tribe (eventually subsumed within Judah) actually become priests? Moreover, could all "levitical priests" actually claim blood descent from the ancient tribe? Some overlapping seems certain. Does the "patrimony" belong, then, in that area of overlap?

Prophecy (18:9-22)

The importance of prophecy for the Deuteronomic school has already been referred to (see Introduction, 14-15, 20, and above on 13:1-5).

Deuteronomy 18:9-22 brings prophecy into focus by contrasting two possible methods of ascertaining the divine will and the details of the divine plan for the future. One way is divination; the other is prophecy.

Divination is illicit, in that it seeks to wrest the divine secrets by the use of human manipulatory skills. Prophecy alone is licit, because it listens for what God's self is saying and seeks to conform human thinking and behavior to God's plans for the present and the future. False "prophecy" is manipulative and therefore nothing but a subtle kind of divination.

To dabble in divination is to fail in covenant loyalty. (The temptation has been present since Mosaic times; Exod. 7:11, 22; 8:7, 19.) For Yahweh is gracious and may be relied on to reveal everything necessary for the covenant people's well-being. More than that is a snare.

18:10a   On "passing the children through the fire," see above on Deut. 12:31. Is it intended here as a means of divination (cf. 2 Kgs. 21:6)? If not, those scholars are probably right who consider Deut. 18:10a an intrusion in the present context.

18:10b-11   Seven forms of divination are listed — "seven" probably symbolizing completeness, a rounded description. These seven fall within two categories: practices concerned with reading or manipulating phenomena of nature, and those attempting to contact the dead.

God does indeed "speak" through natural phenomena (e.g., Reed Sea, Horeb, manna, waters of Jordan). However, in authentic cases the initiative is God's; in divination, the initiative is claimed by the human manipulator. Contacting the dead is an appeal to a spiritual force apart from Yahweh and therefore a departure from wholehearted trust.

All such attempts at divination are "revolting" to Yahweh (vv. 9,

171

12; cf. 7:25). As such they threaten the covenant relation and place
the covenant inheritance in jeopardy (see above on 4:1). God who
"drives out" the Canaanites may also drive out rebellious Israel.

18:13   Hebrew *tamim* (translated "blameless") means "complete," "entire," "fully rounded." It is used in 32:4 of God's work,
and it lies behind the phraseology of Matt. 5:48: "Be perfect, as
your heavenly Father is perfect."

Indeed, that sentence from Matt. 5 may be taken as the definitive commentary on Deut. 18:13: "Draw all your resources from
God in total dependence and commitment, to the point where
the attitude of God is reflected in your total attitude and behavior."

18:14   "God has not *allowed* (Heb. *natan*) you so to do" could
also be translated, "Not thus has God *given* to you."

Both translations are viable: the Great King does not "allow"
his vassal to form any other alliance; and the "gift" of God far
excels anything that Baalism has to offer. He "gives" not divination
but prophecy, that is, insight based on person-to-person relationships. Cf. Adam C. Welch's comment (*The Code of Deuteronomy*,
105): God "made and controlled all things, but His chief work
was man (sic). And when He told His will, He revealed it through
His highest not His lower work."

18:15-19   These verses pick up and continue the narrative of
5:25-29. The material in common is as follows:

Deut. 18	Deut. 5
"Him you shall heed" (v. 15)	"We will hear/heed (you)" (v. 27)
"Let me not hear again the voice . . . or see this great fire" (v. 16)	"We have heard his voice . . . (speaking) out of the midst of the fire" (v. 24)
"They have rightly said all that they have spoken" (v. 17)	"They have rightly said all that they have spoken" (v. 28)

The difference is that, whereas in ch. 5 Moses is called to mediate
the awesome word, in ch. 18 it is "a prophet like Moses" who
conveys Yahweh's message.

We need to remind ourselves of the concrete setting of this Deuteronomic material. Through the device of a thirteenth-century Mosaic farewell speech, an eighth- or seventh-century member of the Deuteronomic school is addressing his own generation. His argument runs thus:

> The Exodus generation could be quite sure that they were hearing the authentic word of Yahweh, because Moses himself was mediating it to them. Can you be so sure today? Indeed you can! Although Moses isn't among you, his God-appointed successors are. When the prophets, preaching in your covenant renewal ceremonies, take the historic torah and apply it to your contemporary situation, God is just as surely addressing you through them, as he addressed the Exodus generation through Moses. Therefore, the onus is on you to hear and obey — or be responsible for your own rejection as covenant people.

Traditionally, this passage concerning the "prophet like Moses" has been interpreted eschatologically. Christian theologians have found its fulfillment in Christ: mediator of the new torah (Matt. 5–7), leader of the new exodus (Luke 9:30-31), and suffering representative (Deut. 1:17; 3:26; 4:21; cf. 1 Pet. 3:18). On the other hand, Muslim theologians have seen its fulfillment in Muhammad, "the seal of the prophets."

The non-eschatological interpretation is to be preferred. It fits the context, that is, the two contrasting ways of seeking to know the will of God for the contemporary situation. Yet it also points beyond its eighth-seventh century fulfillment toward the eschaton. Yahweh does not and will not leave the covenant people without a means of hearing Yahweh's contemporary word. Moreover, contemporization of the torah inevitably means not just bare repetition but also escalation.

For the description of the Horeb experience as "the day of assembly" (Deut. 18:16), see above on 9:10.

20:17   It seems strange that God should be said to commend the people for choosing mediated encounter in preference to direct contact with the divine, so highly valued in texts such as Num. 11:29.

Several factors influence the Deuteronomic theology at this point:

(1) The OT theophanic tradition consistently stresses the awesomeness of direct meeting with God. The encounter is life-threatening (Exod. 33:20; Judg. 6:22-23; Isa. 6:5).

Reticence is therefore adjudged praiseworthy, insofar as it stems from a realization of God's holiness.

(2) The Deuteronomic school place great emphasis on order in worship so as to preserve integrity and purity of faith, hence the insistence on mediation, on centralization of the cult, and so forth. We may ask in general, but specifically perhaps in the case of centralization, whether the price paid was not too high. Centralized worship (and mediated contact?) may be pure, but if it is inaccessible to the people, does not the loss outweigh the gain?

(3) On the other hand, the Deuteronomic school also strongly stress the "re-actualization" that takes place in worship (see above on Deut. 5:1-5). The word read and preached at the annual festival is an echo of the divine voice (Heb. *qol*) "first" heard on Horeb — the voice whose content is torah. This means that there is no necessary conflict between "direct" and "mediated" meeting with God. The difference is, rather, that at the later period Israel's meeting with Yahweh took place within a structured framework, whereas "Horeb" was prior to the structure.

18:19   Rejection of the prophetic word is regarded as parallel to rejection of the priestly-judicial decision and bears similar sanctions (17:12). Both "words" are from God and witness to God's intention.

18:20-22   Criteria for detecting the "false prophet" have been mentioned at 13:1-5. There the context was incitement to apostasy. Here the question concerns prophecy spoken indeed in the name of Yahweh, but not reflecting the will of Yahweh. Such distortion is difficult to detect and to counter. (How does a third party prove that a certain prophet has or has not "stood in the divine council"?). Nevertheless, the Deuteronomic writer insists that the two types of distortion are equally reprehensible and "deserving of the death penalty."

The criterion offered here (18:22) is that "if the prophecy is not fulfilled, then it was false" (see above on 13:1-5, 134). There are, of course, exceptions to this rule: where the threat induces repentance (Jonah 3:10), and where God's patience grants postponement (Jer. 18:7-10; 20:8-9).

Apart from exceptions, however, there is an obvious difficulty with this criterion, namely, that the fulfillment or nonfulfillment usually comes too late for effective response (e.g., 1 Kgs. 22:28).

Nevertheless, this unusual criterion does contain a valuable insight, that the will of God is often known only by hindsight. Believers are frequently called to act on their own conscientious if somewhat diffident assessment of what is wise and right, and only afterwards do they receive confirmation that their choice was pleasing to God.

The prophet whose words are consistently fulfilled will no doubt increasingly enjoy the people's confidence — a situation which brings its own temptations.

On "presumptuous" speaking (Deut. 18:22), see above on 17:12. The phrase "you need not be afraid of him" chimes strangely with the strident call for the death penalty (18:20). Is this a later addition, acknowledging that the requirement of this verse is impracticable — and perhaps unworthy, for all its Yahwistic zeal?

PROTECTION OF INNOCENT BLOOD (19:1-21)

Deuteronomy 19 consists of two major sections: (1) vv. 1-13, concerning the cities of refuge; and (2) vv. 15-21, concerning false witness. The common thread is a concern to prevent the shedding of innocent blood in the name of justice.

Verse 14, sandwiched between the sections, deals with a separate topic. For this reason, scholars have suspected that it may be an intrusion into the context.

The Cities of Refuge (19:1-13)

Preliminary discussion of this topic occurs at 4:41-43 (see above), in the Deuteronomic introduction to the code.

The custom of fugitives taking refuge at shrines is ancient and widespread. It is attested in Phoenicia, Syria, Greece, and Rome.

The earliest stratum of the OT sanctions reprisal, especially in the case of murder, and indeed provides a divine mandate. Such early formulas as Gen. 9:6 make no direct distinction between deliberate and unintentional killing. The primary emphasis at that stage is that the shedding of blood is offensive to the Creator and must not be permitted to extend unchecked.

On that basis arose the distinction between the deliberate and the unintentional. The right of the avenger must be restricted, especially in cases of unintentional killing. Remembering that the avenger in the heat of the occasion could well be incapable of making the distinction, the provision of refuges creates a pause, providing opportunity for the circumstances to be seen more objectively.

In the course of time, the altar of refuge (Exod. 21:13-14; translated "place" here, the term just as frequently means "holy place") became the city of refuge — a form of the institution which seems to have been peculiar to Israel.

Further with regard to origins (cf. Deut. 4:41-43), it is interesting that in the Priestly lists (Josh. 20:1-9; Num. 35:6, 9-15) the six cities of refuge are included among the forty-eight levitical cities. Most scholars doubt that this "levitical city" concept was ever realized historically. However, it may very well be that there was a historical connection between the Levites and the cities of refuge, namely, that from early times the Levites served the altars/shrines which became designated as refuges and continued as the dominant group in the towns which grew up around these shrines.

In principle, Deut. 19:1-13 is an application and expansion, in a later setting, of Exod. 21:13-14.

Further (post-Deuteronomic) stages in the institution's development are described in Josh. 20–21 and Num. 35:9-28.

1. Josh. 20–21 is Priestly, though 20:3-6 may be Deuteronomic material redacted by the Priestly source. The salient emphases are:

(a) The fugitive undergoes preliminary examination by the elders of the refuge. Deliberate slayers are not granted asylum.

(b) Joshua 20:6 describes two different outcomes presumably reflecting two different historical stages:

　(1) The "congregation" (Heb. *'eda*) gives the verdict. Is this body comprised of the people of the fugitive's hometown or the local council of elders?

　(2) The fugitive remains in refuge till the death of the high priest. Does the priest's death atone for inadvertent bloodshed, or does the anointing of his successor mark a new beginning for all citizens?

2. Numbers 35 is later Priestly material, building on Josh. 20–21. In this stage:

(a) Preliminary refuge is granted directly.

(b) After being judged by the congregation, the fugitive must remain in refuge till the death of the high priest.

(c) Failure to remain in the refuge exposes the fugitive — even though adjudged innocent by the congregation — to the retaliation of the avenger.

19:2　The "three cities" intended are probably Kedesh in Galilee (north), Shechem (central), and Hebron (south) (Josh. 20:7; see further on Deut. 19:7-8).

19:3　The term translated "(man)slayer" is Heb. *rotseah* (cf. the discussion on the basic verb form *ratsah* at 5:17).

19:6　The "avenger of blood" is the *go'el haddam*. The verb *ga'al* has no equivalent in the cognate languages, but a survey of its OT occurrences suggests a basic meaning "restore" or "repair," and hence "liberate" or "redeem."

The "avenger of blood" is a close kin of the dead person who restores the disturbed equilibrium and reinstates the wholeness of communal and family relations (even the wholeness of the natural order), which had been impaired by the shedding of blood.

In the later strata of the OT, Yahweh is often described as "go'el," both of oppressed individuals and groups (e.g., Jer. 50:34; Ps. 119:154) and also of the people as a whole (Exod. 6:6; Isa. 41:14; Ps. 74:2).

The phrase "did not deserve to die" is literally "there was no verdict *(mishpat)* of death (attaching) to his/her case."

In the thinking of the Deuteronomic school, the *mishpat* of death in the case of a deliberate slaying is appropriate at two levels. At one level, it is appropriate because such slaying is inimical to the mind of God as expressed in torah. On another level, it is appropriate because the guilty party has transgressed the norms acknowledged by universal human conscience and strikes at the moral order implicit in creation.

19:7-8 The question arises as to the direction in which the "enlargement of borders" is thought to proceed. According to Deut. 1–4, the direction is east to west. Hence, the original refuges are Bezer, Ramoth, and Golan (4:43), and the towns named in 19:2 (see above) are additional. The tenor of Deuteronomy as a whole, however, makes it unlikely that the settlement of Canaan proper is regarded as "enlargement," supplementary to the occupation of Transjordan. In other words, "enlargement" appears to imply a west-to-east movement.

It is clear that the traditions of the Canaan settlement as they have come down to us are highly stylized. Thus it is extremely difficult to reconstruct the historical process on the basis of these accounts. Roland de Vaux *(The Early History of Israel)* suggests the following:

(1) The "Joseph" group, who had experienced "Horeb" under Moses, entered the area of Transjordan situated between the Arnon and Jabbok rivers. This region was already occupied by the Gad clan — who had presumably not been down to Egypt, but converted to Yahwism as presented to them by the Joseph clan.

(2) Sometime later, after the conquest of Canaan proper, some elements of the Reuben clan retreated eastward into Transjordan and fused with the Gad clan.

(3) At a still later stage, "Machir," a branch of Manasseh, crossed from the west and occupied the area of Transjordan to the north of the Jabbok.

If this reconstruction is in principle correct, then the Deut. 1–4 tradition refers to the meeting of the Joseph group with Gad, whereas 19:8 reflects the eastward transmigration of Reuben and Manasseh.

Theologically, the two strands together witness to the occupation of the land (however complicated its process) as gift (cf. Josh. 24:12-13).

In Deut. 12:20 the "enlargement" of borders is promised "to you" (i.e., the desert generation and/or the later festival generation). In 19:8 it is promised "to your ancestors" (i.e., the patriarchs). The two promises are at least five hundred years apart, yet they are one promise — because they are made by the one God to the one people who are the constant object of God's faithfulness.

19:9 Verse 9 is a typical Deuteronomic parenesis or exhortation, reiterating the principle that obedience is essential as response to the covenant of grace (cf., e.g., 7:9-10; 11:22ff.).

19:10 Bloodshed is regarded as defiling the land, and since the land remains the possession of Yahweh, the "tenants" are guilty of insulting Yahweh if they neglect to play their part in correcting the imbalance and removing the pollution. Viewed from another angle, it is also stressed that blood as bearer of the life force is peculiarly God's, so that God's self acts as the avenger of blood (cf. Ps. 9:12; Isa. 26:21).

19:11-13 Deuteronomy 19:11 resumes the statement of casuistic law, begun in vv. 4-6 but interrupted by the intruding parenesis. This continuation (vv. 11-13) reaffirms that the right of refuge is restricted to cases of unintentional slaying. The role of the elders in these matters is obviously ancient (see further 21:1-9). It is noteworthy, however, that in their concern to establish the rule of law in Yahweh's name the Deuteronomic school do not seek to cancel the role of "the avenger of blood" (19:6) — by trans-

179

ferring his functions to the elders, for example — but rather to
delimit and regularize that role. This reluctance to override the
ancient family rights may have both cultic and moral roots. Cul-
tically, members of the family are "one blood." It was deemed
appropriate and/or essential, therefore, that the blood which had
been wronged should, as it were, speak and act in its own defense,
through the family. Morally, the duty of avenging blood was a
particular and forceful expression of the wide-ranging obligation
to family support laid on all members. In this obligation to uphold
one another in life and in death the family is the microcosm of
the covenant people.

Verse 13 rounds off the section by reiterating several familiar
Deuteronomic formulas (see above on 7:16; 13:5; 4:40).

The Ancient Landmark (19:14)

This verse is a miniature example of preached law. The same law
is presented again in different format at 27:17. The parallels
offered by the ancient Near Eeastern codes show, by the severity
of the penalties exacted, that tampering with boundary markers
was a very serious offense. The requirement that the land be
"cleansed" after such a violation (Hittite code 168) indicates that
the offense had cultic-religious implications. A particular parcel
of land, delineated since ancient times, is regarded as a sacral entity,
the violation of which is an offense against the spirit or "god" of
the land.

Whose were the ancient hands that set the marker in place?
(This is an interesting question, in view of the "speech of Moses"
format in which the Deuteronomic code is presented.) Was it the
patriarchs? Or was it the original Canaanite inhabitants? In the
latter case, there is an acknowledged sacredness about the land
which pre-dates Yahwism (or rather, Israel's knowledge of
Yahweh). Or is the speaker a ninth- or eighth-century preacher
who thinks back to the "ancient hands" of the settlers led by
Joshua?

Concerning False Witness (19:15-21)

On this section, cf. 17:6-7.

The core of the material, "a single witness is insufficient to convict an accused person" (19:15a), is expanded in two directions: provision of extra witnesses (v. 15b) and scrutinizing the integrity of the single witness (vv. 16-21).

"False witness" (v. 18) is an ancient concern both in the Near East in general and Israel in particular. The Code of Hammurabi §§ 1-4 broadly applies the *lex talionis* (cf. Deut. 19:21) to such cases. Both the Book of the Covenant (Exod. 23:1) and the Decalogue (Exod. 20:16; Deut. 5:20) prohibit false witness. The later, post-Deuteronomic tradition (cf. Num. 35:30) reiterated Deut. 19:15, adding that those possessing relevant information have an obligation to testify (Lev. 5:1).

19:16 The word here translated "wrongdoing" is rendered "rebellion" at Deut. 13:5 (literally, "turning aside"). The connection is plain: to turn away from God's purpose as presented in torah is to turn away from God's self.

19:17 This verse is a telescoped history. Originally the matter was decided "before Yahweh," that is, by the priestly "mishpat" at the local shrine (cf. 1:16-17). Then with the passage of time the number and variety of officials increased (see above on 16:18-20) so that both priests and judges (either concurrently or successively; cf. 17:9) played a role.

19:19-21 Deuteronomy 19:19-21a reflects familiar Deuteronomic terminology (13:5, 11; 7:16; 19:13).

The *lex talionis* (v. 21b) is formally presented as the application of v. 19. Practically, however, the connection is much looser. The *lex talionis* here is simply used out of context, as an ancient solemnity to close the parenesis with a stress on the extreme seriousness of bearing false witness.

As already noted, the *lex talionis* is evidenced in the ancient Near Eastern sources as well as in early Israelite tradition. Its strongly retributive tone sounds harsh to contemporary ears. Two points should be noted in this regard:

(1) The ancient conviction was that retributive punishment was an effective deterrent for would-be offenders. (Whether it is in fact so in the modern world is another matter.)

(2) The *lex talionis* represented a step forward in the establishment of justice by limiting the reprisal (contrast, e.g., Gen. 4:23-24):

> an eye — and no more! — for an eye;
> a tooth — and no more! — for a tooth.

Unbridled "lashing out" at the offender is banned. Thus, in its context the *lex talionis* is some acknowledgment that human life and physique are to be respected, because they have dignity in the sight of God, the fountainhead of law.

YAHWEH'S WAR (20:1-20)

Deuteronomy 20 covers various aspects of "Yahweh's war" (see Introduction, 15-17).

Verses 1-9 describe the preparation of the battle forces, while vv. 10-12 set the conditions for besieging cities.

Preparations for War (20:1-9)

This section is a mixture of singular (vv. 1, 5-9) and plural (vv. 2-4) grammatical forms, indicating that its structure is composite. Four steps in the formation process can be discerned.

(1) The officer's address to the troops (vv. 5-7 and perhaps v. 9). The title and role of "officer" (Heb. *shoter*) probably dates from the reign of David.

(2) Addition to the above (v. 8, and perhaps v. 9).

(3) The priest's exhortation (vv. 2-4), couched in typically Deuteronomic language (cf. 7:6-16; Josh. 1:9). The Deuteronomic composition, however, probably utilizes traditional material.

(4) Deuteronomy 20:1 is typical Deuteronomic exhortatory language and serves to draw the other threads together into a unity.

20:1 "Horses and chariots" translate as "high military technology," as daunting for the ancient infantry as the modern sophisticated nuclear arsenal is to a small Third World army. The Deuteronomic theologian has the audacity (naïveté, some would say!) to negate this superior might with "Yahweh your God — Yahweh is with you." The struggle Israel is engaged in is "Yahweh's war"; its aim is to establish Yahweh's purpose for and through this strangely chosen people. "Yahweh brought you up from servitude": let that past experience of powerful intervention galvanize Israel's nerve in face of the present challenge.

The exhortation to "not be afraid" of the opposition (typical Deuteronomic language) is balanced by the call to "fear Yahweh" (4:10). This is the great "fear" that drives out all lesser ones.

20:2-4 The term "priest" occurs thirteen times throughout Deuteronomy. In the other twelve instances the reference, either directly or by implication, is to the levitical priests. Thus, we may safely assume the same reference here in 20:2. The vocabulary in which the exhortation (vv. 3-4) is couched is typically Deuteronomic. The phrase "to give you the victory" (v. 4), however, is probably ancient (cf. Judg. 2:16 and *passim*). Indeed, the section as a whole may well comprise traditional "Yahweh's war" material, re-expressed in Deuteronomic language. Furthermore, the preeminence of the priest may represent the ancient order where "sacred" and "secular" authority are as yet undifferentiated.

20:5-7 The dispensation from military service granted to certain categories of men is reminiscent of Judg. 7:2-7, where the number of combatants is deliberately reduced to make it quite clear that the victory is Yahweh's.

The motive for the dispensation adduced here in Deut. 20:5-7 has a "modern" humanitarian ring about it. Nevertheless, beneath this obviously Deuteronomic surface more ancient concepts are submerged. According to ancient thought, every new beginning (new house, orchard, marriage) is an occasion of special vulnerability to spiritual influences, both beneficent and malign. There is a danger, then, that a soldier involved in "new things" could weaken and infect the whole army with his vulnerability. So to avoid this possible contagion, he is excused from duties.

The Deuteronomic re-theologizing of the old material stresses that the enjoyment of house, garden, and marriage is part of Yahweh's gift of life and well-being to those who obey (cf. 28:11; but contrast 28:30).

To "enjoy" the first crop from the vineyard (20:6) is literally to "desacralize" it. The tree whose fruit has never been picked is still in mint condition, fresh from the hand of the Creator. The first harvesting then transfers it to the realm of the everyday. As an acknowledgment that the tree's fertility is the gift of Yahweh, the firstfruits are offered to God. (On the similar concept of "circumcising" the fruit trees, cf. Lev. 19:23-25; see above on Deut. 19:10.)

The phrase "betrothed a wife" (20:7) means literally "paid the (bride) price." The OT in general does not draw an essential distinction between betrothal and marriage. Cf. 22:23-24; Judg. 15:1-2; Gen. 19:14, where in each case "wife/husband" (or equivalent) is equated with "fiancé(e)."

20:8-9 Deuteronomy 20:8-9 is, as indicated, an extension of vv. 5-7 (v. 8a constitutes a fresh introduction, parallel to v. 5a). The threat arising from contagion of fear is somewhat different from the more concrete sources of vulnerability cited in vv. 5-7. Cf. Judg. 7:2-3, where Gideon similarly guards against the individual's fear infecting the group. Such fear is, in effect, the opposite of the numinous fear (cf. Deut. 2:25) prominent in the armory of Yahweh's war. The one hinders Yahweh's victory, while the other achieves it. The "commanders" (Heb. *sar*, literally, "chief," "prince") take their place at the "head" (Heb. *r'osh*) of the people (20:9). Scholars regard the use of the term *sar* here as a reflection of the military atmosphere and structures of David's reign.

Conditions for Besieging Cities (20:10-20)

The section falls into three parts:

vv. 10-14	conquest of distant cities
vv. 15-18	conquest of cities in Canaan proper
vv. 19-20	handling of the trees around the besieged city.

The whole section is in the grammatical singular, giving an impression of homogeneity. The contrasting treatment meted out to towns distant and near-at-hand is reflected in Josh. 9 (JE) and may represent the ancient tradition. On the other hand, however, Deut. 20:15-18 may be from a later and more radical Deuteronomic hand, seeking to tighten up the "overly tolerant" stance of vv. 10-14.

20:10-14   This part in turn includes two topics: (1) treatment of cities that sue for peace, and (2) treatment of cities that resist.

A first reading of vv. 10-14 conveys the impression of a more humane approach to conquest, compared with 7:1-5 and 20:15-18. Only at v. 15 is it stated that vv. 10-14 are in fact of limited application, that is, to distant cities only. It may well be that the *herem* (see above on 2:34) was applied with varying degrees of strictness from time to time and place to place, and that vv. 10-14 were originally meant as a description of conquest within Canaan. If this is so, it would be intriguing to know whether vv. 10-14 are older JE-type material which the Deuteronomic writer (vv. 15-18) is "correcting," or whether one Deuteronomic writer (vv. 15-18) is "correcting" another (vv. 10-14).

The older sources imply (Josh. 16:10; 17:12-13; Judg. 1:28, 30, 33, 35) that forced labor (Deut. 20:11) was exacted from those Canaanites whom Israel could not expel — a situation regretted by the "purist" author of vv. 15-18. This forced-labor system was widened by Solomon (although the Deuteronomist denies this; 1 Kgs. 9:22) to include Israelites also (1 Kgs. 5:13; cf. 4:6). This may have been an emergency, temporary measure during the construction of the temple. However that may be, it is sobering to note how inhumanity "abroad" tends to dehumanize relationships "at home."

The sparing of women, children, cattle, and goods (Deut. 20:14) is in sharp contrast to the rigor of 7:16; 13:15; and so forth. Is there a hint here of theological debate going on within the Deuteronomic school itself — the passion for "strictness," "purity," discipline; and over against the zeal, the insistent question, "Does loyalty to Yahweh, whose second name is Compassion, really require this quenching of humane feeling?"

20:15-18 Deuteronomy 20:15-18 recapitulates 7:1-5. (Some manuscripts add "Girgashites" in 20:17 to complete the parallel.)

Verse 18 (cf. 7:4) is Deuteronomic theologizing. The ancient *herem* was a holocaust offering to the victorious battle-deity. Here its purpose is redefined in terms of absolute commitment to Yahweh and resolute destruction of any hindrance.

To modern thought the desire to safeguard the purity of faith by obliterating all alternatives is wrongheaded and unworthy. The zeal for God's truth is laudable, but the way to truth surely lies through exposure and dialogue rather than confrontation.

20:19-20 Prohibitions against cutting down a neighbor's fruit tree are common in the ancient Near Eastern codes of civil law. The Deuteronomic peculiarity is that the old civil regulation is here applied to war conditions — an indication perhaps of how largely "Yahweh's war" thinking colored Deuteronomic theology. Noteworthy too is the humanitarian and environmental concern evidenced here in pleasing contrast to the rigors of the *herem* as advocated above.

Besides environmental sensitivity there is also enlightened self-interest. It would surely be shortsighted to destroy valuable assets in the land which Yahweh promised (Moses'-speech perspective) would become Israel's, both in the immediate and long-term future. To ruin the sources of sustenance is to mutilate and despise the "inheritance" which is God's gift to the covenant people, and therefore dishonoring to God. In this twin principle of reverence for the land and its resources and responsibility for the future is a foundation for sound ecological concern.

"Are the trees men?" is a whimsical touch that indicates doubts as to whether the uncompromising application of *herem* really is

God's intention. Many a bastion falls to humor that will not fall to polemic!

THREATS TO THE COVENANT (21:1-23)

The chapter consists of five separate units, all concerned more or less explicitly with things that defile the land and therefore threaten the covenant relation with Yahweh, giver of the land.

Concerning Unsolved Murders (21:1-9)

It is clear from 19:1-13 that family responsibility for "avenging blood" is contexted and limited by community responsibility. Similarly here in 21:1-9, it is the community that bears responsibility in regard to "unavenged blood."

The atonement rite described here is clearly ancient. It is of a mystic-magic nature designed to remove the pollution and curse inherent in violently-shed blood.

A comparison with the corresponding sections of the ancient Near Eastern codes highlights this "mystic" quality. In both the Hittite code (I.6, the case of an unknown murderer) and Hammurabi's code (§ 23-24, the case of an unapprehended thief), the community closest to the scene of the crime makes reparation by means of monetary compensation. Deuteronomy 21:1-9, however, deals not with reparation but with removal of pollution and curse — a more ancient and elemental level of concern. Perhaps in stages, the ancient material has been adapted to Yahwism; touches of the process are discernible in vv. 1, 2, 5, 6, 9.

The "elders and judges" (v. 2) who make the initial allocation of responsibility are officials from the central (17:9) or regional (16:18-19) judiciary (according to the Talmud, a commission of three to five members from the central court). Almost certainly this role of central administration is secondary, an adaptation of an originally local rite to the more organized conditions under the Monarchy.

Interestingly, the Samaritan Pentateuch reads *shoter* ("measurer"; see above on 1:15) for *shophet* ("judge") in 21:2 — an indication that there is some hesitancy about the precise wording.

187

This hesitancy suggests that the term may have been added at some stage (cf. 17:9).

The "heifer which has never been worked" (21:3; cf. the tree which has never been harvested, 20:6) is still within the sphere of the sacral, its potency intact and therefore suited to a rite of elemental purification. Similarly, the "valley . . . which is neither plowed nor sown" (21:4) may represent the pristine "innocence" to which the wider polluted area is to be restored. (Alternatively, it may represent the wilderness into which the sin-laden guilt-bearer is discharged; cf. the scapegoat ritual on the Day of Atonement, Lev. 16:10, 20-22.)

The heifer's neck is broken (Deut. 21:4), either to ensure that it remains within the sphere of the sacral (cf. Exod. 13:13) or to prevent its returning, sin-laden, into the midst of the community.

The reference to the Levites (Deut. 21:5) is a later addition. The phraseology ("sons of Levi" rather than "levitical") is unusual in Deuteronomy but typical of the Priestly vocabulary — which probably indicates that v. 5 was added by the compiler(s) of the Deuteronomic history. The Levites' "settling of disputes" is by means of the torah, of which they are guardians. Thus their functions here correspond to those listed at 10:8.

There is a double symbolism in the "washing of hands" (21:6). The performing of this act "over the heifer" is a ritual transferring of the guilt to the victim, while the use of running water symbolizes the floating away of the pollution (cf. Lev. 14:5).

20:7-8 The ancient protestation of innocence (Deut. 21:7) is coupled with a specifically Yahwistic prayer. The covenant people's reliance is not on an ancient mystic-magic rite as such, but on Yahweh's personal powers and graciousness. To "forgive" (v. 8) is literally "to cover" (Heb. *kipper*). The old rite may have intended this "covering" in the broader sense of the life blood vivifying and restoring nature, or in the more specific sense of animal blood "covering" the victim's blood or "covering/substituting for" the perpetrator's blood. Yahweh, however, is able to "cover" directly, without being bound to the necessity of a mediating rite (32:43b). Ultimately, then, it is not the ritual that is efficacious but Yahweh's self.

The section ends (21:9) as it began with typical Deuteronomic preaching-exhortatory phrases: Doing the "straight," "upright" thing is *the* effective way of covering innocent blood and thus of restoring nature's harmony. Is the "innocent blood," in modern terms, that of the poor, the unemployed, the victim of prejudice, racism, war, greed? The community is responsible under God for restoring creation's balance.

Women Prisoners of War (21:10-14)

There is a uniformity about this passage which probably marks it as a straight Deuteronomic composition. Originally connected with the "Yahweh's war" material (ch. 20), it now sits in a context of family-household legislation (21:10-21).

The woman prisoner concerned here must be a foreigner (20:14), for the Canaanite women were to have been totally annihilated (20:16). The postexilic reticence about marrying foreign women (Ezra 9:2-3; 10:2-3; Neh. 13:23-24) has not yet surfaced in Deut. 21:10-14. The assumption is that foreign women can be sagely assimilated to the faith life of Israel (in a way that the closer Canaanites could not). There is little threat to the purity of the faith, in that the prime instructor of the young generation is not the mother so much as the congregation. The key factor is the attendance of husbands and fathers at the festivals (16:16) and the passing on of that festival teaching in catechism and household instruction (6:20-21).

The shaving of hair and paring of nails (21:13) mark a definitive break with the old way of life and a preparation for entering the new.

The space given for weeping is not primarily a period of mourning (though it is perhaps to be assumed that the woman's father has died in the *herem;* 20:13, 15). Rather, it is given in compassionate consideration of the large adjustment she must make, and the accompanying trauma. It is an acknowledgment, too, that her former life is ended and a new life is to begin (cf. Ps. 45:10). The hints of compassion breaking through the brutality of the age reflect an awareness of divine compassion, however limited by the thought climate of the times.

"Let her go" (Heb. *shilleah,* Deut. 21:14) is elsewhere (24:1; Isa. 50:1; Jer. 3:8) the technical term for "divorce," and that is presumably its meaning here. Divorce entails the handing over of a certificate which clarifies the woman's status and thereby guarantees her citizenship. This became hers in the act of marriage and is not to be withdrawn.

What constitutes the "humiliation"? The marriage itself was honorable. Is it then the subsequent change of attitude: "I find no delight in her"? Or does *'innah* ("humiliation") refer to the wider emotional strain to which the woman has been subjected?

Feminists will find much that is objectionable in this text. Legitimately so. Yet there are within it seeds of empathy which betoken awareness of human dignity, and the dignity of women in particular. Massively patriarchal as the society was, the inner dynamic of Yahwism introduced into it the latent possibilities of a wider understanding.

The Inheritance of the Firstborn (21:15-17)

Several ancient Near Eastern codes deal with the question of multiple marriages and seek to ensure a just share in inheritance for all the children concerned. Nevertheless, the special status of the firstborn is also widely attested. The specific concern of Deut. 21:15-17 for the firstborn is no doubt rooted in ancient nomadic custom, when strong, undisputed leadership was essential for the clan's survival. The "double portion" (2 Kgs. 2:9) would then be a resourcing, to finance or support this necessary strong leadership. The emphasis on the preeminence of the firstborn persisted in Israel in connection with an ancient strand of Israel's covenant theology, that "birthright" and "blessing" belong together (Gen. 27:36; 48:18; cf. 2 Kgs. 2:9).

The "blessing" entails the privilege and responsibility of becoming bearer of the covenant promise (Gen. 21:12; 25:31-34). The firstborn is thereby responsible before Yahweh for the faith obedience of the extended family. On that pattern, the nation of Israel is described as "firstborn among the nations" (Exod. 4:22; Jer. 31:9) — not by right, but by inestimable privilege (Deut. 7:7-8).

On the ancient offering of the firstborn sacrifice, see above on 12:6; 15:19-23.

The "right" of the firstborn (21:17) is, in Hebrew, "mishpat" — a "decision," rooted as it were in the natural order of things (see above on 19:6). This ancient understanding, grounded in a sense of the firstborn's essential leadership and preserving role as described above, became enshrined in ancestral law and subsequently incorporated into torah — and thus into the covenant tradition.

In dealing with the rights of the firstborn, 21:15-17 also touches in passing on the question of polygamy.

Monogamy is not explicitly required in the OT, though it is implicit in such passages as Gen. 2:18-24; Mal. 2:14-16. Here in Deut. 21:15-17 and elsewhere, the tensions to which multiple marriages give rise are simply noted without overt comment and left to bear silent testimony. In practice, economic conditions through much of the OT period (as in much of the contemporary Muslim world) ensured that polygamy was the exception rather than the rule — it takes substantial resources to support a multiple household.

A Disobedient Son (21:18-21)

This law also has its parallels in the ancient Near Eastern codes. According to the Code of Hammurabi, the natural child who rebels is disinherited and the adopted child is punished by mutilation. By comparison, the punishment advocated in 21:18-21 is even more severe, namely, the death penalty. This severity is an expression of Israel's (in particular, the Deuteronomic school's) determination to safeguard Israel's covenant with Yahweh. It is implicit here that "rebellion" included carelessness toward, or rejection of, the Yahwistic faith which the parents are mandated to pass on. From this point of view, this passage is an extension and application of the Fifth Commandment (see above on 5:16). Cf. also the provision that the child who strikes (Exod. 21:15) or curses (v. 17; Lev. 20:9) the parent should be put to death.

To "chastise" (Deut. 21:18) in Hebrew is the verb *y-s-r*. It is used of Yahweh's moral- and faith-disciplining of Israel (4:36;

191

8:5) and of the elders', teachers', and parents' training of the young in the ways of Yahweh ("instruction," Prov. 1:3 and *passim*).

Chastisement includes both healthful advice and (as here) physical correction. It also implies that the rebellion is not merely against authority as such but against the teaching which that authority commends.

As at Deut. 5:16, the mother equally with the father (21:19) is responsible for the education of the young. (Cf. also the role of the congregation; see above on v. 10.) Here the mother presumably stands as second witness (cf. 20:15). That the "elders" as traditional clan leaders are in the judicial role (cf. 19:12; 21:4, 6) is an indication that the provision is of ancient origin — though more advanced than, e.g., Gen. 38:24, where the head of the family takes the law into his own hands.

The execution is carried out by the general citizenry (Deut. 21:21), on the grounds that such rebellion is a poison which threatens communal life and endangers the common covenant.

Implicit in the phrase "all Israel shall hear, and fear," is the understanding that this drastic action will be an effective deterrent (cf. 13:11). History proves such hopes illusory: awareness cannot be imposed, but rather elicited by teaching, persuasion, prayer, and example.

In fairness it should be noted that there is no known example from Israel's history of this discipline's being practiced. It is an expression of theological zeal rather than a literal prescription.

Burial after Execution (21:22-24)

The "crime punishable by death" (21:22) is, literally, the "crime whose verdict *(mishpat)* is death" (see above on 19:6).

"Hanging on a tree" is not the method of execution; rather, it is the exposing of the body to shame after the sentence has been carried out. According to the Mishnah, this shaming applied only to those stoned to death (for blasphemy or apostasy). The "tree" may be either a growing one or a timber pole. The Mishnah assumes the latter, and adds that it was equipped with a crossbar for the hands (this no doubt reflects later usage).

To expose a corpse to birds of prey (Gen. 40:19) was a frightening atrocity, because it was believed to cause the victim to enter the afterlife in a mutilated condition. The Deuteronomic history relates several incidents where the corpse is exposed (Josh. 8:29; 10:27), in the way that Deut. 21:23 alludes to. Interestingly, these accounts show signs of Deuteronomic editing. Other unedited accounts (2 Sam. 21:8-14) do not mention the exposure of corpses. Was Deuteronomy drawing on some special source at this point?

"A hanged person is accursed by God" (Deut. 21:23). The primitive thinking behind this formulation is that the deity is deeply offended by the crime for which this shameful exposure is the punishment, and that the exposure is designed to allay the divine wrath. In the present context, however, the primitive has been overlaid with a different motif, namely, that prolonged exposure defiles the land and sets up a spreading contagion which threatens the land's fertility and endangers the population's well-being. It has already been noted (see above on 14:1-2, etc.) that contact with the cult of the dead is regarded as inimical to Yahwism. In the later Priestly source, any contact with carcass (Lev. 22:8) or corpse (Num. 5:2) is considered defiling, and it may be that this thought is already reflected here. Yahweh is the living God; it is unbecoming, then, that signs of death should be flaunted on the face of the land which is Yahweh's inheritance.

Morally and theologically, this could be extended to include all the unjust and inhumane practices that tend to death — exploitation, oppression, discrimination, including racial, class, and sectarian prejudice.

In the NT, Deut. 21:23 is cited at Gal. 3:13. The curse of God rests on the sign of death. This curse is no "detachable" force, external as it were to the being of God. Rather, it is God's implacable hostility to all the signs of death — a hostility taken up in the being of God (as reflected in the man Jesus), absorbed, transmuted, and re-issuing as divine energy for the affirmation and redemption of life.

RESPECT FOR LIFE AND RELATIONSHIPS (22:1-30)

The chapter divides into two broad sections. The first (Deut. 22:1-11) is an intertwining of two general themes: social and conservation concerns (vv. 1-4, 6-7, 8), and prohibitions against mingling various natural entities (vv. 5, 9-11).

The second section (vv. 13-30) deals with five cases of aberration in sexual relationships.

Verse 12 contains a short ritual provision that has no obvious connection with the context.

Neighborly Help (22:1-4)

Verse 1 corresponds to Exod. 23:4. This apodeictic law is then "preached" in Deut. 22:2-3, and applied more broadly to include not only the local "enemy" (Exod. 23) but any fellow Israelite "brother or sister," and clothing as well as livestock. Implicitly there is concern also for the well-being of the animal.

The "garment" (Deut. 22:3) did double duty as wrap (sarong, lavalava) by day and blanket by night, so that its loss entailed privation (cf. 24:12-13).

Deuteronomy 22:4 is parallel to Exod. 23:5 (broadened to include ox as well as ass). The fallen donkey was presumably laden, so helping to raise it would include the time-consuming chore of unpacking and repacking. Besides concern for the neighbor, this provision surely implies compassion for the animal also.

Transvestism (22:5)

We may safely assume that this prohibition has cultic undertones.

Within Canaanite fertility worship, cultic prostitution — both male and female (1 Kgs. 14:24; 2 Kgs. 23:7) — was a recognized ritual for stimulating the fertility of nature. Archaeology attests that at several places throughout the ancient Near East such rites included a male-female exchange of clothing. Deuteronomy 22:5 then has nothing to do with unisex jeans, but aims to preserve the purity of Yahwistic faith by checking the encroachment of such distortions as the manipulative fertility rites.

Positively stated, the theological thrust of v. 5 is that Yahweh has created male and female with specific and complementary characteristics so that in their relationship the two constitute the full expression of humanity. To blur the intersexual distinction which Yahweh has established strikes at the natural order and harmony willed by the Creator.

The Bird and Its Nestlings (22:6-7)

There is no discernible cultic background to this requirement as there is with the superficially similar prohibition of boiling a kid in its mother's milk (14:21). Rather, the concern here is conservationist, tinged with the compassionate and the prudential. Reverence for Yahweh involves compassionate reverence for all Yahweh's creatures, with a careful husbanding of the natural resources which Yahweh has bestowed. In the long term, care for the environment is in humanity's own best interest (cf. 5:16 and elsewhere: "that it may go well with you"). Yahweh does not issue commands for commands' sake; Yahweh's will is the creature's true well-being.

The Rooftop Parapet (22:8)

For an approximate parallel, cf. Hammurabi's code § 229. The difference is that, whereas Hammurabi's regulation is civil, the biblical provision is cultic: "that you may not bring the guilt of blood upon your house." Such bloodguilt must be removed by means of specific cleansing rites, somewhat similar perhaps to that for "cleansing the diseased house" (Lev. 14:49-53). Though that is the background for the Deuteronomic writer, the focus has obviously shifted from the cultic to the humanitarian. The householder is to be responsible for the safety and well-being of his fellows, especially members of the family. It will be remembered that the roof is flat and used for relaxation and socializing.

Mingling Two of a Kind (22:9-11)

The compactness and uniformity of style suggests that these three sentences already formed a unit before being incorporated into their present setting.

The basis for this prohibition on mingling two of a kind is that the mingling blurs the orderly distinctions which God has built into the structures of creation, and therefore makes light of God's wisdom. Some scholars speculate that behind this is an ancient animistic belief that each natural species is generated by a particular spiritual genius, and that the mixing is dishonoring to and resented by these spirits. If that is so, then the ancient belief has here been "demythologized" and integrated into Yahwism.

When the crop "becomes holy" (Deut. 22:9 RSV mg) it can be eaten only by the priest. The primitive animistic root of the idea would be that the product of different "gods" or spirits becomes "sacred" when combined, and too dangerous for human consumption. On the more rational Deuteronomic level, v. 9 becomes a warning against greed: to "force" the land by overproduction is counterproductive in the long run.

Maimonides (12th cent. A.D.) bases v. 10 on the distinction between the "clean" animal (ox) and the "unclean" (donkey). Donkeys were not offered in sacrifice to Yahweh (Exod. 13:13), but (probably) to some Canaanite deity. Most likely, however, the Deuteronomic writer is more concerned with the humane quality in the regulation: to plow with two animals of unequal strength is cruelty to the weaker. An alternative interpretation is that "yoking" (plowing) has to do with mating, so that donkey and ox are not to be brought together for breeding purposes. This explanation indeed fits the context rather better than that of unequal strength.

Hebrew *sha'atnez* (="false weaving"?) or "mingled stuff" (Deut. 22:11) is an obscure foreign term, possibly indicating originally a web used in magic ceremonies. Yahwism has no truck with magic which is at base manipulative.

Tassels (22:12)

According to Num. 15:37-41 (P) the tassels are "to remember all the commandments of Yahweh," the many threads bound into one symbolizing the torah, as being many commands bound into one. Once again, this is an obvious demythologization of something ancient and animistic.

One suggestion is that the tassel originally represented brooms, sweeping aside the harmful spiritual influences so that rituals could proceed safely. In their "Yahwized" form they then come to state a conviction that only obedience to Yahweh's word can oust malign spiritual influences.

In the later development it became increasingly apparent that these tassels affixed to the outer garment marked Jews in a very demonstrative way, attracting unwelcome attention in days of persecution. They were therefore transferred to an inner garment and eventually to the prayer shawl *(tallit)* to become, along with the *tephillim* (see above on Deut. 6:8-9), a specific reminder at times of devotion.

"Tokens of Virginity" (22:13-21)

General parallels to the provision in this section are to be found in the Code of Hammurabi §§ 127, 131, 132. A comparison reveals two main differences:

(1) The punishments stated in Deuteronomy are heavier (a heavier emphasis on "Yahweh's holy people"?)
(2) Deuteronomy shows more concern for the woman's rights and reputation (cf. Introduction, 15).

22:14-15 Verse 14 states literally that the man has levelled "wantonness of words" at the woman; it is not her conduct but his accusations which are "shameful." True or not, however, the charges are destructive. Indeed, throughout the OT name and personhood are intimately associated, so that change of character induces change of name, and vice versa. To damage one's name is to damage one's character.

The term "tokens of virginity" (vv. 14, 15) is usually taken as referring to the bloodstained sheet from the bridal bed. Gordon J. Wenham (*"Bᵉtûlāh,"* 331), however, suggests that the reference may be to the inner garment, stained with menstrual blood, which the woman wore immediately prior to marriage. This latter would certainly be more accessible to the bride's parents (v. 15) — though both suggestions encounter the difficulty that such a "token" would be easily counterfeited or "manufactured." Perhaps the point is that the use of such a token as proof will always make the woman's defense an easier matter. Modern medical science, of course, would deny that the absence of blood in this case is proof of blameworthiness. Bleeding is not invariable at first intercourse. Thus, the obligation to provide proof would be vicious, if such "proof" were not so easily accessible to the woman.

22:18-19 The penalty for making a false accusation is "discipline" (flogging? v. 18), as well as a hundred-shekel fine (v. 19). The fine is to be understood in the light of v. 29, where the bride-price is quoted at fifty shekels. It may well be that the husband brings the false accusation with intent to defraud. Should he simply divorce his wife, he would lose the bride-price he paid, but if he "proves" misconduct his fifty shekels will be returned. The false accusation is then an attempt to steal, and stolen property is to be returned twofold (Exod. 22:4). In effect, then, his crime (and punishment) is double: his attack on his wife's good name and his designs on his father-in-law's money.

This passage illustrates a rather advanced system of justice. This judicial procedure with its accompanying peace and security is acknowledged as a gift from God — which is not to claim that the system is perfect and eternally definitive.

22:20-21 In the presumably (and hopefully) rare case in which the charge is held to be proven, the death of the young woman is regarded as cleansing her parents' home from the guilt-pollution arising from her act. As in the case of the disobedient son (21:18-21), the parents are the prime witnesses and the entire population the executioners, because the guilt is seen to threaten the whole community.

"Folly" (Heb. *nebalah*) is used both for sexual transgression (Gen. 34:7; Jer. 29:23) and for misappropriating *herem* goods that rightly belong to Yahweh (Josh. 7:15). In essence it describes the transgression which places in jeopardy Israel's existence as the covenant people. The definition gives rise to the question: what are the "follies" which destroy contemporary humanity's relationship with God — and in particular, that of God's modern covenant people, the Church? How may those "follies" be corrected?

Adultery (22:22)

This sentence is a casuistic supplement to the Seventh Commandment (Deut. 5:18; see above) naming the penalty for transgression. Parallels are found in several of the ancient Near Eastern codes. In comparison with these, the biblical version tends to place primary responsibility for the transgression on the male — though both suffer the same punishment. The ancient Near Eastern codes tend to ascribe the evil initiative to the woman.

Rape of an Engaged Woman (22:23-27)

As already mentioned (20:7; see above) the OT draws no essential difference between engagement and marriage. Accordingly, here the "betrothed virgin" (22:23) is described as the neighbor's "wife" (v. 24). This section is therefore an extension of v. 22. As with the ancient Near Eastern parallels, the biblical version also takes into account the circumstances in which rape occurs. Where there is opportunity to call for help and the woman fails to do so, her complicity is assumed (v. 24); otherwise, she is regarded as innocent (vv. 26-27). The place of execution is the "gate of the city" (v. 24), the traditional place of judicial decisions (but see above on 17:5).

Inquiry into the ancient Semitic roots of these regulations involves a deal of conjecture. Did those roots concern the necessity of "covering" guilt incurred against primary sources of fertility, lest the mysterious forces of life be antagonized? However that may be, for the Deuteronomic school the accent is on the cruciality of the husband-wife relationship for the well-being of society (5:18).

Rape of a Virgin Who Is Not Engaged (22:28-29)

The ancient Near Eastern parallel (Middle Assyrian code) covers a wider range of questions than does Deut. 22: Is the rapist married or unmarried? Is the virgin's father willing to accept the *fait accompli* and give her in marriage? It is also more directly punitive than vv. 28-29. The corresponding passage in Exodus

(Exod. 22:16-17) also covers the unwillingness of the virgin's father. Had such refusal become rare by Deuteronomic times?

To contemporary thought, the resolution of the matter appears as a blatantly all-male decision. Even the rider that "he may not divorce her" (Deut. 22:29b) pays no regard to the woman's wishes or feelings — though in the context of the times the motive was humane, in that it aimed to provide her economic security. What shall we say? The Deuteronomic provision is not absolute and once-for-all revelation, but rather a cross section in the ongoing revelation of God's intention for the human family. The process still continues, and we are caught up in it. It demands of us our very best by way of thought, energy, action, openness, and receptivity.

Marriage with a Father's Wife (22:30)

The brief statement is unclear as to its precise reference. Does "father's wife" refer to the younger man's mother or stepmother? Also, does the prohibition apply in the father's lifetime or after his death?

The ancient Near Eastern parallels allow (with or without penalty) marriage with a stepmother, after the father's death. It seems likely, therefore, that what is envisaged in v. 30 is intimacy with a stepmother during the father's lifetime.

According to A. D. H. Mayes (*Deuteronomy*, 313), the prohibition is directed against the ancient practice of taking over the fathers' wives and concubines as a means of claiming the primary inheritance. This usually happened after the father died (2 Sam. 3:7; 1 Kgs. 2:22), but sometimes during his lifetime (Gen. 35:22; 49:4; 2 Sam. 16:22).

A contemporary application of this prohibition would be against the using of other people sexually, emotionally, economically, or howsoever, for personal aggrandizement or for the advantage of one's group, class, or race.

LAWS OF PURITY (23:1-25)

The chapter consists of seven units, two longer and five shorter. The two longer, Deut. 22:1-8 on "membership in Yahweh's as-

sembly" and vv. 9-14 on the "purity of the camp," relate to the
"Yahweh's war" theme. The second part of the chapter, vv. 15-25,
describes various attitudes and qualities characteristic of Yahweh's
people, and thus extends the general theme of vv. 1-14.

Those Debarred from Yahweh's Assembly (23:1-8)

The passage is obviously composite. It consists of several layers
round an ancient core:

- Debarred categories (vv. 1, 2a, 3a)
- Short comments on the debarment (vv. 2b, 3b)
- Longer sermonic exposition of the debarment (vv. 4-6)
- (Presumed) lifting of two earlier debarments (modelled on the
  style of vv. 1, 2a, 3a) (vv. 7-8)

At first sight it may appear that the debarments are based on
chauvinist prejudices. Closer inspection, however, indicates that
the root reason in each case is cultic, and that therefore the issue
at stake is loyalty to Yahweh and the integrity of Yahweh's worship.

23:1   The crushing of the testicles (v. 1) was an operation performed on small boys at various places in the ancient Near East,
preparing them as eunuchs for service in shrine or palace. The use
of the term "eunuch" in connection with the Israelite Monarchy
(Heb. *saris;* normally translated "officer," e.g., 1 Sam. 8:15) shows
that the custom was known in Israel. Thus the debarring of
eunuchs from Yahweh's assembly is primarily aimed at preventing
the associated alien religious rites from infiltrating the worship of
Yahweh.

To this ancient basic motive, the Deuteronomic school would
add two factors: (1) to mutilate the human body is to demean
God who created humanity for fruitfulness (Gen. 1:28); and (2)
the practice is also an affront to human dignity, concern for which
is a prime Deuteronomic emphasis.

23:2-3   The "bastard" (Heb. *mamzer,* Deut. 23:2) is literally the
"isolated," "ostracized." The only other occurrence of the term in

201

the OT is Zech. 9:6, where it means "people of mixed race." If that is its significance in Deut. 23:2, the motive for exclusion is probably to prevent the paganism inherited through the non-Israelite parent from infiltrating Israelite worship. The original motive for debarring Ammonites and Moabites (v. 3) was probably similar. Nehemiah obviously interpreted the prohibition in this way (Neh. 13:1-3). The earlier popular record, on the other hand, rejects Ammon and Moab as "born out of incest" (Gen. 19:37-38) — presumably an oblique allusion to the "depravity" of pagan worship and practice.

23:4 That "they did not meet you with bread" is scarcely the original reason for the animosity against Ammon. Archaeology attests that, after a break in the evidence lasting several centuries, the Ammonites reappeared on the scene in the 13th cent. B.C., in an area overlapping with Sihon's Amorite kingdom (Deut. 2:26-37). Israel under Moses is warned not to violate Ammonite territory (2:37). It was not until two centuries later that tension did in fact arise between Ammon and Israel (e.g., Judg. 10:7-8), and it is this that is reflected in the ancient debarment.

The little we know of Ammonite religion suggests that fertility rites were prominent. This paganism obviously became a temptation to Israel (Judg. 10:6).

Moab occupied the area south of Ammon, between the Arnon and Zered rivers. In the 13th cent. the Moabites were in transition from a seminomadic to a settled lifestyle. They saw Israel's supposed incursion as a mortal threat, hence their intransigent reaction (Deut. 2:9). There were further clashes with Moab during the period of the Judges (Judg. 3:12-13).

Moab's religion closely resembled the Canaanite practice. Their supreme god Chemosh ("sun"; cf. Heb. *shemesh*) had affinities with Canaanite worship of Ashtar ("morning star"). Fertility rites were also featured, as in Ammon and Canaan.

It is implicit in Deut. 2:28-29 that Moab did in fact supply Israel with food and drink on their conquest trek. Perhaps 23:4 intends that they should have donated these supplies out of compassion rather than having sold them.

It is noteworthy that the debarment of Moab was not applied

in historical practice, for King David's grandmother was a Moabitess (Ruth 4:17-22).

23:5-6 Drawing further on the Balaam tradition (cf. Num. 22–24), the exposition notes that "God turned the curse into blessing for you" (Deut. 23:5). The ancient understanding is that powerful words (of curse and blessing) once uttered cannot be recalled, but henceforth have an objective life and influence of their own. So God's way of averting the evil planned by "Moab" through Balaam is not to neutralize the curse but to prevent its being uttered — indeed, to cause a blessing to be uttered in its place (Num. 23:5-10).

Modern understanding does not objectify language in quite this way. Nevertheless, it is sobering to be reminded that words once spoken cannot be recalled and assuredly influence the mental and spiritual condition of those around us. It therefore behooves us to ensure that our words constantly befit our state as people of faith.

The phrase "you shall not seek their peace or their prosperity" (Deut. 23:6) occurs in Ezra 9:12 in the context of covenant-making, so it may be interpreted quite concretely both in Ezra and in Deuteronomy: "Do not enter into covenant with them."

23:7-8 To "abhor" (Deut. 23:7) is literally to "regard as revolting." On the corresponding noun, see 7:25.

That Edom and Egypt, prominent among Israel's traditional enemies, are here regarded so favorably is surprising. Obviously the formulation here is from a period in history when relations with these nations were good.

The old patriarchal narratives indeed describe Jacob-Israel and Esau-Edom as "brothers" (Gen. 25:29-30). However, something similar could be said of Ammon (Gen. 19:38) and Moab (v. 37). Like Moab, Edom also hindered Israel's conquest trek (Num. 20:14-21). Furthermore, like Ammon and Moab, Edom also fought Israel at times (1 Sam. 14:47; 2 Sam. 8:14; 1 Kgs. 11:15). Why then the difference? As stated above, the only satisfactory answer is that the formulations crystallized at a period or periods when relations with one pair were bad, and with the other pair (i.e., Edom and Egypt) good.

203

In the postexilic period contact through trade brought about a warmer appreciation of Egypt. For impressive testimony to this and to the effect that ordinary "secular" relations can have on the development of theology, cf. Isa. 19:18-25.

"You were a sojourner (Heb. *ger*) in Egypt" (Deut. 23:7). On *ger* see above on 1:16.

There is an interesting parallel between 23:8 and 5:9. The effects of sin persist till "the third and fourth generations," whereas the effects of foreignness dissipate by "the third generation" — in minimum time, one could say. This is then an expression of real openness and tolerance.

Purity of the Encampment (23:9-14)

This section is perhaps even more directly connected with the "Yahweh's war" theme than the previous one. (See the Introduction, 15-17, on Deuteronomy's concern with "Yahweh's war.") The connection between 23:1-8 and 9-14 is clear. When the covenant people assemble for war, both their undivided commitment (vv. 1-8) and their ritual purity (vv. 9-14) are essential. Only so can their spiritual energy potential be intact and full, a fitting instrument for Yahweh to use in Yahweh's enterprise.

23:9 Hebrew *mahaneh* (vv. 9, 10, 11, 12, 14) can be translated "camp" or "army," according to context. The concern is not with the setting as such, but with the people.

"Evil" (Heb. *ra'*, v. 9) covers a wide range of meaning. While the basic reference is to moral evil, it can also mean "disaster" (Amos 3:6), "woe" (Isa. 45:7), "harmfulness" (cf. Isa. 7:15).

Here in Deut. 23:9 the sense is "anything that brings about misfortune." (Implicitly, the misfortune is seen as an expression of divine displeasure.)

23:10-11 The reference is to a nocturnal emission of semen (cf. Lev. 15:16). Sexuality is within the realm of the sacral, as being close to the mysterious sources of life and creation. Any "abnormality" here forms a dangerous gap through which harmful spiritual forces may infiltrate. Loss of the fluid also signifies a dangerous lessening of "spiritual" potential in face of the oncoming military encounter. "Cleanness" is restored "when the sun goes down" (v. 11), that is, at the beginning of a new day (counting from evening to morning; Gen. 1:5, 8, 13).

23:12-14   As noted above, "camp" includes the notion of people on the move — a mobile God in the midst of a mobile people. Because in all their activity the people depend so totally on God's resource-full presence, there must be a scrupulous avoidance of anything that might cause them to forfeit that presence. In the exposition of this utterly relevant principle, two quite primitive concepts are pressed into service. The first is the idea of God's physical presence in their midst: "God walking in the camp" (cf. Gen. 3:8; 2 Sam. 7:6-7). The second is that, in walking, God might foul the feet in human excrement and take offense. (There persists a popular belief in some societies today that "spirit possession" results from a spirit's taking offense at being unwittingly contaminated with human waste.) This is a highly anthropomorphic picture! Implicit, too, is the understanding that God is concerned with the whole of human life, including hygiene and sanitation.

The use to which the Deuteronomic preacher-scholar puts these ancient concepts is striking. From within the shadow of disaster-by-exile he looks back at the idealized beginnings of the covenant people, marked as he sees it by tender sensitivity to every slightest indication of the divine will. "If *we* were so sensitive, we would not be facing the current crisis. Our 'contaminating' behavior is in danger of forcing God to withdraw and leave us to fight our battles unaided." When the people do not obey, God withdraws (Ps. 60:10; Jer. 7:5-7 JB; Ezek. 10:18-19).

The Fugitive Slave (23:15-16)

This passage is in marked contrast to the ancient Near Eastern parallels. Hammurabi's code, for example, lays down that the penalty for aiding, harboring, or concealing a runaway slave is death. Deuteronomy 23:15-16, on the contrary, requires that the fugitive be sheltered and protected.

The objection has been raised that the Deuteronomic provision is impractical. Once widely known, the terms of this law would spell the end of slavery in a very short time.

Obviously, however, not every case of slavery is intended here. Rather, the law concerns specifically the person enslaved in foreign parts and then fleeing to Israel for asylum.

Isolated texts (e.g., 1 Sam. 30:15; 1 Kgs. 2:39-40) indicate that slaves were sometimes handed back across international borders. Archaeology attests that some ancient nations had ex-tradition agreements with their neighbors. Thus the Deuter-onomic provision represents an advance in humanitarian feeling. It may not, however, be radically new. A special provision at the conclusion of Hammurabi's code (§ 280) states: "If a person purchases a slave while travelling abroad, and then on return to his own land discovers that his newly-purchased slave is in fact a citizen of the homeland, who had been enslaved but then sub-sequently fled to foreign parts, only to be re-enslaved there, then the slave is to be granted freedom forthwith."

The chain of circumstances involved would obviously make the case a rare one. The Deuteronomic provision has the merit of broadening the issue by offering asylum to all fugitive slaves from outside Israel.

Deuteronomy 23:16 implies that the fugitive is accorded status as a sojourner (*ger*). "Do not oppress" in context means "do not re-enslave." As noted at 1:16, the *ger* was peculiarly vulnerable to exploitation. Deuteronomy 23:16 states the principle that the whole nation of Israel is to be his place of refuge. ("You," though singular here, refers not to the individual but to the community.)

Might a contemporary ideal for the people of God be that the "enslaved" internationally should find asylum in the community of faith?

Cult Prostitutes (23:17-18)

On the general background for this passage, see above on 22:5.

The Hebrew technical terms (*qedeshah,* female; *qadesh,* male) mean "holy," referring to those who have so "sanctified" them-selves to the service of the fertility shrine. As frequently stated, such activity is inimical to Yahwism, for in the first place it implies that the deity seasonally grows weak and needs human stimulus to excite and reinvigorate it. Yahweh, on the contrary, is the reinvigorator of weak humanity (Isa. 40:28-29) who personally needs no such stimulus.

In the second place, as frequently stressed, Baalism is manipulative, seeking to bend the divine forces to human intention, whereas Yahwism seeks to submit all human forces (including sexual potency) to Yahweh's intention, to become part of Yahweh's structuring of a well-ordered world.

"Dog" (Deut. 23:18) is descriptive of the male prostitute. It may be a term of opprobrium as frequently in the OT (1 Sam. 24:14; 2 Sam. 9:8; 16:9; 2 Kgs. 8:13; Isa. 56:10-11). On the other hand, it may be an honorific term, as in several other Semitic languages:

- The palace official is "the king's dog guarding his house faithfully." (Amarna Letter 60)
- The Assyrian temple ministrant is "Marduk's faithful little dog."
- Personal names from Babylon bear the prefix Kalb (="dog"); e.g., Kalbi-Sin ("servant of the Moon"), Kalbi-Shamash ("servant of the Sun").

It may be, therefore, that "dog" in the context of Deut. 23:18 means "servant of the shrine."

Is the prohibition in v. 18 addressed specifically to the prostitute ("do not offer the reward of your activity . . .") or to society at large? In other words, does the money remain polluted, even after it has changed hands several times? If so, this would be a powerful statement of communal responsibility for all social wrong and religious abuse. The community's means of exchange (of social intercourse!) becomes polluted by every act of prostitution, "sacred" or "secular."

Collecting Interest (23:19-20)

These verses occupy an intermediate status between the simple statement of Exod. 22:25 (E) and the more detailed exposition of Lev. 25:35-38 (P).

In Leviticus "interest" (literally and appropriately, "bite") is redefined as "increase," perhaps as a curb on those who use casuistry to circumvent the plain sense of the regulation. The increased use of exhortation in P, too, is possibly an indication that the condition of the poor has worsened in the interim.

It is noteworthy that throughout the OT period "trader" in Hebrew is "Canaanite" *(kana'ani)*. Hebrews were slow to learn the art. It is probable, therefore, that the interest prohibited in Deut. 23:19-20 is not that on commercial transactions, but interest within the neighborly circle, on the emergency day-to-day needs of family and fellow citizen. "Foreigners," on the other hand, came to Israel expressly to trade and by definition owned sufficient capital. They therefore needed no special consideration such as is envisaged here.

The lesson is urged (v. 20b) in the typical language of Deuteronomic exhortation.

Vows (23:21-23)

The topic of vows, their appropriateness, and their fulfillment, belongs in general to the wisdom tradition (cf. Eccl. 5:4-6; Ps. 76:11; Prov. 20:25), rather than the legal. However, there is indeed an overlapping between wisdom and preaching, and we have noted repeatedly that Deuteronomy is "preached law."

Possibly Deut. 23:21-23 has been drawn into its present context through association with v. 18: "Certain funds may be illicit for the paying of vows, but the vows themselves stand."

Vows are basically of three types:

(1) Bargaining: "If you do this, then I will do that" (e.g., Gen. 28:20-22)
(2) Thanksgiving: for blessings received (e.g., Deut. 12:6, 11, 17)
(3) Pledge of self-denial (e.g., 1 Sam. 14:24)

Deuteronomy 23:21-23 covers all three forms.

On v. 22 (reluctance to make vows), cf. Eccl. 5:5: "It is better that you should not vow than that you should vow and not pay."

Integrity of speech is part of the total integrity which God requires of the covenant people. Like to like, God's integrity toward humanity is perfect, and covenant relationship with God implies that the divine nature should begin to reflect in the covenant people.

Hospitality: Enjoyed But Not Abused (23:24-25)

The aim of this provision is to combine humanitarianism and justice.

The underlying principle is that the land of Israel belongs to God (see above on Deut. 4:20) and is given as inheritance to the covenant people. Though the land is apportioned to the tribes and clans (Josh. 13–21), yet the right of the individual farmer is not so absolute that he or she can legitimately deny a share in its produce to the hungry. "This is my land" really means "This land is entrusted to me." On the other hand, the farmer does also have rights vis-à-vis the fruits of his or her toil.

In contemporary industrialized society the principle extends to include the natural resources which industry utilizes. The industrialist does not have absolute right over these resources; rather, they are entrustment from God, who remains the true owner (Ps. 24:1).

On the other hand, the passage also addresses those who seek to "rip off" the modern welfare state. "The humanitarian provisions serve your need, not your greed." Accept what you need with dignity as a God-given right, but do not "put in the sickle."

MARRIAGE AND COMPASSION (24:1-22)

Broadly, the chapter falls into two sections: Deut. 24:1-5, concerning marriage and divorce, and vv. 6-22, a chain of units on the general theme of compassion for the underprivileged.

The reference to leprosy (vv. 8-9) is probably intended as a threat of God's punishment on those who fail to show the required compassion. The stress on individual responsibility (v. 16) is a reminder that the call to compassion cannot be avoided. Several thin linguistic threads throughout the chapter strengthen the impression that the whole is at best a loose unity:

- "Sin/guilt" (Heb. *het*, vv. 4, 15, 16)
- "Remember" (Heb. *zakar*, vv. 9, 18, 22)
- "Bless" (Heb. *barak*, vv. 13, 19)

No Remarriage of Divorced Partners (24:1-4)

Nowhere in the OT is Israelite divorce procedure explicitly spelled out. The reason for this is presumably that divorce is part of the inherited Semitic practice which is everywhere taken for granted (Lev. 21:7, 14; 22:13) but not really approved (Mal. 2:13-16) or taken up as a conscious element of Yahwism.

Deuteronomy 24:1-4 relates to a specific category within divorce, namely, the husband who dismisses his wife, and then, after her second marriage has terminated, wishes to remarry her. This is prohibited, no doubt with the aim of forcing the affronted husband to weigh the consequences carefully before rushing into divorce. (Interestingly, Islamic *shari'a* law seeks to ensure the same careful consideration by the opposite method, that is, by insisting that the divorced wife *must* have been married to a second husband before her first husband may remarry her.)

The ancient Near Eastern codes attest that divorce normally involved a monetary settlement; this presumably was also the case in Israel, though it is nowhere stated. The fate of the children of a broken marriage is likewise unclear. All that is certain is that they remain their father's heirs.

According to v. 1a the right of the husband to divorce his wife is absolute. We noted some small beginnings of concern for the woman's predicament (e.g., 22:19: "he may not put her away . . ."). This is reinforced in 24:1a, b: "because he has found some indecency in her." In other words, divorce is not to be based on mere whim ("she finds no favor"), but on serious grounds. The determining of the "serious grounds" is, however, still subjective. That it is not a case of sexual misdemeanor is clear from 22:20-22: the penalty for that is not divorce but death.

The "bill of divorce" (24:1b) also protects the woman from subsequent charges of "adulteress" should she remarry. Although not explicitly stated, the letter may well have been officially witnessed — which would further safeguard the woman's position.

On "send her away," see above on 21:14.

He may not remarry her "after she has been defiled (Heb. *tame'*)" (24:4). In what sense is the woman "defiled"? Is it by the first husband, who in effect "sent" her to seek another partner? Is it by the second husband, who took another man's wife? At any rate, this law permits the divorce: why then call it "defilement"? More likely "defiled" means "taboo" *(haram)*; by virtue of the divorce she is now "forbidden" to her first husband.

Jeremiah (Jer. 3:1) makes striking use of the prohibition outlined in Deut. 24:1-4 in order to attack the facile view that repentance is easy, and always available at the whim of a sinful people. Their sin is repudiation of their Partner, and this brings about divorce. Moreover, divorce is final — unless there be a stupendous grace initiative from their Partner's side, radically superseding the law.

The phrase "bring guilt on the land" (Deut. 24:4) implies a unity of all God's creation. By virtue of that unity, "inanimate" nature is implicated in human rebellion (Gen. 3:17-19) and again joins in the rejoicing (Isa. 55:12-13) when God acts to redeem humanity and restore the creation (Isa. 35).

The Bridegroom Freed from Military Service (24:5)

For the Deuteronomic writer, this verse is primarily a provision for "compassionate leave" (Deut. 24:5b).

To die childless was a bitter fate in Israel (hence, e.g., the provision for "levirate" marriage, 25:5-10). This possibility is also guarded against in 24:5. But behind this again there is probably a more primitive thought: marriage is a peculiarly sensitive time, in that it marks the stirring of sexual energies with their sacral quality.

Through the medium of this sensitivity, negative spiritual forces may infiltrate the family, clan, and army. To guard against this infiltration into the combat which is itself sacral activity, the newly-married is temporarily retired. Implicit in this specific provision is the more universal understanding that all sexual activity is sacred to God and that its pleasurableness is grounded in God's design. Sexual pleasure therefore entails sacred responsibilities.

Taking of Pledges (24:6, 10-13, 17b)

It is legitimate to require security for a loan, only one should let
the manner of taking it conform to the norms of compassion and
respect for human dignity.

Poor Israelite families ground corn and baked bread daily, so
that to take both millstones or even the upper rotating one (the
"carriage") as security would impose suffering (24:6).

On the cloak that is taken in pledge (vv. 12-13, 17b), see 22:3.
Compassion requires that the cloak be available as a blanket. It is
sufficient incentive to remember and repay the debt if the pledge
must be re-surrendered each morning. (On the infringement of
this principle, cf. Amos 2:8; Job 22:6.) The widow (Deut.
24:17b) is particularly vulnerable and should not be subjected
even to the inconvenience of this daily re-surrendering of the
security. The provisions of vv. 10-11 are designed to preserve the
debtor's dignity. The debtor's self should select the article to be
pledged, and freely hand it over without any demeaning invasion
of privacy. The poor are still human beings, whose blessing (and
curse) are powerful (v. 13; cf. 23:4). To behave empathetically to
the poor is "righteousness before Yahweh" (cf. 6:25).

The Evil of Kidnapping (24:7-9)

Deuteronomy 24:7 reinforces the Eighth Commandment (5:19).
Kidnapping (for selling into slavery; cf. Ezek. 27:13) was condemned throughout the ancient Near East in general. Here the
text stresses that such behavior — above all toward a brother or
sister of the people of Israel — is incompatible with the people's
covenant status. It is an "evil" to be "cauterized" if the covenant
is to remain intact. This is impressive insistence on the dignity
and freedom of the person!

Deuteronomy 24:8-9 was probably introduced here to underline the hatefulness of kidnapping and similar inhumanities. As
God acted against Miriam (v. 9), so God will certainly take action
against blatant covenant-breakers. Verse 8 then functions as background to v. 9.

Incidentally, v. 8 provides interesting testimony as to the relation of theology and medicine. The priest doubles as diagnostician. Nowadays theology and medicine are separate sciences, yet both are from God and should therefore be mutually supportive.

Paying Wages on Time (24:14-15)

The daily grinding and baking (v. 6) depend on the daily wage to purchase the grain — a hand-to-mouth existence! Cf. the prayer for "daily bread" (Matt. 6:11). Awareness of our common dependence on God's bounty should determine our compassionate attitude toward our fellows. God is their defender (Deut. 24:15b) — as ours! — whether they belong to our racial stock or not (*ah,* "brother," or *ger,* "sojourner").

Personal Responsibility (24:16)

In the midst of a stress on collective responsibility (here in the immediate context and generally throughout the Deuteronomic code; 13:12-17; 21:1-9, 22-23; 23:9-14; 24:4b), 24:16 strikes the note of personal responsibility. This is a closing of the door, lest individuals be tempted to opt out: "I endorse the principle, but my personal exception won't matter, just this once!" Personal and corporate responsibility belong together as two sides of one moral coin.

On the citing of 24:16 in the Deuteronomic history, cf. 2 Kgs. 14:6.

Sojourner, Fatherless, Widow (24:17-22)

The "justice" due to the marginalized is Yahweh's decision (*mishpat*) in their favor. Cf. Deut. 24:13: caring for those in need is "righteousness before Yahweh." Together vv. 17-18 form a typical Deuteronomic parenesis, summarizing the compassionate provisions of the preceding verses. Verses 19a, 20a, 21a have been attracted as an addendum to this summary and bound to it by a threefold repetition of the refrain: "it shall be for the sojourner, the fatherless, and the widow."

It may be that vv. 19-22 represent a piece of demythologization in the interests of social concern. The remnants of the harvest "forgotten" and left in field and orchard may well have been intended in primitive times as offerings to the gods or goddesses of grain, vine, and olive, to entreat their continuing favor (cf. the Javanese rice offerings to Dewi Sri). The Deuteronomic school in banishing the gods and goddesses suggest that the "forgotten" sheaves and fruit be now deliberately intended for the poor.

MISCELLANEOUS LAWS (25:1-19)

Like the previous chapter, Deut. 25 consists of a number of separate units. Some thought connection is discernible between the first two units (vv. 1-3, v. 4) and again between the third and fourth (vv. 5-10, vv. 11-12), but otherwise there is no apparent common theme.

The impression is that at the end of the code (chs. 23–25) relatively short pieces which defy integration into larger wholes are simply tagged on.

Corporal Punishment (25:1-3)

In the ancient Near Eastern codes, physical punishment is stipulated for a wide range of offenses: libel and defamation, causing physical injury, fraud in financial and property matters.

Though these verses attest that corporal punishment formed part of Israelite justice also, yet the specific cases to which it was applied are never mentioned. Perhaps 22:18 contains a hint of the matter: the Hebrew word *yisser* used there literally means "discipline" and may well be accurately translated "flog." According to the (second-century A.D.) Mishnah (*Makkot* iii.1-9), scourging is applied in every offense whose punishment is not otherwise stipulated.

The salient feature of Deut. 25:1-3 is the concern to preserve human dignity in what can so easily be a brutalizing process. The guilty party is "your brother" (v. 3), and is to be beaten with a maximum of forty strokes (thirty-nine to be on the "safe" side; cf. 2 Cor. 11:24), "lest he be degraded — in your eyes." That last point is significant: the effect on the guilty is to be strictly monitored, but so is the effect on the judiciary, witnesses, and general public.

The judge not only gives the verdict but supervises the carrying out of the sentence (Deut. 25:2), to ensure that the process is as humane as possible. The strokes are "proportionate to the offense," and so controlled that any tendency to vindictiveness and lynch law is excluded.

This instruction is surely not to be seen as providing a mandate for corporal punishment in modern educational and penitentiary institutions. Rather, it is a powerful call to imbue inherited structures and processes with genuine humaneness and in so doing transform them.

Do Not Muzzle the Ox (25:4)

Surrounding nations seemingly did muzzle their working animals, and Israelites would be tempted to copy this "economical" practice, which prevented the animals from tasting the grain they were trampling. But v. 4 counters the urge by stressing that the compassion that is shown to human beings should be extended to animals as well. Cf. 5:12-15 ("extend the sabbath rest to your animals"); 22:4-6.

This concern for domestic animals arises out of the awareness that God is Creator of all creatures and cares for their fate. Accordingly, to treat every creature with due respect is a mark of reverence for the Creator. Further, the gratitude for freedom from Egyptian servitude should be reflected in the treatment of the animals in Israel's fields.

In the NT (1 Tim. 5:18; 1 Cor. 9:9) "the unmuzzled ox" is used allegorically to press the right of the clergy to financial support as they process the spiritual harvest. Indeed, Paul (1 Cor. 9:9-10) goes so far as to set aside the literal meaning in favor of the allegorical: "Is it for oxen that God is concerned?" The Deuteronomic code would reply unequivocally, "Yes, Paul, it is!" — without invalidating the ecclesiastical principle that Paul is seeking to establish.

Deuteronomy 25:1-3 and 4 therefore have in common the compassionate regard for one's fellow creatures, be they human or animal.

A Man's Duty to a Dead Brother (25:5-10)

The practice of so-called levirate marriage (Latin *levir,* "husband's brother") was not peculiar to Israel, but was known throughout the ancient Near East and indeed in Asia-Africa and South America.

In all probability the practice is part of Israel's pre-Mosaic heritage. In the early period its aim was threefold: to perpetuate the deceased's name and clan, to preserve the balance in land inheritance, and to provide for the widow.

An early example of levirate marriage is recorded in Gen. 38:1-11. A comparison of this text with Deut. 25:5-10 yields the impression that the custom was weakening by Deuteronomic times. Earlier the duty had been compulsory (Gen. 38:8-11) at the father's bidding, and noncompliance brought death (v. 10). Later the initiative has passed to the "levir" (is the levir's father already deceased in this particular case?), and a certain element of choice is involved (Deut. 25:5b, 7). The penalty for noncompliance too has been softened from death to public shame.

The custom presumably applied specifically in the context of the extended family, where three or four generations dwelt under one roof (cf. 5:16). Psalm 133 also reflects the decline of the custom, and seeks to shore it up by praising the institution of the extended family.

A further stage in the decline of the levirate principle's application ensued with the Priestly enactment that daughters have the right to inherit their father's estate (Num. 27:1-11). The book of Ruth (Ruth 3–4) describes a variant of the levirate law, where the *go'el* ("redeemer") is not the deceased's brother but his next of kin, and where the levirate agreement also involves land-redemption rights.

The perpetuation of the individual clan and tribe (cf. Deut. 24:5) was important for the "balance" of Israel (cf. Judg. 21:3). According to the "amphictyonic" theory (applied to Israel originally by Martin Noth), there were a number of tribal confederations in the ancient Near East unified around a central shrine whose upkeep was tended in rotation by each tribe in turn. Clearly the confederation ("amphictyony") would fall into disarray should one tribe disappear.

While the amphictyonic theory is now generally abandoned, still the OT in general does reflect the conviction that the structure of Israel is important to God. The number of tribes within the whole is not fortuitous, but is under God's protection and concern. This concern for completeness ("reluctant that any should perish") is then extended to the clans within the tribes and individuals within the clans, hence the care lest a "name be blotted out of Israel" (Deut. 25:6b).

The concern was all the more poignant at a period when hope of personal survival beyond death had not yet emerged, so that one's "name" (i.e., personality) was conceived as being perpetuated in one's children. To be childless was equivalent to having one's "lamp snuffed out." The role of the elders (vv. 7-9) is an indication that the material is ancient (cf. 19:12; 21:2).

25:9 It is clear from Ruth 4:7-9 that the handing over of one's sandal was symbolic ratification of a land transaction. In very early times one attested one's right to a parcel of land by ceremonially treading its boundaries (Gen. 13:17; Deut. 1:36; 11:24; Josh. 1:3). Later, the actual treading was replaced by the sandal symbolism (cf. Ps. 60:9, where God lays claim to Edom).

It is a strong surmise that the levirate marriage has special relevance in cases where the deceased was head of the clan. In marrying the widow, the younger brother would then inherit the responsibilities of clan head, including stewardship of the clan lands.

When the widow therefore removes the younger brother's sandal, the symbolism is that he is unworthy to be family protector and steward. This is strengthened by the detail that he does not hand over his sandal voluntarily, but has it removed by the one who bears the brunt of his unfitness, namely, the widow of the deceased head.

The public shaming implicit in this act is reinforced by the person's being spat upon (cf. Num. 12:14; Isa. 50:6). In ancient belief, spittle and other bodily fluids contained a person's life potential, and were therefore powerful vehicles for imparting blessing or curse.

25:10   Ironically, the one who refuses to perpetuate his brother's name thereby succeeds in perpetuating for his own descendants the opprobrium he has earned by his selfish individualism.

In ancient society the levirate marriage was considered important in preserving the clan cohesion and strength on which their survival depended. Theologically, the custom attests Yahweh's concern for the preservation, wholeness, and balance of the covenant people. Indeed, Yahweh's care extends to each member of the people. This care of Yahweh is the basis for belief in eternal life — the love that never lets go (Jer. 31:3). The experience and conviction of such care then become an incentive for the people of God to cherish their fellow believers throughout life — and beyond, to provide for their widows and fatherless children.

Acts of Indecency Forbidden (25:11-12)

The Middle Assyrian code (§ A.8) provides the nearest ancient Near Eastern parallel to this law: a woman who damages a man's testicle will have her finger cut off — or both eyes gouged out, if both testicles are damaged.

The concern is not so much with immodesty as with jeopardizing the man's chance to produce progeny. This is probably the case in Deuteronomy also (hence the connection with Deut. 25:5-10). There is also the added dimension, that this indecent behavior degrades the sexual processes (i.e., the processes of creation) and sullies the dignity of a fellow human being. Reference has already been made at 23:10-11 to the sacral nature of sexuality. Touching or damaging another's genitals transgresses the bounds of the sacral and so insults Yahweh, Creator of humanity and Chooser of Israel.

Deuteronomy 25:11 begins literally, "when men fight together, a man and his brother." The last phrase, referring to "brother," may have been added to strengthen the connection with vv. 5-10.

The ancient Near Eastern codes frequently prescribe punishment by mutilation. Apart from the *lex talionis* (see above on 19:21), 25:12 is the sole example of such a prescription in the OT. As already suggested, the *lex talionis* was probably never intended to be applied literally in Israel. Rather, it is a solemn traditional formulation used to add weight to the exposition of the law's requirement.

Thus this sole instance of mutilation highlights both the seriousness of this particular act and the humaneness of the OT code(s) in general.

Honest Weights and Measures (25:13-16)

Cf. Lev. 19:35-37; Amos 8:5.

In typical Deuteronomic style, this section is again a combination of law and exhortation.

In ancient Near Eastern kingdoms there was an effort to standardize weights and measures by royal decree (cf. 2 Sam. 14:26, "the king's weight"). In the absence of a standards control system, however, cheating was easy and rife. Because gold and silver coins were not of uniform weight either, the coinage as well as the goods was weighed in concluding a transaction. In such circumstances it was a simple matter for the unscrupulous to weigh the goods with a "small" shekel (Deut. 25:13) and the coinage with a "large" (or are "small" and "large" technical terms, so that the deceit referred to here is the switching of the "small" shekel [11.4 g. (.4 oz.)] and the "large" [2.2 g. (.8 oz.)] in mid-transaction?).

Similarly with measures (v. 14), the "ephah" varied from 13–23 l. (3.5–6 gal.). Might the Israelite trader have been as adroit as the Javanese, slipping his thumb surreptitiously into the "ephah" so that the measure which looked full at purchase turned out later to have contained only two-thirds?

The temptation to "use" the loopholes in the economic system is a perennial one. All such "dodges" are in principle ruled out of court by this passage.

"Wipe Out the Remembrance of Amalek" (25:17-19)

These verses are tacked onto the Deuteronomic code, which has in fact ended at 25:16. (Chapter 26 is not so much law as liturgical response to the preceding body of laws.)

According to Gen. 36:12, Amalek is the grandson of Edom

219

and so "family" to Israel (cf. Deut. 23:7). The vehemence of the
anti-Amalekite feeling is therefore surprising.

Deuteronomy 25:17-19 obviously reflects the old tradition recorded in Exod. 17:8-16. That passage describes an historic military
clash (Exod. 17:8-13), supplemented with a summary of subsequent encounters between Amalek and Israel down the centuries
(Exod. 17:14-16). The series of encounters begins at the Exodus
and ends with Amalek's final overthrow in the reign of Hezekiah
(1 Chr. 4:41, 43). Strikingly, every contact listed in the series is
negative (Judg. 10:12; Num. 13:29; 14:25, 43, 45; 1 Sam. 15:1-
33; 27:8-9; 30:1-20; 2 Sam. 8:12). It is this "summary of the
centuries" from Exod. 17:14-16 that colors Deut. 25:17-19. The
detail of Deut. 25:17-19 differs somewhat from Exod. 17. The
latter describes an open clash (Exod. 17:9), whereas Deuteronomy
speaks of guerrilla sniping (Deut. 25:18) — presumably to
heighten the sense of atrocity and indignation. (The details of this
"heightening" are probably freely adapted from 1 Sam. 30:1-3.)

According to Deut. 25:18, Amalek "did not fear God." For
Israel, to "fear Yahweh" means to obey Yahweh's revealed torah.
Amalek does not know Yahweh's name or torah, but "he" does
know God — through the laws of universally accepted morality and
universally acknowledged human conscience (cf. Amos 2:1: the
inhumanity of one pagan people against another still comes under
the judgment of the universal God whom Israel calls Yahweh).

The function of Deut. 25:17-19 in this "late final" position is
perhaps twofold:

(1) It forms a contrast to 25:5-10. Yahweh is concerned (v. 6)
that no name be "blotted out of Israel." But Amalek, who
opposed both the universal sense of God and God's specific
purpose for the covenant people, *is* to be "blotted out
without trace." Yahweh is both God of covenant grace and
God of universal justice.

(2) It strikes again a note that has been prominent throughout
the Deuteronomic code, namely, "Yahweh's war." This is
basically a note of empowerment: "Whatever the current
odds, nothing can ultimately defeat those who submit
themselves in willing obedience to Yahweh's purpose."

ROUNDING OFF OF THE
DEUTERONOMIC CODE (26:1-15)

As noted above, the code has in fact ended at 25:16. Description of the covenant ratification follows at 26:16. Included here are liturgies expressing gratitude and heartfelt acceptance of the code's essence.

What then is the function of 26:1-15? After all, the offerings of firstfruits (26:1-11) and tithes (vv. 12-15) has already been expounded at 14:22-29; 15:19-23. The answer is probably that these offerings are a grateful acknowledgment that Yahweh has delivered the promised gift, namely, the freedom to be a people, and the land on which to enjoy that freedom.

The annual repetition of the offerings reminds Yahweh's people that their life constantly depends on Yahweh's promise and guidance.

It is noteworthy that the vocabulary and phraseology throughout 26:1-15 show marked and detailed resemblance to that used in the successive introductions to the code now found in chs. 12, 6, and 4. The number and closeness of these correspondences suggest that 26:1-15 was deliberately designed to match the opening(s), in order to highlight the all-roundedness of the code as a covenant document. (We can also assume, incidentally, that the composition of 26:1-15 came rather late in the process of compiling Deuteronomy — i.e., after chs. 12, 6, and 4.)

In our earlier discussion (on 14:22-29) we concluded that "tithing" was in fact a spelling out of the prescription for the "firstfruits" offering. The intention of the two terms is the same; they simply reflect different stages in the historical development. This is then presumably the case in 26:1-11, 12-15.

The Offering of the Firstfruits (26:1-11)

The passage is not homogeneous. In v. 4 the priest accepts and places the offering; in v. 10b it is the worshipper who places it. Furthermore, the accompanying confession of faith is duplicated, occurring both in v. 3 and in vv. 5-10a.

These divergences imply that 26:1-11 was composed in stages.

221

The confession in vv. 5-10a obviously contains ancient material (see below).

Presumably an early Deuteronomic writer has edited this ancient stuff into the form of vv. 1-2, 5-11; and a later hand from the same school has added vv. 3-4, highlighting the role of the (levitical) priest (a specific Deuteronomic concern, as frequently noted).

26:3-4 The brevity of the confession in v. 3 and its use of typical Deuteronomic language suggest that its function is secondary, that is, merely to introduce the role of the priest. In the finished form of Deuteronomy the "firstfruits" are the priests' portion (18:4). Here (26:4) they are offered to Yahweh — implying (1) that the priest receives his livelihood from Yahweh and (2) that in giving for the support of the "clergy" the worshipper is giving to Yahweh.

26:5 To "make response" (literally, "answer and say") is a technical phrase introducing solemn or official material, in this case the formal, longer confession. Gerhard von Rad put forward the view that at base 26:5-10a forms an ancient "credo," recited in premonarchic times at Gilgal as part of the rites commemorating Yahweh's promise of land to the patriarchs and the gift of that land to their descendants (cf. 6:20-24).

Hebrew *obed*, translated "wandering" in 26:5, is elsewhere rendered "perished" (Job 4:11; 29:13), "broken" (Ps. 31:12), and "lost" (Ps. 119:176; Jer. 50:6). Its use here pictures Jacob wandering aimless like a lost sheep, having loosed his previous home ties and not yet found new ones in the God-promised homeland.

The overall phrase "A wandering Aramean was my father" (Heb. *arammi obed abi*) has a poetic conciseness which gives the impression of an ancient cultic-credal formulation. Remembering too that Israel was frequently at war with Aram-Syria throughout the period of the Monarchy (e.g., 2 Sam. 8:5; 1 Kgs. 11:25 and *passim*; 2 Kgs. 5:7 and *passim*), it seems practically certain that the phrase originated prior to these wars, that is, in ancient times. The "Aramean," as indicated above, is Jacob — designated "Aramean" in reference to his sojourn with his uncle "Laban the

Aramean" (Gen. 25:20; 28:5; 31:20-24; cf. Hos. 12:12). That
Jacob is mentioned so specifically, rather than "the ancestors" in
general, is an indication that the material is from a northern
Israelite source.

The phrase "harsh bondage" (Deut. 26:6), not otherwise used
in Deuteronomy, is typical of the Priestly postexilic source, and
unlikely to be ancient. The language of vv. 5b, 8-9 is typical of
Deuteronomic exhortation.

In summary, then, the so-called credo clearly incorporates ancient liturgical language from the Feast of Weeks celebration (cf.
16:9-12) — material heavily reworked by the Deuteronomic
school.

Von Rad, however, draws wider consequences from this credo.
Since (in its present Deuteronomic form) the passage does not
mention the giving of torah at Sinai-Horeb, he concludes that the
primitive Festival of Weeks celebrated at Gilgal was not acquainted
with the Horeb-Torah tradition. Recent scholarship questions von
Rad's assumption at this point. It seems safer to assume that from
the beginning the celebration of the Feast of Weeks included a
remembrance both of the liberating Exodus and the entry into
Canaan, on the one hand, and the historic law-giving at Horeb,
on the other. In other words, the call to celebrate and to obey
were intimately linked from Israel's beginnings.

Von Rad also notes that in its current form 26:5-10 resembles
in structure the typical psalm of thanksgiving: experience of difficulty, call for help, experience of salvation. It is indeed possible
that the psalm structure has influenced the shape of the credo.

The Offering of Tithes (26:12-15)

Assuming that "firstfruits" and "tithes" are in principle equivalent
terms — though from different periods in the history of the development of the cult — we meet a superficial difficulty in v. 12,
namely, that firstfruits are (presumably) offered annually whereas
the "tithe" is paid every "third year." For the resolution of this
difficulty, see the discussion on 14:22-29.

The first impression from v. 12 is that the tithe is divided *in
toto* among the four categories of needy people — Levites, so-

journers, fatherless, widows. In fact, however, the wording does
not necessarily exclude the participation of the worshippers and
their family, as described in 14:22-29. Certainly the balance is
different — probably indicating changing circumstances in changing times. This distribution in the third year is a local activity
("within your towns"). The concluding worship, however, is
"before Yahweh," that is, at the central shrine (26:13; cf., e.g.,
14:23). The act of worship includes a solemn affirmation that the
tithe requirements have been conscientiously fulfilled — an affirmation which then forms the basis of a plea for God's ongoing
blessing.

To "remove" the sacred portion (26:13) is to "cauterize," to
"destroy entirely" (Heb. *bi'er;* see above on 13:5). In the context
of 26:13, the use of this term implies that there is a sacral-taboo
quality inhering in the tithe goods which would bring a curse on
those who withhold the tithe for their own use. For the well-being
and safety of their own households, worshippers should surrender
the entire tithe according to the prescriptions laid down. "Forget-
ting" here is not lapse of memory, but the willful overlooking of
acknowledged duties. It is the opposite of the dynamic "remembering" called for in 7:18 (see above).

26:14 The threefold declaration of innocence in 26:14 has the
ring of an ancient formula, originating presumably in times when
the whole tithe was a direct offering to God. The underlying
principle is that the whole tithe offering becomes "polluted" when
any part of it is used wrongfully. Such pollution threatens the
well-being of the family or community concerned. The "mourning" referred to may be for the death of a family member, or it
may be a ritual mourning in connection with the fertility cult
where the god(dess) of fruit, grain, or fecundity is regarded as
dying in autumn (cf. Zech. 12:11; Ezek. 8:14). Archaeological
finds attest a communal meal associated with this fertility cult
ritual weeping.

Whether in connection with personal or ritual mourning, the
Deuteronomic school and indeed the OT tradition as a whole
forbids all association with the cult of the dead. Such association
is incompatible with a total dedication to Yahweh. The people

who trust Yahweh may not rely on any other spiritual force apart from Yahweh.

This theological thinking is undergirded by a primitive natural aversion in the face of death. Because Yahweh is the living God and source of life, death appears as an affront to Yahweh's nature. Thus not only is the cult of the dead compromising, but all contact with a (nonsacrificial) carcass or corpse is seen as defiling (cf. Hag. 2:13).

For the various causes of "uncleanness," see above on Deut. 12:15. Uncleanness, from whatever cause, was regarded in ancient times as an infection which would spread to the whole, and in this case render the entire tithe unacceptable.

The same would apply to "offering any of it to the dead" and the accompanying "polluting" contact with the dead. The "offering to the dead" may be either:

(1) An offering to the spirit of the deceased, wooing the deceased to reveal the fate awaiting the living (cf. 18:11), or food presented as sustenance for the deceased's journey into the world of the dead (cf. Tobit 4:17; Ecclus. 30:18-19).

(2) An offering to "the dead gods," gods of fertility who have no relevance or significance for Yahweh's people (cf. Ps. 106:28, where "eating sacrifices offered to the dead" and "attaching themselves to the Baal of Peor" are paralleled).

In either case, it is a matter of relying on a spiritual force other than Yahweh — a stance which defiles both the worshippers and their entire offering.

On the "voice (Heb. *qol*) of Yahweh," cf. Deut. 8:20.

26:15 That God should "look down from thy holy habitation" is consistent with the Deuteronomic "name" theology (see above on 12:5). God who fills the heavens is nevertheless surely present among the covenant people.

The text implores God to "bless thy people Israel and the ground which thou hast given us." It is impressive that the individual worshipper should have such a strong sense of membership in and oneness with the entire covenant people. The individual offering is an integral part of Israel's total harvest thanksgiving. The land which the individual family farms is part of Israel's God-given land of promise. The obedient devotion of "Israel" is the obedience of each citizen, one by one. When, on the other hand, one citizen neglects his or her duty to Yahweh, the life of the whole nation is compromised.

CONCLUSION OF THE SECOND SPEECH

Deuteronomy 26:16–28:68

This also constitutes the covenant ratification. As in each other major section of Deuteronomy, so here too the material is diverse. Within the subsections there is also evidence of development processes at work and compilation from a variety of sources.

COVENANT RATIFICATION FORMULA (26:16-19)

In the Introduction (4-10) we noted that, in the stages of its production, the book of Deuteronomy has been successively structured as code of law, vassal treaty, and farewell speech. Where does Deut. 26:16-19 fit into all of this? While it may perhaps be read as conclusion to the Deuteronomic code, or as part of the final peroration of the second speech of Moses, its closest and most natural association is with the vassal treaty, namely, as the declaration of the treaty ratification. This is undoubtedly its original function.

The language of v. 16 is typical Deuteronomic exhortation (cf. 4:1, 14; 6:5).

The threefold stress on "this day" (26:16, 17, 18) is in keeping with the atmosphere of solemn covenant ratification. As frequently noted, there is a strong stress on "contemporization" throughout Deuteronomy. The historic Horeb covenant-making is "this day-ed" at successive annual festivals. The "re-present-ation" of covenant ratification is the climax of the celebration, as the congregation are called to meeting and response: "Here and now, you are standing in the presence of Yahweh on Horeb; this day Yahweh is entering covenant with you." (We are reminded of the re-present-ation of the Last Supper in the ongoing eucharistic practice of the Christian Church.)

227

26:17-18 "You have declared this day concerning Yahweh that Yahweh is your God, . . . and Yahweh has declared this day concerning you. . . ." The specific and unique nuances of the language give the impression that these twin sentences comprise an official ratification formula rooted in ancient tradition. Some scholars suggest that this formula was used by Josiah in the covenant renewal (presumably based on the text of Deuteronomy) as described in 2 Kgs. 23:1-3. This does not of course necessarily imply that the formula originated with Josiah.

The phrase "have declared . . . concerning" translates literally as "have caused . . . to say" (cf. the NJB: "have obtained this declaration from . . ."). In human-to-human terms this means something like "have put under oath": "You have taken Yahweh's oath that Yahweh will be your God; and Yahweh has taken your oath, that you will be Yahweh's people."

Applied to God in this way, the language is bold indeed. The faithfulness of Yahweh's covenant keeping has never been in doubt; it is the human party who needs to be "bound over" by solemn oath. The use of this human-to-human terminology does, however, make the double point very effectively: on Yahweh's side the covenant is immovably steadfast, yet it is also conditional on Israel's faithful obedience.

The solemn formula (Deut. 26:17a, 18a) is set in typical Deuteronomic parenesis (vv. 17b, 18b-19; cf. 4:1-2; 5:33; 7:6; 8:20), the effect of which is to "compromise" the balanced exactitude of the official formula with a strong stress on the importance of human accountability.

The phrase "high above all nations" (26:19; cf. 28:1) is unusual. "High" (Heb. *'elyon*) is a divine cultic title, "the Most High" (e.g., Gen. 14:18-22; Ps. 7:17; 46:4; 82:6). Hence it is transferred to the anointed Davidic king as Yahweh's representative (Ps. 89:27). It is likely that Ps. 89 was used in the Jerusalem cultus in connection with the king's role in covenant renewal. In that case, it is probable that the Deuteronomic writer here has deliberately transferred the title from king to people, as a corrective to the "royal covenant" that was traditional in Jerusalem. It is the people who are *'elyon* by virtue of God's gracious election. The primary covenant is not that between Yahweh and king, but that between Yahweh and people.

228

"In praise and in fame and in honor" (Deut. 26:19b) is probably also "royal-covenant" language (cf. Ps. 89:16-18), which in Deut. 26:19 (as also in Jer. 13:11) is transferred unambiguously to the covenant people.

CONCLUSION OF THE SPEECH (27:1-26)

Formally we have classified Deut. 27 as part of the conclusion to Moses' second speech. In fact, of course, the connection is rather loose, even artificial.

Moses is three times referred to in the third person (vv. 1, 9, 11), indicating that the material originated in another milieu and was only subsequently forced by the editor into the speech format. Chapter 27 does not constitute a unity, but is composed of four separate units: vv. 1-8, 9-10, 11-13, 14-26. In the finished form of the material as we have it, the unifying factor is that all these units refer to rites and ceremonies at Ebal and Gerizim, the twin mountains which cradle Shechem. Significantly, v. 7 in particular is directly reminiscent of the worship circumstances described in ch. 12 (12:6-7, 11-12, 17-18, 26-27), which feature thanksgiving and communion at a central shrine. In our discussion of ch. 12 we concluded that the compiler of that chapter interpreted the "one place of worship" as the Jerusalem temple. In the Introduction (20-21), however, we saw that the Deuteronomic traditions probably originated in northern Israel and moved south as a result of the fall of Samaria in 722 B.C. On this basis, some scholars suggest that the "one place" may originally have had a northern reference, namely, Shechem. If that is the case, it would seem likely that ch. 27 embodying these Shechem traditions was added to the corpus of Deuteronomy sometime after the completion of chs. 12–26, with its implicit "Jerusalem" reference.

An exhaustive study of the problems associated with Deut. 27 would require a separate volume. Here it must suffice to draw attention to a group of texts which discuss or allude to a rite or rites similar to that described in this chapter. These texts are Exod. 24:1-11; Josh. 24:1-28; 4:1-10; Deut. 11:19-32 (and Josh. 8:30-35, which is a rescript of Deut. 27).

In the finished form of these texts, the rite or rites they describe are variously located at Sinai-Horeb, Shechem, and Gilgal. To what extent are these in fact separate rites — or variations stemming ultimately from a common original?

A general comparison of the texts strengthens the impression that they stem from a common stock.

(1) Both Deut. 27 and Exod. 24 are highly composite. Their seeming aim is to combine elements from the liturgies of Shechem, Gilgal, Jerusalem, and possibly other shrines as well, and relate the whole back to the definitive salvation experience under Moses (whether at Horeb or on the plains of Moab). These composite traditions arose from the desire of the compiler in each case to trace back to Moses all the wealth of liturgical variation which had emerged at the local shrines during the previous generations.

(2) In our discussion on Deut. 11:26-32, we noted the probability that Shechem traditions were at one stage transferred to Gilgal and vice versa, so that "Ebal" and "Gerizim" came to function not merely as locations but as symbols of "curse" and "blessing."

(3) "Sacred" stones are also a feature common to this group of passages. The "twelve pillars" of Exod. 24:4 are reminiscent of the "twelve stones" set up at Gilgal (Josh. 4:2-8). Seemingly an originally Gilgal element has been read back into the Exod. 24 Horeb account, in order to attest the authentically Mosaic nature of the Gilgal ritual.

What of the "large stones" (plastered and inscribed) set up at Shechem (Deut. 27:2-4)? Are these the Shechem equivalent of the Gilgal stones?

Then, too, is the "great stone" of witness at Shechem (Josh. 24:26-27) a variation on the same theme? Here and in Exod. 24, the torah inscribed in a book is the prime witness to the covenant, so that the stone becomes a secondary witness. In Deut. 27:2-3 (cf. Josh. 8:32) the stone, actually inscribed with torah, is the primary witness.

Memorial Stones and Altar on Mt. Ebal (27:1-8)

As noted above, this is a separate section within the chapter. Indeed, unevennesses within the section have caused some to question whether Deut. 27:1-8 is itself a unity (the "stones" to be written on [v. 8] are not the altar stones [vv. 5-6] but the standing stones of vv. 2-4. Does this indicate that vv. 5-7 are an insert)?

27:1 Here, for the first time in Deuteronomy, the elders stand with Moses as co-mediators of the law. This contrasts with 5:23-24, where they stand over against Moses, voicing the mind of the people. Elsewhere, too, their role is as representatives of the people (19:12; 21:2-6, 19-20; 22:15-18; 25:7-9), who together with the people are subject to the torah. Interestingly, the only other comparative text which assigns a mediating role to the elders is Exod. 24:1-9 (see above, 230). The tradition reflected here obviously differs somewhat from mainstream Deuteronomism. (Some LXX manuscripts smooth the unusualness by transposing: "Moses commanded the elders . . . and the people.")

27:2 If the phrase "the day you pass over" is to be taken literally (cf. Josh. 4:3, "tonight"), then the site indicated is Gilgal. The journey to Shechem is too far. Otherwise the phrase must be interpreted generally, "when you pass over." The number of stones to be set up is unspecified. The Gilgal tradition, however, stipulates "twelve" (Josh. 4:2).

27:3 This verse plainly implies that the whole Deuteronomic code is to be inscribed on the standing stones. Some scholars, doubting the feasibility of this, have suggested that a summary is intended — the Decalogue or the Shechemite "twelve curses" (Deut. 27:15-26). This is unnecessary, considering that the whole Code of Hammurabi is inscribed on a single pillar.

27:4 It is problematic whether the original version of 27:1-8 intended to locate "Mount Ebal" at Shechem or at Gilgal (see above, 230). It is also strange that the torah stones should be set up on the "mount of cursing" (v. 13), for is not the torah a ground for rejoicing (v. 7)? Interestingly, the Samaritan Pentateuch (followed by the Old Latin) reads "Gerizim" (the mount of blessing) here. Previously scholars assumed that after the rup-

ture between Jews and Samaritans in the 4th cent. B.C. the
Samaritans altered the Masoretic reading in order to validate their
new temple on Mt. Gerizim. More recently, the contrary opinion
is gaining ground, namely, that the Jews altered the reading to
"Ebal" in the interests of anti-Samaritan polemic. If "Gerizim" is
indeed the original reading, the effect is to present the torah as
"blessing" — an emphasis in keeping with the tone of Deuteronomy as a whole (e.g., 4:7-8).

27:5-6 The unevenness in the composition of 27:1-8 lends
some plausibility to the interpretation that the "words of this law"
(v. 8) were written on the altar stones (vv. 5-6). (The parallel
account in Josh. 8:30-35 is even more ambiguous in this regard.)
It is preferable, however, to regard Deut. 27:1-8 on this point as
parallel to Exod. 24, where the standing stones (Exod. 24:4) are
quite separate from the altar (v. 5).

On the stipulation that the altar stones be unhewn, cf. the
ancient "law of the altar" in Exod. 20:24-25. It is stated there
that the stones must be in their natural condition, uncontaminated
by human artifice. Further, the ancient law obviously envisages a
multiplicity of altars and sacred sites ("every place where I cause
my name to be remembered," Exod. 20:24) — unlike Deut. 12.
Similarly, 27:5-7 makes no mention of a "unique altar" in "one
place." Does this imply that the author who added ch. 27 to the
corpus of Deuteronomy had a rather different theological perspective from that of the compiler of ch. 12?

27:7 The "peace offering" (Heb. *shelem*) is (surprisingly) not
mentioned in the descriptions of sacrifice in ch. 12 (12:6, 11, 14,
17) or elsewhere in Deuteronomy, though it occurs frequently
throughout the remainder of the Deuteronomic history. This perhaps strengthens the possibility that ch. 27 employs a special
source.

It is noteworthy, too, that the *shelem* features also in Exod.
24:5. (See above on the similarities between Exod. 24 and Deut.
27.)

The term *shelem* is an ancient one known in inscriptions from
Ugarit and southern Arabia. Traditionally scholars linked the term

with *shalom* ("peace"), and saw the sacrifice as concerned with atonement (peace with God) or communion (peace and fellowship with people). For all practical purposes, it was regarded as synonymous with Heb. *zebah* (sacrifice in general). More recent scholarship, however, interprets *shelem* in terms of completeness — "the final offering," concluding the whole burnt offering rite.

It remains an open question whether the flesh of the *shelem* was burned or eaten. Possibly the *shelem* began as a specifically royal offering which was democratized in the process of its development.

Eating and rejoicing go together, as in Deut. 12:7, 18, and so forth. The eating is also reminiscent of Exod. 24:11. To eat together "before Yahweh" in festival is to celebrate one's membership in the covenant people and symbolically to taste Yahweh's (harvest) generosity and Yahweh's gift of land and freedom.

27:8 The command to "write" (Heb. *be'er*) "the law plainly" picks up Moses' intention at the beginning: He "undertook to explain *(be'er)* this law" (Deut. 1:5). Every time the torah is read and expanded in festival or in home catechizing, the historic Horeb words are re-presented and the ongoing relationship with the covenant God is confirmed.

Affirming the Covenant Ratification (27:9-10)

These verses are distinct from 27:1-8 and may well form a continuation of 26:16-19.

As the elders in 27:1 acted as co-mediators, so here do the levitical priests (v. 9). Nowhere else in Deuteronomy are Levites associated with Moses in this way — though interestingly there is a parallel between their role here and that of the "young men" in Exod. 24:5. (Exod. 24 could not yet speak of "Levites," for only in Exod. 32 were the Levites formally chosen for priestly duty.) In Deut. 27:14 also, the Levites seem to function as Moses' assistants. This is the grandest status claim so far made on behalf of the Levites. At the same time, Moses remains preeminent: he is (by implication) priest, as well as prophet and lawgiver.

There is a widespread and ancient belief that silence (v. 9b) is

233

vital at the climactic moments of contact with the sacred (Zeph. 1:7; Zech. 2:7; cf. Latin *favete linguis*). The sound of a voice can dissipate the spiritual potency of the occasion and indeed unleash threatening spiritual forces.

This ancient understanding has of course been modified in the present context. The accent is no longer on averting spiritual threat, but on realizing the sacred solemnity of the moment in which Israel became (and liturgically becomes once more) the special possession of all-holy Yahweh.

"This day you have become Yahweh's people. You shall therefore obey . . ." (Deut. 27:9-10). As noted on 5:6, the order of clauses is "evangelical." Obedience is not a way of becomimg accepted, but a grateful response to prior acceptance.

Ceremony on Ebal and Gerizim (27:11-13)

These verses are obviously not continuous with 27:14-26, but describe a distinct ceremonial of covenant solemnization.

The passage gives the impression that six tribes (or their representatives) pronounce the blessings on covenant obedience, while the other six pronounce the curses on covenant infringement. Whether the curses follow the blessings en bloc or alternate one by one is unclear. In either case, the procedure differs from that of vv. 14-26, where the Levites pronounce the curses and the people as a whole respond, "Amen" (v. 14). Note too that in v. 12 Levi is listed as one tribe among the six, whereas in v. 14 Levi stands over against "Israel."

In the introduction to ch. 27 we discussed the location of Ebal and Gerizim. It is unclear whether vv. 12-13 originally located them at Shechem or at Gilgal.

As to the naming of the twelve tribes, a comparison of the various OT lists reveals significant variations.

The accounts within the JE source (Gen. 29:31–30:20; 35:22-26; 49:3-27) group the twelve according to the wives of Jacob:

Sons of Leah:	Reuben, Simeon, Levi, Judah, Issachar, Zebulun
Sons of Bilhah:	Dan, Naphtali

Sons of Zilpah: Gad, Asher
Sons of Rachel: Joseph, Benjamin

We have already suggested (Deut. 19:7-8) that the accounts of Israel's ("Jacob's") tribal structure are highly stylized. "Leah" seems to stand eponymously for an original tribal alliance which never experienced slavery in Egypt, the Bilhah ("concubine") group for the fringe members of that alliance, Rachel for the group which did experience slavery and exodus, and Zilpah (also a concubine) possibly for those regarded as the fringe-members of Rachel.

The other characteristics of the JE description are that Joseph is undifferentiated into Ephraim and Manasseh, and that Levi is counted as a territorial tribe.

The grouping of the tribes in 27:11-13, on the other hand, is based not on eponymous ancestry but on the location of their territories. As Gerizim is located southwest of Shechem, so the tribes of the south and west stand there. Ebal is to the northeast, so the northern and eastern tribes stand there. Interestingly, Levi is still regarded as "territorial," and "Joseph" is still undifferentiated.

Of the remaining OT lists, Deut. 33 (of unknown provenance) subsumes Simeon within Judah, and retains Joseph and Levi as units. Genesis 35:22ff. (P) follows the "Jacob's wives" pattern of JE, but places Rachel next after Leah. Num. 1:5 15 (P) follows Gen. 35:22ff., but eliminates territorial Levi, differentiates Joseph, and mixes the children of the concubines. Num. 1:22-42 (P) follows Num. 1:5-15, except that Gad replaces Levi among the sons of Leah.

27:12 "Crossing the river" may well have formed part of the ongoing liturgical reenactment of the land occupation. Such a reenactment would more likely be sited at Gilgal than at Shechem.

"Stand upon Mount Gerizim to bless" contrasts with Deut. 11:29 ("set the blessing on Mount Gerizim"), which implies that the tribes stand facing the mountain and proclaim their blessings towards it, thus making the mountain a repository of blessing. Joshua 8:33, on the other hand, implies that the "blessers" stand with their backs to the mountains and place their blessing (curse) directly on the people.

Does the variety of explanation mean that the precise details of the ceremony have been lost in the mists of antiquity? Even though that may be, the abiding impression is still valid — that of a whole nation responsible before God for its own covenant obedience, and deeply aware of the consequences of rebellion. They are aware, too, that the very land which their covenant God has given to them stands around them (symbolized by the ever-lasting hills) as perpetual witness to the covenant and repository of blessing and curse.

The Twelve Curses (27:14-26)

As noted, this section is discontinuous with Deut. 27:11-13.

The term "cursed" (Heb. *arur*) used throughout the passage has authority overtones. It is used with God, ruler, or sovereign assembly as subject, to isolate and distance the guilty party and consign them unprotected to the realm of the malign. The term *qelalah,* used for "curse" in v. 13, is sometimes used in the same context as *arur* (e.g., 28:14-15), but normally implies concrete — and therefore "survivable" — disaster, rather than the "definitive" distancing implied by *arur*.

Viewed from the perspective of form criticism, sentences 2-11 (i.e., 27:16-25) in this "Dodecalogue" series exhibit a uniformity of style and content, whereas numbers 1 and 12 (vv. 15 and 26) are longer in form and more summarizing in content, and are probably later additions. However, even the remaining ten sentences (vv. 16-25) form neither a comprehensive nor a specialized series and are unlikely to be an original unity. Probably the compiler of Deut. 27 was the one who assembled the series, incorporating larger and smaller pieces of ready-made material that lay to hand. Sentences 6–9 (vv. 20-23) were obviously an already-existent specialized series (on sexual aberrations), and numbers 10-11 (vv. 24-25) may be a fragment of a similar series (on physical assault; Heb. *hikkah*). Sentence 2 (v. 16) is an ancient version of the Fifth Commandment (see above on 5:16; cf. Exod. 21:17). Number 3 (Deut. 27:17) is a variant of 19:14, and number 5

(27:19) is formed from typical Deuteronomic parenesis. Sentence 4 (v. 18) — otherwise unknown — may have been attracted into association with number 5 by the wordplay between "justice" (Heb. *mishpat*, v. 19) and "blindness" (*'iwwer*, v. 18) such as we find in 16:19 ("justice" becomes "blind").

Some scholars have noted the explicit reference to "secrecy" in 27:15, 24, and suggest that "secrecy" may be the common thread uniting the twelve sentences. By their nature, indeed, many of the condemned actions will certainly have been performed in secret. But on the whole, the evidence is too slender to support the conclusion that "secrecy" is the guiding motif.

Many also see this Shechem Dodecalogue, placed at the end of the Deuteronomic code, as a deliberate counterbalance or reinforcement of the Decalogue (5:6-21) which opened the presentation of the code. This attractive suggestion is supported by what was said earlier in this section about the weighty significance of the term *arur* ("cursed"). The authoritative tone of the term implies that the Dodecalogue is not so much a sanction appended to the torah code, but (like the Decalogue in ch. 5) an actual proclamation of the torah in summary form. The detailed exposition (chs. 12–26) then is bracketed in a reinforcing summary.

By responding "Amen" to each sentence, the entire people undertake responsibility for upholding and "policing" the covenant stipulations. Indeed, the "Amen" acts as a kind of trigger, releasing the "excommunication" against the offender.

The language of 27:14 is distinctive ("Levites," "men of Israel," "loud voice"), signifying that the passage is from a distinctive source. The introductory statement in v. 15 (curse no. 1) locates *the* sin par excellence (cf. ch. 4) and condemns it in all its forms, whether carved (4:16, 23, 25; 5:8) or molded (9:12, 16) images. On the polemic note, cf., e.g., Isa. 44:9-10; Jer. 10:3-4.

To "dishonor" father and mother (Deut. 27:16) is to "treat them lightly" — the Hebrew term for which is closely akin to "curse" (*qelalah*, v. 13). See further the discussion on the original form of the Fifth Commandment (5:16).

Sensitivity toward the needs and feelings of the blind (27:18) is reflected also in Lev. 19:14; Job 29:15.

In the mini-series on sexual aberration (Deut. 27:20-23) v. 20

repeats 22:30 (see above). The prohibitions in 27:20, 22 originally reflected the conditions of the extended family. The debarring factor was not genealogical proximity but living under one roof. The survival of the family was a major concern (see above on 5:16). For that purpose conscientious adherence to a strict sexual ethic was essential. The ancient Near Eastern codes (Code of Hammurabi §§ 157-58) also legislate on these points, as on the matter of bestiality (27:21; cf. Hittite code II.187-88, 199). In Deut. 27 the prohibition of bestiality is inclusive and absolute, whereas in the Hittite code it applies only to those types of animal offered in sacrifice. In early Israel the prohibition would reflect the aversion to "confusing the patterns of creation by mixing the species" (see above on 22:5, 9-11). Later sensitivities would connect it with the insight that humanity is created in the image of God.

On "secret slaying" (27:24, 25), cf. 21:1-9. It may be said that the two passages present alternative methods of dealing with unavenged blood. The more ancient method (ch. 21) uses a ritual of guilt transference, whereas the later method (ch. 27) is to place the unknown perpetrator under the faith community's ban. The underlying concern is the same, but the change in procedure indicates a development in theological reflection and understanding.

Bribery (v. 25) was obviously an endemic problem throughout Israel's history. What was earlier condemned in officials (16:19) is here forbidden to every citizen: "like people, like priest."

Deuteronomy 27:26, as noted, is a summary of the Dodecalogue, and by extension of the whole code. Paul uses it so to focus his faith-law antithesis (Gal. 3:10). It may be apposite to comment, however, that Paul's polemic is not against the Deuteronomic school, but against a Judaistic legalism six hundred years later. The radical unity between "cleaving to Yahweh in trust" and "obeying Yahweh," which is the heartbeat of Deuteronomy, is also central to Paul's theology.

COVENANT SANCTIONS (28:1-68)

In the Introduction II (4-8) we discussed the legal code and the covenant treaty frameworks that were imposed on the Deuteronomic material at certain stages in its development. We noted also the role of sanctions (i.e., curses and blessings) within both frameworks. This is the function of Deut. 28 within the code-covenant which is Deuteronomy.

It is noteworthy that curses (vv. 15-68) preponderate over blessings (vv. 1-14), although the blessings do precede the curses. In the corresponding ancient Near Eastern texts the same pre-ponderance normally occurs, and in the extant examples curse always precedes blessing.

"Curse" was thus the primary sanction. Indeed, some scholars conclude that originally only curses were mentioned — the bless-ings being a later development.

Against this background the noteworthy feature of Deut. 28 is not the preponderance of curse but the relative prominence of blessing — the more so in that the chapter in its finished form is obviously colored by the bitter experiences of suffering in exile — interpreted as God's "curse" on the people's disobedience.

In the Introduction (8) we also mentioned the rise of Assyrian power (accompanied by conquests and treaties) in the 8th cent. B.C. as the probable factor which triggered Deuteronomic interest in the treaty form. From this point of view it is noteworthy that there are close and extensive parallels between the sanctions appended to the vassal treaty of Assyrian king Esarhaddon (681-669) and those of Deuteronomy (see the detailed notes below).

Deuteronomy 28 falls into three main sections:

- Blessings (vv. 1-14) and curses (vv. 15-46).
- A warning sermon (vv. 47-57)
- Concluding warning (vv. 58-68).

The material utilized in the chapter can be traced to five main sources.

(1) A succinct and well-honed series of blessings (vv. 3-6), matched exactly by corresponding curses (vv. 16-19). This has all the appearance of ancient, inherited material.

(2) A looser series of blessings (vv. 7, 12a, b, 13aα, 13aβ) and corresponding curses (vv. 25a, 43, 44a, b, 23-24). These too have an ancient ring.

(3) Citations from other parts of Deuteronomy, and pieces of Deuteronomic parenesis. The following is a list, by no means exhaustive, of the major citations:

28:10	"all shall see . . . and fear"	4:6
v. 14	"turn . . . to the right hand or to the left"	5:32
v. 20-21, 27-28, 35, 59-61	"diseases of Egypt"	7:15
vv. 29, 31	"no one to help you"	20:4
vv. 30, 39	"houses and vineyards"	6:11; 20:5-6
v. 30	"another will/will not lie with her"	20:7
v. 46	"signs and wonders"	4:34; 7:19; 26:8
v. 47	"joyfulness and gladness"	12:7, 12, 18; 14:26; 16:11, 14; 26:11; 27:7
vv. 51, 53-54	"grain, wine, oil"	7:13-15
v. 62	"as the stars of heaven"	1:10
v. 64a, c	"scattered . . . to serve other gods, of wood and stone"	4:27-28
v. 64b	"from one end of the earth to the other"	13:7

The Deuteronomic parenesis fills the interstices between citations: e.g., 28:1-2, 8-10, 13b-15.

(4) Echoes, reminiscences, and citations of other OT passages (admittedly, it is occasionally difficult to determine whether Deut. 28 or the look-alike is prior, or whether both depend on an antecedent source). A representative list, again not exhaustive, includes:

28:14	"turn to the right hand or to the left"	Josh. 1:7, etc.
v. 20b	"evil of your doings"	Jer. 4:4; 23:2, etc.
vv. 21, 27, 28-29, 35, 38	"plagues of Egypt"	Exod. 9:3, 9-10; 10:4, 21ff.

v. 26a	"corpses become carrion"	Jer. 34:20
v. 26b	"no one to frighten them away"	Jer. 7:33; Mic. 4:4, etc.
v. 28	"madness, blindness, confusion of mind"	Zech. 12:4
v. 29	"groping at noonday"	Isa. 59:10; Job 5:14
v. 29aβ	"prosper/not prosper in your ways"	Josh. 1:8
v. 32	"eyes fail with longing"	Lam. 4:17
v. 35	"boils from sole to crown"	Isa. 1:6; Job 2:7
v. 36	"sweep away your king"	1 Sam. 12:25
v. 38	"poor harvests"	Hag. 1:6
v. 48	"yoke of iron"	Jer. 28:14
v. 48	"hunger"	Isa. 8:21
v. 49	"enemies speaking a strange language"	Isa. 28:11; 33:19; Jer. 5:15
v. 49b	"swift as the eagle flies"	Jer. 48:40
vv. 55, 57	"eat one's children's flesh"	2 Kgs. 6:28-29
v. 62	"as the stars of heaven"	Gen. 15:5-6
v. 67	"Would it were morning"	Job 7:4

(5) Finally, as already noted, there are ancient Near Eastern parallels — whether conscious and direct citations from contemporary sources, or (much more likely) dependent in common on ancient traditions.

The overall impression is that the compiler(s) ransacked the storehouses of Israelite and Semitic tradition to produce covenant sanctions whose seriousness would have maximum impact in the "almost-too-late" circumstances of the impending or actual exile.

The Blessings (28:1-14)

Verses 1 and 2 are introductory and typical parenesis. For the phrase "God will set you high . . . ," see above on 26:19.

The aspects of blessing mentioned in 28:3-6 are representative, and together portray total all-around well-being — such as Baalism illusorily offers and Yahweh genuinely intends for humankind

241

in general and the covenant people in particular. "Basket and kneading-trough" represent Yahweh's kindly concern for the entire provisioning process, from sowing to harvest, to milling and baking, to table (cf. 26:2). Likewise, "coming in" and "going out" (28:6) are representative of total activity (see above on 6:9).

Yahweh, the controller of nature's processes, is also controller of battle and the turns of history (28:7).

Verses 8-10 constitute a "recall to Horeb." The land and its fruitfulness are a covenant gift. Once again eternal oath and solemn condition stand together: "Yahweh swears faithfulness . . . if you obey."

Just as the sandal passing symbolically over the land is a firm guarantee of ownership (25:9), so the solemn pronouncement of Yahweh's name over the covenant community (28:10) seals it as Yahweh's possession.

Interestingly, v. 11 is a preached version of v. 4. The ancient formulas are not only repeated but urged and applied.

The rain (v. 12) in its season (cf. 11:14) is "wealth," in that it releases the fertility of the fields. It is given from the "treasure house of the heavenly palace" — graphics of Yahweh's universal sovereignty.

On "lend but not borrow" (28:12), cf. 15:6.

Deuteronomy 28:13b-14 reiterates and reinforces the opening parenesis (vv. 1-2) and is clinched with the command, typical of the Deuteronomic history (e.g., Josh. 1:7; 23:6; 1 Sam. 6:12; cf. Deut. 5:32; 17:11, 20, which are also presumably Deuteronomic), not to "turn aside . . . to the right hand or to the left," but to hold dead center in undeflectable obedience.

The Curses (28:15-46)

28:15-16 Deuteronomy 28:15 picks up and reverses the phrase which has bracketed the blessings: "If you obey all the commandments . . . blessings. But if you do not obey . . . curses." In vv. 15-16 the two terms expressing "curse" (*arur* and *qelalah*) are used together (see above on 27:14ff.). Thus they embrace both the devastation and barrenness of city, field, and flocks, and also the divine self-distancing which is sensed as lying behind these physical phenomena.

Deuteronomy 28:16-19 is the reverse of vv. 3-6, with only minor variations in order.

28:20 The "confusion" (Heb. *mehumah*) of v. 20 is the "numinous panic" which forms one of the weapons in "Yahweh's war" (1 Sam. 5:9, 11; 14:20). As formerly it supported the covenant people against the opposition (Deut. 7:23), now it is turned against the covenant people in their apostasy.

"Me" at the end of 28:20 is obviously Yahweh (cf. also v. 68). The seemingly unconscious shift into speech of Yahweh in the first person witnesses to the perceived intimacy between Moses and Yahweh and to the writer's consciousness of Yahweh's voice echoing in the form of written words.

28:21-25 The irony of v. 21! Because Israel failed to "cleave" (Heb. *dabaq*) to Yahweh (see above on 4:4), disease will "cleave" to Israel. In rejecting the source of well-being, one chooses misery.

Seven sicknesses are listed in 28:22, the number seven being symbolic of "totality."

On "heavens . . . like brass" (v. 23), cf.:

- The sanctions (Lev. 26:3-39) attached to the Holiness code (Lev. 17–26 P), especially Lev. 26:19-20
- The drought, sensed as divine punishment on apostasy, under King Ahab (1 Kgs. 17–19)
- The sanctions attached to Assyrian king Esarhaddon's vassal treaty: "May the gods harden your land like iron . . . and rain not fall as if the heavens were brass."

"Dust from heaven" (Deut. 28:24) is a death-dealing parody of the life-giving rain (cf. Exod. 9:8-9). In natural terms, this is the sirocco, the hot, dry, dust-laden wind blowing off the deserts of Arabia to the east.

Deuteronomy 28:25 reverses v. 7. "Seven" again symbolizes "totality" (see v. 22).

28:26-35   These verses are closely parallel, both in content and in sentence order, to the "Esarhaddon" sanctions (cf. v. 22 above, and the introduction to ch. 28). See Moshe Weinfield, *Deuteronomy and the Deuteronomic School,* for details.

We have also noted parallels with the "plagues of Egypt" tradition in Exod. 7–12.

This richness of parallels both from within Israel and beyond suggests not so much direct literary dependence, as utilization of a common stock of ancient Near Eastern curse and treaty sanction material.

Since the Hebrews regarded the human being as a body-spirit unity, abuse of the corpse would jeopardize the well-being of the person in death. The thought of the corpse becoming carrion was therefore revolting (Deut. 28:26; cf. 2 Sam. 21:10).

Deuteronomy 28:31-33 is generally reminiscent of Job 1:13-19. Behind the lack of help (Deut. 28:31) is the absence of the Helper (Heb. *moshia'*), whose desire in fact is to raise up assistance in every time of need (cf., e.g., Judg. 3:9, 15).

28:36   "You and your king" (Deut. 28:36) echoes the negative or critical assessment of kingship which we have seen to be typical of the Deuteronomic school (17:18-20).

28:42-43   Deuteronomy 28:42 describes a further ironic reversal of covenant blessings: the land from which the Canaanites were driven out in order that Israel might possess it (Heb. *yarash,* "inherit"; see above on 4:1) now sees the apostate Israelites driven out to exile, so that locusts "inherit" it.

The irony continues (28:43)! The sojourners (1:16) who once sought protection in Israel are now in the position of strength. But the pinnacle of irony and of pathos is reached in 28:45-46: "All these curses shall come upon you . . . as a sign and a wonder . . . for ever." In God's intention, "signs and wonders" are to be grace-filled interventions on the covenant people's behalf (e.g., 4:34; 6:22; 7:19; 26:8). But through the people's recalcitrance grace turns (or seems to turn?) to its opposite, and these grace-negating curses become the "sign and wonder" — a perpetual pathos, speaking mutely of what might have been. Yet is there a glimmer of hope even in that, that negative though it has become, the "sign" still stands?

A Warning Sermon (28:47-57)

The aim of the sermon is to contrast two alternatives: the rejected option of serving Yahweh willingly, out of love and gratitude; and the imminent alternative, forced servitude to conquering aliens. Israel's freedom has been based on grace (7:7-8). To reject the grace is to fall back into servitude.

"Joyfulness" has been the keynote of covenant celebration (e.g., 12:7, 12, 18) — rejoicing in the harvest bounty of a fertile land. The joy turns sour when covenant obligations are rejected and the covenant protection therefore withdrawn, so that an inherently weak people are left to pit their puny natural resources against overpowering odds. The danger "foreseen" (Mosaic speech perspective) in 6:12 has materialized: abundance has resulted in pride and arrogant "forgetfulness."

Israel's prophetic tradition has consistently proclaimed that Yahweh is creator and controller both of nature and of history. Yahweh "anoints" kings (1 Kgs. 19:15), "uses" armies (Isa. 10:5), "rebukes" international atrocities (Amos 2:1), guides the destinies of every nation (Amos 9:7), and intends international peace (Isa. 19:23-25). The Deuteronomic school were likewise convinced that Yahweh was "saying something" to Israel through the (imminent or actual) Babylonian invasion. Nations and governments are morally responsible for their political decisions, yet their free decisions become raw material in the overall fabric of Yahweh's purpose. So Babylon, sovereign political agent, is also Yahweh's instrument in Yahweh's dealings with Israel.

The graphic portrayal of the invasion is heavily reminiscent of Isaiah (Isa. 29) and Jeremiah (Jer. 4–6). The description of the famine occasioned by the siege (Deut. 28:53-57) probably draws on 2 Kgs. 6:24-30. The siege itself is a further example of reversal irony. Once the hearts of the Israelites melted, when faced with Canaanite cities "fortified up to heaven" (Deut. 1:28). But God pitied their weak timidity and made them inherit the land which they were unable to take by their own unaided

strength. Now in their God-forgetting pride they occupy fortifications similar to those which once intimidated them (28:52).
But it is to no avail. If they forfeit Yahweh's favor and empowerment, they are defenseless.

Apart from the OT parallels already cited, vv. 53-57 also show
similarities with the "Esarhaddon" sanctions (see above on vv. 22,
26-35): "In your hunger, eat the flesh of your son . . . (In her
hunger), the mother will lock the door against her daughter. . . ."

In some modern cultures, the placenta (v. 57) is regarded as
one's "little twin" or companion-in-birth. It must therefore be
buried with due honor and its burial-place carefully guarded
from violation. To eat the afterbirth would therefore be akin to
cannibalism.

Here we may perhaps push the Deuteronomic school's thought
a little beyond their intention without doing violence to their
basic theology. Thus, behind the cumulative horrors of the siege
portrayal is an understanding of Yahweh as the cohesive force who
keeps humanity human. When the grace-full restraints of covenant
presence and covenant relation are removed, city becomes jungle
and "humanity" preys on "humanity" — even on one's own offspring. This is surely the ultimate "sanction"!

Concluding Warning (28:58-68)

The opening of this section (v. 58) echoes the opening and closing
of the previous two sections (vv. 1-2 and 13-14, vv. 15 and 45).
But there is a difference: there the living "voice" (vv. 1, 15, 45)
is resounding in the words; here it is very much a case of "book-
ness" (vv. 58, 61).

The "voice" is not entirely silent (v. 62), but it is now secondary
to the written word. This stress on writtenness is one of the signs
that the material we are dealing with here belongs to the latest
strata of Deuteronomy (cf. 17:18; 31:24; 26; 29:27; 30:10).

"The words of this torah which are written in this book"
(28:58) is interesting phraseology. Obviously the writer has
forgotten the Mosaic speech framework, according to which the
speech's content is not written down until 31:9, 24-25.

On "this torah" (*hattorah* in the definitive sense), see above on

4:8, 44. The concept of "one written torah" is the product of the interweaving of several older and new strands in Israel's covenant and legal tradition:

(1) Several Deuteronomic texts regard the Decalogue as the original covenant document — and therefore the basic torah (e.g., 10:1-5). Note also that according to 31:24, 26 the "book of the law" is stored *alongside* the ark of the covenant, whereas the Decalogue is *inside* it, in the "core" position.

(2) In the old Elohistic tradition Moses wrote a "book of the covenant" (Exod. 24:4, 7) on Horeb. This book is identified as Exod. 20:22–23:19, of which the Deuteronomic code (Deut. 12–26) is, as we have seen, a later expanded version. Thus the code qualifies also as *hattorah*.

(3) Elements in the Deuteronomic preaching (e.g., Deut. 4:8) imply that "the torah" includes not only the Deuteronomic code (chs. 12–26) but also its parenetic introduction (chs. 4–11). Thus, in practical terms Deuteronomy as a whole is described as *hattorah*.

To "fear" Yahweh's name (28:58) is to fear Yahweh's self, for "name" mirrors character and personality (cf. 5:11). Yahweh's character is revealed in the *torah* (or "signpost") erected to guide the covenant people's behavior. Thus the intention and purpose of the torah is to conform the people's character to that of their God. "Fear" in this context then implies awed awareness of the privilege involved.

Hebrew *pala'*, used in 28:59 to describe Israel's afflictions as "extraordinary," normally means "wonder" and applies to God's saving acts on Israel's behalf. Thus its use here contains a further hint of the "ironic reversal" which pervades this chapter. Saving "wonders" are God's "proper" work; "extraordinary" curses are God's "strange" work (cf. Isa. 28:21).

The suggestion (Deut. 28:60-61) that disease is God's punishment needs to be seen in the double context of (1) the treaty sanctions tradition, with its inherited vocabulary, and (2) the wider OT tradition, with its acknowledgment that the righteous also suffer sickness (Job, Isa. 53, Ps. 22). Undoubtedly there is a connection between obedience and health, but this is quite clearly apparent only from the universal and eschatological perspective. When the first three petitions of the Lord's Prayer have been definitively answered, disease will presumably have ceased — an "end" or eschaton not to be expected as the climax of a historical evolution, but awaited as a crowning gift of grace at the fulfillment of time.

Deuteronomy 28:62 continues the "reversal" pattern (cf. 1:10; 10:22; 26:5). The following verse (28:63) is perhaps the most chilling in the OT: "God will take delight in . . . destroying you"! The comparable reference in Isa. 30:32 is to the punishment of Israel's enemies; but here God is pictured rejoicing at the destruction of the covenant people! The reference stands alone in the OT. The truly representative note is struck rather in Ezek. 18:32: "I have no pleasure in the death of anyone; so turn and live"; and in Jer. 32:41: "I will rejoice in doing them good." What is the ground of God's "rejoicing" in Deut. 28:63? That God's plan for a renewed creation shall succeed, even though Israel may have to be set aside as an unusable instrument!

Deuteronomy 28:65 threatens "no rest for the sole of your foot." The feet which trod and claimed the land (11:24-25) by Yahweh's blessing are now forced into withdrawal and wandering by the cancellation of that blessing.

28:68   Return to Egypt (cf. Hos. 11:5) signifies a return to the situation which Israel experienced before Yahweh called them — as if the covenant has been cancelled, as a total failure. God is then (by implication) pictured as choosing a new instrument to complete the plan which Israel rejected.

The "ships" may refer to the slave-trading vessels of the Phoenicians (cf. Ezek. 27:13; Joel 3:6). Alternatively, scholars have suggested that the text be amended and that "ships" (Heb. *'oniyyot*) be read as "sorrows" (*'aniyyot*). This is an attractive suggestion.

As in Deut. 28:20 (see above) the "I" who speaks is Yahweh.

Finally comes the ultimate degradation. Having suffered the humiliation of not only being offered (15:12) but actually offering themselves for sale as slaves, the people come to the bitter realization that nobody wants them. They are rejected merchandise, thrown into the leftover bin after the sale is over.

The story has turned full circle; the nation whom Yahweh lifted from slavery are by their own choice once more reduced to slavery. No one does it to them — least of all Yahweh. On the contrary, they do it to themselves.

THE THIRD
SPEECH OF MOSES

Deuteronomy 29:1–30:20

Like Deut. (1–4) 5–28, this section is structured both as speech of Moses and as covenant treaty (or covenant renewal liturgy).

As "speech," it is stage III of a marathon discourse. As covenant material, it is presumably intended to describe a ceremony on the plains of Moab, in which the Horeb covenant is renewed at the conclusion of the forty-year wilderness wanderings. (There has been some scholarly debate as to the precise reference of 29:1, numbered 28:69 in the MT. Does the phrase "these . . . words" refer back to chs. 12–28, thus presenting those chapters as the text of the plains of Moab covenant as well as of the Horeb covenant? Or does the phrase point forward, identifying chs. 29–30 as outline of the plains of Moab covenant renewal? Consensus seems to be gathering for this latter conclusion.)

There is a superficial difficulty in regarding Deut. 29–30 as a description of covenant renewal, namely, that the material does not present itself as a clear and complete structure. An attempt to categorize the various units within the two chapters yields the following result:

29:2-8	Narrative of previous relations between Great King and vassal
29:9	Basic principle of the covenant
29:10-15	Formula of covenant ratification
30:15-18	Sanctions: blessing and curse
30:19-20	Summoning of witnesses

It will be noted that the above outline bypasses 29:16–30:14. This block consists of preaching and exhortatory fragments, which pick up specific elements of the covenant making:

29:16-17	A fragment of "previous history"
29:18-21	Curses
29:22-29	Witnesses (albeit somewhat generalized)
30:1-5	Blessings (which will follow the covenant renewal)
30:6	Basic principle of the covenant
30:7-10	Blessings
30:11-14	Exhortation to fulfill covenant obligations

253

The outstanding omission apparent in the above outline is that precisely the specific detailed covenant stipulations are not mentioned. Recognizing that, some scholars have suggested that Deut. 29–30 is a liturgical framework, and that the specific stipulations (presumably identical with chs. 12–26) are to be inserted between 29:9 and 10.

This suggestion would be convincing if Deut. 29–30 did in fact present a clear and complete structure. Since this is not the case, however, it is safest to assume that the two chapters are intended as a literary composition rather than a report of an actual historical occurrence.

Compared with the heavy gloom of ch. 28, there is (relatively speaking!) an atmosphere of light relief in chs. 29–30. The aim of the compiler is to stress that "curse" is not the last word. Though the curse of the covenant sanctions has befallen the people, yet the possibility of restoration remains open for those who repent.

A detailed study shows clear parallels between chs. 29–30 and chs. 1–4. Since chs. 1–3 (4) are presumably the work of the Deuteronomic historian, it is probable that chs. 29–30 are also.

OPENING EXHORTATION
Deuteronomy 29:1-15

INTRODUCTION TO THE
COVENANT RENEWAL IN MOAB (29:1)

In this late strand of the Deuteronomic material, a basis is forming for the concept of canon. The word "covenant" is used here with such stress on its verbal content that "covenant" is the virtual equivalent of "torah" (cf. 1:5).

PREVIOUS HISTORY OF
YAHWEH'S RELATION TO ISRAEL (29:2-8)

The experiences of the ancestors are so re-presented to successive generations in the liturgy that exodus, covenant making, and land occupation become contemporary realities — calculated to stimulate faith and quicken obedience. However, "to this day" (29:4) the desired quickening has not been achieved.

"To this day"? We shall find reasons for concluding that the material of chs. 29–30 comes out of the Exile (see below on 29:22-29; 30:1-10). Does the writer mean that *from* "this day" realization has at last dawned, and healthful changes are now in train? Or does he mean that *at* "this day" obduracy still reigns? Commentators tend to the second, more pessimistic explanation. That "Yahweh has not given you a mind . . . eyes . . . ears" (29:4) sounds at first hearing like divine determinism. Cf., however, the notes on 2:30, "Yahweh hardened Sihon's spirit."

Every effectual giving of a gift involves both a donor and a recipient. No matter how willing the donor may be, the operation fails if the recipient rejects the offer. This is the mystery of "conditionality of the everlasting grace covenant" stated afresh.

Again in 29:5-6 the "I" of Yahweh's direct address breaks through the mediacy of Moses' speech (cf. 28:20, 68). Lack of wheat fields or vineyards did not prevent Israel's eating and drinking to the full (8:15b, 16) — and proving God's kindly provision in the process.

As noted in the introduction to chs. 29–30, there are close parallels between chs. 1–4 and 29–30. This is obvious in 29:7-8, which clearly summarizes 2:26–3:17 (2:32-33; 3:13-14, in particular).

That this parallelism is not fortuitous but a deliberate structuring becomes increasingly apparent as the two chapters unfold:

29:10-15	parallels 4:1-2, 4-5 (obedience is essential)
29:16-21	parallels 4:15-19 (idolatry is disastrous)
29:22-28	parallels 4:6-8 (other nations acknowledge Israel's unique relation)
30:1-10	parallels 4:25-31 (new obedience and restoration)

The overall effect of this massive bracketing is to set the covenant stipulations and their attendant sanctions within the context of grace-responsibility-grace. The responsibilities attached to privilege are awesome, but the last word is grace.

29:9 Obedience brings "prosperity." The Hebrew word translated "prosper" *(sakal)* has an interesting semantic range. From a basic "look," it extends to "pay attention," "understand," "be wise," "succeed," and "prosper." It is common in the Wisdom Literature ("be wise"), but in Deuteronomy occurs only in the latest strata (29:9; 32:29). The "wisdom" nuances surely emerge here in 29:9: to obey Yahweh's torah is the true wisdom, which alone leads to life in its fullness.

FORMULA OF COVENANT RATIFICATION (29:10-15)

It is striking that the phrase "this day" (v. 10) occurs no fewer than five times throughout Deut. 29 (cf. vv. 12, 13, 15, 15, 18). See above on 5:3.

29:10-11 These verses read like a roll call: "heads . . . elders . . . officers . . . men . . . women. . . ." The text may indeed reflect the ordering of the festival assembly for covenant reading and renewal. On "heads," "elders," "officers," cf. 20:9; 21:19; 1:15.

The "little ones" or "toddlers "(29:11), though not yet at the age of understanding, are an integral part of the congregation — as are the sojourners also. The women too are specifically listed as members of the assembly. This is in contrast to the older tradition (Exod. 23:17; Deut. 16:16): "Three times a year shall all your *males* appear."

That every man, woman, and child should attend the centralized festival is obviously a theologically idealized requirement. Its intent is to stress that every citizen without exception is under obligation to heed and obey Yahweh's torah.

The "hewers of wood and drawers of water," that is, assistants in the sacrificial and purificatory rites at the temple, are most probably Gibeonites, and therefore foreigners. Their presence in Israel, let alone as servants of the sanctuary, is in conflict with the *herem* insisted upon at 7:1-5. The tradition of Josh. 9 (the historicity of which is the subject of scholarly discussion) describes how the Gibeonites tricked Joshua into granting them covenant immunity, and how he then "compromised" by making them temple servants. It is these "marginalized" people to whom Deut. 29 grants "sojourner" status within the assembly of Israel.

29:12 The phrase "enter into the sworn covenant" translates literally as "cross over into the covenant and the oath." In general terms, "crossing over" may signify Israel's shift in status — formerly slaves but now covenant people! More specifically, some scholars have connected the term with the ancient covenant-making rite described in Gen. 15:17-18: a flaming torch (representing Yahweh) "crossed over" between the pieces of sacrificial flesh. In this awesome image of Yahweh invoking provisional curse on Yahweh's self, Yahweh's absolute faithfulness in promise is dramatically portrayed. Interpreted in terms of this ancient ritual, then, Deut. 29:10-12 would mean "You stand ready to invoke provisional curse on yourself: 'may I be slaughtered like the sacrificial offering if I do not keep my covenant promises to God.'"

257

The term "oath" (Heb. *alah*) used here does indeed signify a conditional curse, either imposed or self-administered: "Cursed be you/I, if you/I break this agreement." The term has ancient roots, even though its use in the OT is confined to the later books. That the composite expression "covenant and oath" (RSV "sworn covenant") is used three times in ch. 29 whereas it never occurs in chs. 1–28 is probably connected with the virtual absence of specific "curse" material in chs. 29–30. In other words, "covenant and oath" is shorthand for "the covenant content of chs. 12–26, reinforced by the sanctions of ch. 28."

29:13 "You are Yahweh's people, Yahweh is your God" (29:13a) parallels the covenant ratification formula of 26:17-18 (see above). Deuteronomy 29:13b then proceeds to stress the unity of the Horeb and patriarchal covenant(s) (cf. 4:31, 37; 10:15; 13:17). Such direct linking of the two covenants is in fact quite rare in Deuteronomy; almost all Deuteronomic references to the patriarchs concern the promise of land rather than the explicit covenant relationship.

29:14-15 Moses is portrayed here as incorporating yet-unborn generations in the Moab (and Horeb) covenant-making. Through this device the Deuteronomic author wishes to assure the generation(s) living under the cloud of exile that the lapse of seven hundred years has not weakened or vitiated their participation in Yahweh's covenant, or blunted the necessity of their assent to the covenant conditions.

COVENANT RESPONSIBILITIES

Deuteronomy 29:16-28

FRAGMENTS OF HISTORY AND WARNING (29:16-21)

On 29:16-17, cf. 7:25-26. The thoughts are the same; the vocabulary is now typically Deuteronomic. Regarding idols of silver and gold, the "detestable" is no more acceptable through having become aesthetically pleasing. Rather, its allure makes the corruption all the more subtle and sinister.

The corruption just described is blatant and external. In contrast, the "root" (29:18) is hidden, "underground." Cf. the suggestion above, that 27:14-26 focuses on "secret" violations of the covenant. Not only here, of course, but throughout the entire corpus of Deuteronomy it is stressed that Yahweh is concerned, not with bare outward conformity, but with obedience from the whole heart, mind, and will.

Several interpretations are offered for the proverbial saying in 29:19b, "the sweeping away of moist and dry alike":

(1) The "secret offender" of v. 19a may still be speaking: "When the floods cover the whole land, soil that was formerly moist will be indistinguishable from soil that was formerly dry. Even so, my deeds will be undetected."

(2) The sentence may be a reply to the secret offender: "This attitude of yours will cancel out all your good deeds, just as a drought 'cancels out' all the watering which the garden has received."

(3) "Moist" and "dry" may refer to watered and unwatered plants. Just as a blight wipes out both, so the "secret offense" will wipe out both the innocent and guilty mem-

259

bers of Israel. No sin is purely private: it inevitably involves the community.

The third possibility suits the context best, and therefore seems preferable.

Verse 20 is vividly anthropomorphic: Yahweh's nostrils smoking with anger (Ps. 18:8), Yahweh's face flushed with jealousy (Deut. 4:24). Ominously, the anger originally directed against the covenant community's oppressors is now levelled at the offender within the community itself. The sharpness of the anger is proportionate to the vastness of the grace rejected.

For the horror of having one's "name blotted out," see above on 25:6. In this, too, a fate originally intended for Israel's opponents (7:24) is ironically applied to the covenant people themselves (cf. 9:14).

IINDIRECT WITNESSES
TO THE COVENANT (29:22-29)

This section is a fragment of exhortatory preaching on the theme of the covenant curses. It is likely that the passage reflects firsthand experience of exilic conditions.

29:22-23 The mention of "afflictions and sicknesses" (29:22) recalls 28:59, 61, the difference being that there it is the people who suffered sickness, whereas here it is the land. The author's intention in this is to stress that rebellion against God destroys not only personal well-being and social structure, but the whole order and harmony of creation (11:17; cf. Gen. 3:17-19). By way of concrete example, one thinks of modern humanity's tendency to blatant materialistic self-sufficiency — a form of rebellion — and its disastrous repercussions in matters of ecology.

The reference to "Sodom and Gomorrah" (Deut. 29:23) recalls Gen. 19:24-28. The companion cities, Admah and Zeboiim, are mentioned earlier (Gen. 10:19; 14:2, 8). As these notorious cities were blighted for the behavior of their inhabitants, so was the land of Israel. The mention of Admah and Zeboiim alone in Hos. 11:8 (a northern source) has led to the conjecture that Sodom and Gomorrah originally featured specifically in the southern (J) source, and Admah and Zeboiim in the northern (E) source.

"Sowing with salt" (Judg. 9:45), as a symbolic "cursing with infertility," is attested in the ancient Near East as an action taken against cities who broke their covenant with the Great King. This may be implied in Deut. 29:23: the land is sown with "brimstone and salt" for the people's rejection of Yahweh.

29:24-28 There is a striking parallel between vv. 24-28 and the account of Ashurbanipal's (seventh-century) conquest of Arabia (*ANET,* 300): "Whenever the inhabitants of Arabia asked each other: 'On account of what have these calamities befallen Arabia?' (they answered themselves) 'Because we did not keep the solemn oaths (sworn to) Ashur, because we offended the friendliness of Ashurbanipal. . . .'" The closeness of the parallel indicates that both are drawing on a recognized formula for stating the consequences of covenant-breaking. Cf. also 1 Kgs. 9:8; Jer. 16:10-11; 22:8.

The unusual phrase "forsake the covenant" (Deut. 29:25) really implies "forsake the covenant Giver." "Transgression" is seen in personal, not legal terms.

"Gods whom they had not known" (v. 26) could also be translated "gods who had not known them." Deuteronomic usage in general supports the first (RSV) alternative, but the second is worth pondering. (In either case there is comparison and contrast between "gods" and Yahweh.) It is fundamental to the grace-covenant concept that our knowing God depends on God's prior knowing us.

Regarding Yahweh's "allotting" gods apart from Yahweh's self to certain nations, see above on 4:19.

"As at this day" (29:28) implies that the exile is current reality. Has the author overlooked that the speakers in this paragraph are "your descendants" and "foreigners" (v. 22)? Do the descendants view the devastated land in imagination from their place in exile? Also, do the foreigners quote "this book" (v. 27) to explain the devastation? We have noted frequent indications that on occasion both the "covenant treaty" and the "speech" structure sit lightly on the material.

29:29   Verse 29 fits loosely in its context. Its "timeless-wisdom" quality distinguishes it from the typical "at-the-moment" Deuteronomic exhortation. Its use of the first person plural attracted the attention of the Masoretes, who accentuated the phrase "to us and to our children" with dots over each letter. Their reason for doing so was perhaps to stress the direct contemporaneity of the covenant for every generation.

It is a feature of both chs. 1–4 (5) and chs. 29–30 (which we saw are closely related) that Moses frequently speaks in the first person plural. As 5:3 brings that tendency to a climax in chs. 1–4 (5), so 29:29 brings it to a climax here in chs. 29–30: "To us and to our children! — Not with our ancestors, but with us! . . . all of us! . . . here! . . . alive! . . . today!"

There is an evident affinity between 29:29 and 30:11-14. Some scholars indeed would see the two as halves of an original whole, severed in order to frame 30:1-10 (with its hope of restoration). The intention of such a framing would be to ground the hope of restoration in the constantly-renewed contemporaneity of the covenant — that is, in the faithfulness of God. Whether or not that is so in detail, the affinity makes 30:11-14 a useful clue to the interpretation of 29:29. The emphasis of 30:11-14 is that Yahweh's torah is not some obscure secret knowledge but guidance open and accessible, easily understood and practiced. Implicit is the conviction that the people's future — peace and prosperity, or disaster — does not depend on mysterious secret factors but entirely on their posture of obedience toward the torah which Yahweh has provided. This is the clue to the interpretation of v. 29: God alone knows what developments will take place in international politics and so forth. But Israel's future is not determined by these developments. Yahweh is capable of controlling all such factors. Yahweh undertakes to order the unknown, provided the covenant people are faithful to their sole responsibility — which is to follow Yahweh's will as presented in the torah.

CONCLUDING EXHORTATION

Deuteronomy 30:1-20

REPENTANCE AND RESTORATION (30:1-10)

As noted above (on 29:7-8), 30:1-10 parallels 4:25-31. In contrast to ch. 28 with its repeated insistence that Israel has come to the end of the road (28:20, 22, 24, 25, 45, 51, 61, 63), these two passages share the hope that Yahweh will again restore the exiled people, providing they turn back to Yahweh. Both passages give the strong impression of being addressed directly to the conditions of the Exile.

As noted in the introduction to chs. 29–30, these two chapters are presented as the transcript of a covenant renewal ceremony in the plains of Moab. Nevertheless, the material is not complete in itself. As already noted, the specific covenant stipulations have to be supplied from chs. 12–26. Similarly with the "curse" material, the allusions in chs. 29–30 require filling out from chs. 27–28.

In the same way, the blessings mentioned in 30:1-10 are not self-contained, but dependent on earlier chapters. Just as the curses of ch. 28 consist in part of a reversal of covenant blessings (removal from the promised land, 28:25, 36, 64), the blessings of 30:3-5 in their turn constitute a reversal of those reversals. Verse 6 goes on to promise by way of blessing that the requirements of 10:12-16 will be actualized. Finally, 30:9 is a provisional, preached form of blessing, dependent on 28:11.

The precondition of restoration is genuine repentance. Strikingly, the phrase "with all your heart and with all your soul" occurs three times within these verses (30:2, 6, 10). Yet there is also compassionate acknowledgment that genuine repentance is beyond the unaided capacity of the people, hence the promise of

divine enablement. Whereas 10:16 commands Israel to "circum-
cize the foreskin of your heart," 30:6 promises that God's self will
do this for them — making possible the love that is required of
them (cf. 5:6, where demand is preceded by a reminder of the
liberating grace already lavished). The reference is to "your hearts
and the hearts of your offspring"; according to the speech-of-
Moses format, those directly addressed are thirteenth-century
Israel. From the perspective of the Deuteronomic compiler of ch.
30, the "offspring" ("seed") of that thirteenth-century generation
are his own contemporaries, experiencing with the compiler the
bitterness of exile. To them he declares, "The ancient promise
stands. We are the 'seed' of the ancestors. God will enable us too
to repent."

The promise (v. 9) that "Yahweh will again take delight" in
Israel balances and cancels the dreadful statement at 28:63.

The passage concludes with a reiteration of the solemn reminder
that grace is not automatic. Its purpose is to evoke loving obedience. Where the response is not forthcoming, grace is frustrated.

THE ACCESSIBLE TORAH (30:11-14)

We noted above the obvious connection between 29:29 (see
above) and 30:11-14. Like 29:29, 30:11-14 is clearly influenced
by the wisdom tradition.

An ancient Near Eastern parallel occurs in the Akkadian (late
2nd millennium) "Pessimistic Dialogue" (*ANET,* 438): "Who is
tall enough to ascend to heaven? Who is broad enough to embrace
the earth?" The meaning of this proverb is that awareness of our
human finitude should encourage us to accept our fate with
humility and resignation.

If this saying is parallel with Deut. 30:11-14, the contrast is
striking. Pessimism based on the blindness of fate and awareness
of human incapacity is countered by the optimism of Israel's faith.
The still-dark future is in Yahweh's caring hands. Moreover, the
covenant people *have* the capacity to achieve what is required of
them, for they possess a completely sufficient map for the way,
namely, the God-given torah.

The needed torah is "not in heaven" (v. 12). According to

1 Kgs. 22:19-20, Yahweh's *torah* ("guidance") does indeed originate in heaven (see above on Deut. 13:1-5, 134). But through God's intimates, the prophets, it has been brought from there and mediated to the people. Moses, the first and greatest of the prophets, has entered the very presence of God, received the torah, and made it henceforth continuously accessible (see 5:24-31). Its sufficiency means that Yahweh's people will never be at a fatal loss.

The "word is very near" (30:14); having achieved written form, it is read and expounded at every festival. The "nearness" of the torah is in fact a mode of Yahweh's nearness (see above on 4:7-8).

"It is in your mouth" — first at the liturgical reading in the context of centralized festival, and again at home, in the process of catechizing the family. It is also "in the heart" — here in the sense of a dynamic remembering, which shapes and motivates current behavior.

"You can do it." The torah does not contain some esoteric or eschatological ethic incapable of being practiced. It is within the capacity of ordinary people here and now.

In citing Deut. 30:11-14, Paul (Rom. 10:4-10) applies to Christ what is said here about the torah. Thus for Paul, Christ is the quintessence of the mind and intention of God which came to expression (according to the Deuteronomist, completely sufficient expression) in the torah. Paul, we may imagine, would contend that even the most perfect scripting of the words most clearly and sensitively overheard in the "divine council" are approximations to the "Omega point." In Christ the "Omega point" (to borrow Teilhard de Chardin's well-known term) itself appears, tantalizingly beckoning to ever new unfoldings of insight and intention.

SANCTIONS: BLESSINGS AND CURSE (30:15-18)

As with Deut. 30:1-10, the material here is not self-contained, but refers back to chs. 27–28.

As frequently throughout Deuteronomy, "life" (30:15), the ultimate blessing, is linked to obedience (v. 16). To obey the torah is to obey Yahweh, whose word it is. "Life" is normally equated with "length of days" (v. 18), hence the primary reference is to natural life in the physical world. But because it is life in the presence of Yahweh, the physical is shot through with a spiritual dimension.

In the same way, "death" refers primarily to physical decease. In the Deuteronomic code, death is the "shortening of days" in punishment for violation of covenant stipulations. But because the covenant is Yahweh's, the violations are seen as rebellion against Yahweh. In that context death too takes on a spiritual dimension — untimely death, marked by rupture of relationship with Yahweh. This is the ultimate curse.

The temptation to turn to "other gods" (v. 17) during exile is to be seen in the light of ancient belief (only ancient belief?) that the defeat of a people by superior forces meant that the god of the conquered had been defeated by the god of the conquerors. With Yahweh's temple in ruins, the might of Marduk must have appeared formidable.

SUMMONING OF WITNESSES (30:19-20)

On the significance of calling the created world as witness, cf. 4:26.

Deuteronomy 30:19-20 is reminiscent of 11:26-28. As the general parenesis (chs. 5–11) is closed with a statement of blessing and curse (11:26-28), so too the code proper (ch. 28) and now the Moab covenant presentation also (30:19-20). Indeed, this final blessing-curse formula rounds off chs. 1–30 as a whole.

The people are urged to "choose life" (30:19). Elsewhere in Deuteronomy, with one exception the verb "choose" always has Yahweh as its subject: It is Yahweh who chooses the ancestors, Israel, their descendants, and the place of worship. The covenant is grounded in Yahweh's initiative. Here the stress is on the necessity for human response. "Life" is virtually a title for Yahweh: to choose life is to choose obedience to the torah and to the prophetic voice which continuously contemporizes torah — that is, to choose Yahweh, whose mind and intention are expressed through both torah and prophets.

ADDENDA

Deuteronomy 31:1–34:12

SUCCESSOR TO MOSES

TIME OF TRANSITION (31:1-30)

Deuteronomy 31 consists of three interwoven strands:

(1) The first part (vv. 1, 9-13, 24-29) describes Moses' writing of the torah, and the handing over of the completed text to be stored alongside the ark of the covenant and read at intervals of seven years on the occasion of the Feast of Booths.
(2) The second part (vv. 2-8, 14-15, 23) concerns the appointment and commissioning of Joshua as Moses' successor.
(3) The third part (vv. 16-22, 30) is an introduction to the Song of Moses (32:1-43).

The composition and interrelation of the three strands in ch. 31 is not completely straightforward. We shall see below that the first and second strands are composite. There is also a similarity of mood between the first and third strands — though their themes are different. There is indeed a disconcerting switching of themes throughout the chapter: Torah (vv. 9-15); Song of Moses (vv. 16-22); Torah (vv. 23-29); Song of Moses (v. 30).

Some scholars have put these two factors together (the similarity of mood and switching of themes), added a third (i.e., that in Hebrew script *torah* and *shirah*, "song," are similar), and concluded that originally vv. (9-15,) 16-30 addressed one theme only. Most of these scholars suggest that wherever the word *torah* appears in vv. (9-15,) 24-29 it substitutes for an original *shirah*. Some take the opposite view, however, that where *shirah* occurs in vv. 16-22 the original reading was *torah*.

However that may be, the final redactor obviously had clear reasons for casting the material in its canonical form. There seem to be two basic motives:

(1) He wishes to stress that Moses was not an isolated phenomenon in the history of Israel's faith, but that his work continued through a legitimate succession — specifically and in the first instance through Joshua. (In this, ch. 31 picks up 3:28.) To enhance the authority of Joshua, his appointment (31:7-8) and commissioning (vv. 14-15, 23) are recounted in close association with the authoritative torah originally entrusted to Moses (vv. 9-13, 24-29). Further, the introduction to the Song (vv. 16-22) is inserted within the account of Joshua's commissioning (vv. 14-15, 23), thus creating the impression that it was the commissioning which inspired the Song. In this way the whole of 31:2-29 becomes an exposition concerning the appointment of Moses' successor.

(2) The redactor's second motive is to introduce the Song of Moses, both as a summary of salvation history and as a warning against apostasy. It may be said that the witness of Moses the prophet (ch. 32) is made to parallel the witness of Moses the lawgiver (chs. 5–30). Indirectly, it may also be said, the Song functions to facilitate Joshua's leadership task, by reminding the covenant people of their tendency to rebel and their obligation to obey. If that is so, then the whole of 31:1–32:52 may be said to constitute a bridge between the book of Deuteronomy ([1–3] 4–30) and the book of Joshua (i.e., volume 2 of the Deuteronomic history).

Joshua, Moses' Successor (31:1-8)

31:1 The text of Deut. 31:1 is disputed:

• Moses continued to speak . . . (RSV; cf. JB)
• Moses went and spoke . . . (NJV)
• Moses finished speaking (NEB)

270

The NEB follows the reading of the Qumran text and of the LXX. The implication is that 31:1 is the conclusion of ch. 30.

Both the RSV and JB are based on the MT. Hebrew *halak* normally means "go," but can indeed mean "continue" (cf. Gen. 32:1; 15:2). Context must decide which is the more appropriate meaning.

In favor of "continue" is the fact that Moses' speech does indeed continue in the following song (Deut. 32) and blessing (ch. 33).

"Go," however, is a strong contender, if 31:1 is regarded as linking back with 5:30–6:1. The Exodus parallel makes the connection clear. According to the Exodus account the people hear the theophanic voice delivering the Decalogue, and immediately request that henceforth the word be mediated to them by Moses (Exod. 20:18-21). Accordingly, Moses alone received the Book of the Covenant (Exod. 20:22–23:19), complete with its sanctions (23:20-33). After having received this material, Moses then "leaves" the presence of God and "comes" (Exod. 24:3) to detail the covenant document to the people.

Correspondingly in the Deuteronomic version, Moses is appointed covenant mediator (Deut. 5:24–6:1), receives the code as covenant document (chs. 12–26) together with its accompanying sanctions (chs. 27–28), then "goes" (31:1) to convey the content of the covenant to the people.

31:2 Moses' age is 120 years (v. 2; cf. 34:7). In the historical framework of the Deuteronomistic history, "forty years" stands for a complete generation (e.g., Judg. 3:11; 5:31b), or for the time in office of a great leader — Eli, David, Solomon, Joash, and Moses himself (e.g., Deut. 2:7).

That Moses' life span is precisely three times forty years may be symbolic of his preeminence (cf. his threefold speech; see Introduction, 9-10).

To "go out and come in" may be intended in the general sense (cf. 28:6), but more likely refers to military leadership (1 Sam. 18:13-16).

31:3 Yahweh's "going before" (cf. Deut. 9:3), symbolized perhaps by the carrying of the covenant box (cf. 10:1ff.?), is the theological reality behind Joshua's leadership. Indeed, every leader that emerges among the covenant people is to be an expression of Yahweh's leadership.

31:5-8 Deuteronomy 31:5 repeats 7:2 and recalls the command to apply the *herem* (see above on 2:34).

The language of 31:6-8 is typically Deuteronomic (cf. especially Josh. 1). Deuteronomy 31:7-8 reechoes the thought of v. 3, that human leadership (ideally) is a mode of divine leadership.

Similarly, divine encouragement (v. 23) comes to expression through human encouragement (v. 7); the identical words are spoken alternately by Moses and Yahweh.

Verse 8 repeats and reinforces v. 6: "Do not fear (on this concrete occasion)" (Heb. *al-tire'u*, v. 6) becomes "put away fear forever" (*lo' tira'*, v. 8). Each concrete exercise of courage strengthens the settled capacity for courage.

Provision for the Periodic Public Reading of the Torah (31:9-13)

Strictly speaking it is only here at last (v. 9) that words become book. Previous references to "the book" (28:58, 61; 29:20, 21, 27; 30:10) are indications that the compiler at those points has forgotten the speech-of-Moses format in which the material is being presented.

In our discussion on 10:1-5, we noted that the Deuteronomic school deliberately "demythologized" the covenant box or ark (Heb. *aron*) by insisting that its sole function was as receptacle for the summary of torah on the stone tables. Hence in their terminology the ark became "ark of the covenant" *(aron habberit)*. It will be seen that "covenant" here has become synonymous with torah — an indication that the material is from the latest strands of Deuteronomy.

That the "elders" are present at 31:9, yet have to be summoned at v. 28, indicates unevenness in the material. Their mention alongside the priests is to stress the complementarity of civic and liturgical leaders. Having been celebrated at the festival (under priestly leadership), the torah is carried home to be taught and applied (under local leadership).

31:10-11 The ancient Near Eastern treaty texts prescribed that the treaty be read periodically to the vassal's subjects. It is entirely credible that the torah text did indeed have an important role in the Israelite festivals. Only here in v. 10 are the details stated, that the reading is at seven-year intervals, and that it takes place at the Feast of Booths. Much remains obscure. Was the Decalogue, as a summary of the torah, read annually at the six intervening festivals? Or was it used every year as a convenient teaching instrument?

Who is the individual (v. 11, "you [singular] shall read") charged with the public recital of torah — the king, the high priest, or some other covenant mediator?

31:12-13 "Hear, learn to fear Yahweh, put into practice." The heart of obedience to the torah is the "fear of Yahweh." Torah is perceived not as moral or religious regulation, but as expression of Yahweh's mind. To honor the words is to relate to Yahweh's self, whose words they are.

Moses and Joshua before Yahweh (31:14-15)

Unlike the remainder of this strand (vv. 1-8, 23), vv. 14-15 are not couched in Deuteronomic language, but rather reflect the old Elohistic style. The affinity with Exod. 31:7-11; Num. 11:24-29; 12:1-8 (all from E) is obvious. In contrast to the Priestly tradition, which places the tabernacle in the midst of Israelite encampment, the tent of meeting in the Elohistic tradition is outside the camp. Nor does Yahweh dwell in the tent of meeting (cf. Yahweh's constant presence in and through the ark), but descends to enter relationship with whoever comes out to meet Yahweh there.

It is clear from Exod. 31:7-11 and from Deut. 31:14-15 that those seeking Yahweh stand inside the tent, while the theophany takes place outside, at the tent opening. This has given rise to the conjecture that the tent functions like the "cleft of the rock" (Exod. 33:21-23) where Moses took shelter from the overpowering glory of Yahweh. The cloud (Deut. 31:15) likewise veils God's glory, lest worshippers be overwhelmed.

The pillar of cloud is an extension of the Horeb theophany. As

Yahweh appeared on Horeb enveloped in cloud at that first definitive encounter, so the pillar of cloud accompanying Israel on their
ongoing journey symbolizes the fact that Yahweh does not remain
static and aloof on the sacred mountain, but is continuously
present with the covenant people. Yahweh's presence is always
accompanied by the symbolic veiling, out of compassion for the
people's creaturely frailty.

Introduction to the Song of Moses (31:16-22)

As noted above, the insertion of Deut. 31:16-22 in its present
context implies that the Song (ch. 32) was revealed to Moses in
the theophany at the tent of meeting.

The origin and age of the Song will be discussed in ch. 32. It
is clear, however, that it was inserted into Deuteronomy at a late
stage — probably *the* latest stage — in the redaction process. This
means that the introduction to the Song in 31:16-22 is a late
insertion into this chapter. It is striking that the editor who made
the insertion used *torah* language to introduce the Song. Like the
torah, the *shirah* ("song") must be:

- "written" (31:19, 22; cf., e.g., 27:3, 8; 28:58, 61)
- "taught" (31:19, 22; cf., e.g., 4:1, 5, 10, 14; 5:31)
- "placed in the mouth" (31:19, 21; cf. 30:14; Josh. 1:8)
- "established as a witness" (31:19, 21; cf. v. 26)

On the significance of this paralleling, see the introduction to ch.
31, 270.

The tranquil description (v. 16) of death as "sleeping with one's
forebears" or "being gathered to one's people" (32:50) is typical
of the early OT (cf. Gen. 15:15; 35:29; Judg. 8:32). In this mode
death is regarded not as a tragedy but as a fitting conclusion.
Possible survival beyond death is not an issue. Several passages
indeed imply that dying is the end of personal existence (2 Sam.
14:14; Job 7:21; Ps. 39:13). More generally, however, an at-
tenuated version of the self is thought to persist in Sheol (Ps.
49:14; Isa. 14:9ff.; 38:10ff.; Ezek. 32:21ff.). The view of death
as "appropriate conclusion" depended on three conditions: that

(1) the deceased had reached mature years, (2) was leaving descendants to perpetuate his or her name, and (3) was accorded a fitting burial.

Strikingly, in Moses' case only the first of these conditions is cited. In years, indeed he reached the divinely appointed limit (Gen. 6:3; cf. Deut. 34:7). But his descendants (Exod. 2:22) play no role in the Deuteronomic tradition, and his "grave" is unknown (Deut. 34:6). These very "deficiencies," however, become marks of Moses' preeminence:

- It is the torah, not children, that perpetuates his name.
- His unknown grave testifies to his intimacy with Yahweh: buried by divine hand, not by human.

There is, however, a more sombre aspect to the OT understanding of death. The linking of death and disobedience (Gen. 2:17; cf. Deut. 30:19-20) implies that death is an undesirable. Also, the rejection of the cult of the dead (14:1-2) suggests that a spiritual force is active there which is inimical to the Creator's intention. Yet the world of the dead is within Yahweh's control (Amos 9:2; Ps. 139:8; Prov. 15:11). From that understanding springs the conviction that death does not dissolve but rather enhances the relationship between God and God's covenanted ones (Isa. 25:8; 26:19; Dan. 12:2).

"Playing the harlot" (Deut. 31:16) implies unbridled sexual license and is a reference to Israel's indulgence in the fertility religion with its practice of cultic prostitution. Had the "covenant" been specifically pictured here in terms of marriage bond, the specific term for "adultery" would no doubt have been used.

There is an ironic "tit for tat" in vv. 16-18: "they will forsake me" (v. 16) and "I will forsake them" (v. 17); "I will hide my face" (vv. 17, 18) because they have "turned (their face) to other gods" (v. 18).

To "hide the face" means to disclaim all concern or responsibility for the fate of the other (cf. Isa. 53:3). Throughout the OT the "face of God" is the source of human well-being. As the sunlight makes the earth beautiful and productive, so the "light of God's face" enables and enhances human life (Num. 6:26; Ps.

4:6; 44:3, 15c). Conversely, the hiding of God's face because of human sin means that help ceases and human life withers (Ps. 13:1; 104:29; Isa. 54:8; Ezek. 39:23ff.). This is total deprivation. As the face reveals the personality, so the face of God represents the being of God. The withdrawal of the Creator's self, if permanent, would mean dissolution into nothingness. God's withdrawal even for a moment is a horrendous prospect. Mercifully in the Song, the threat of "hiding the face" (Deut. 32:20) is transmuted into vindication and compassion for the powerless (v. 36).

To describe the evils and troubles of exile (31:17) as "coming upon" or "finding" Israel, is virtually to personify the evil. Implicit in this is the understanding that such troubles are the result of a curse which, once uttered, assumes an independent — almost "personal" — existence. Another aspect of the same thought complex is that there is no such thing as a spiritual vacuum; at the withdrawal of Yahweh, malign "forces" will occupy the space (cf. Luke 11:24-26). Still, the compiler undoubtedly shares the basic Deuteronomic conviction — that all "forces" are ultimately in Yahweh's control.

The command to "write" (Deut. 31:19) is grammatically plural, suggesting that Joshua is involved with Moses in the process (cf. 32:44). On the temptation to "forget" (RSV "despise"), see 6:3, 10-15: to "break the covenant" is not mere legal transgression, but personal affront to the Covenant-Giver (31:20).

Hebrew *yetser*, translated "purpose" (v. 21), is elsewhere rendered "imagination" (Gen. 8:21), "mind" (Isa. 26:3), "frame" (Ps. 103:14). Overall it may be taken to describe that faculty of human existence which is the source of intentions. The concept underwent development in the intertestamental period, and in later rabbinic Judaism was used in attempts to explain the origin of human sinfulness. According to Deut. 31:21 Israel's *yetser* has tended to rebellion throughout their history as a covenant people.

Appointment of Joshua (31:23)

As already noted, v. 23 links back to vv. 2-8, 14-15. The promise earlier made by Moses (vv. 7-8) is here reiterated by Yahweh's self. There is a slight difference of emphasis: "you shall go with this people into the land" (v. 7) stresses Joshua's membership in the covenant people, whereas "you shall bring the children of Israel . . ." (v. 23) accents his leadership of them. As in 17:15, the good leader arises from the ranks of the led and retains his or her awareness of continuing to belong to their company.

Storage of Torah Text (31:24-29)

This section links back to 31:9-13, and probably linked forward originally to 32:45 (a connection now broken by the insertion of the Song (32:1-43).

According to ancient Near Eastern custom, the original copy of the vassal treaty was stored in the central shrine of the kingdom, indicating that the god of the shrine was guardian of the treaty. Possibly the covenant box (31:26) is here regarded as the inner sanctum of Yahweh's temple, so that placing the torah text before the ark stresses Yahweh's guardianship of the covenant. Further, the ark of the covenant contains the Decalogue. The placing of the Decalogue and code side by side may therefore be intended to affirm the basic identity of the two. The Decalogue summarizes the code; the code expounds the Decalogue. Equally with the Decalogue, the code is the authentic Horeb covenant document: to obey its stipulations is to obey Yahweh.

The idea of the torah as "witness" probably developed from 31:19, where the Song is witness. So long as torah was an echo of Yahweh's voice it was integral to the covenant relation. Now in its written form it stands as it were alongside the covenant partners as a distinct entity. This emphasis belongs to the latest strand of Deuteronomic theology and helps lay the foundation for later Jewish (and Christian) biblicism.

By contrast, v. 28 once again describes the covenant-making in terms of living voice, and cites creation (see above on 4:26) as witness.

On "evil that befalls (literally, 'meets')" (31:29), cf. v. 17. Implicit is the understanding that such "evil" is no unavoidable fate but is the direct result of Israel's opting for disobedience: "evil meets you because you *do* what is evil."

THE SONG OF MOSES
Deuteronomy 32:1-52

COVENANT LAWSUIT (32:1-47)

The origins and age of the Song are problematic. The finished text presents itself as a mixed literary form. But there are indications that either its original author or its final redactor intended it as a *rib*, or accusation of covenant violation, formally levelled by Yahweh against the covenant partner Israel.

Various scholars have suspected that the finished text of the Song includes several interpolations. Opinions differ as to the precise identification of these additions. This much seems fairly clear: that an original, which levelled the accusation against Israel alone, has been modified to include a denunciation of Israel's enemies as well. This has been achieved by the insertion of 32:26-27, 30-31, 36. As a result of these additions, reproaches which once applied to Israel now more naturally refer to the enemy (see the detailed exposition). The effect is to portray Yahweh not as Accuser alone, but as Accuser and Defender of the covenant people.

The *rib* form is exemplified in such prophetic texts as Isa. 1:10-20; Mic. 6:1-8; Jer. 2:4-13 (cf. also Ps. 50). Its characteristic shape is:

I. The court scene is set (The Great King is normally represented by an intermediary.)

II. The case for the Plaintiff:

    A. Witnesses are summoned ("heaven and earth")

    B. The accused is arraigned

    C. The charge is stated:

        1. It is usually in question form

   2. Excuses are disallowed
   3. Details are spelled out
 D. The verdict is pronounced

Deuteronomy 32 (vv. 1-19 in particular) follows this general scheme:

 I. (absent)
II.

   A. v. 1
   B. (absent)
   C.
      1. vv. 4-6
      2. vv. 7-14
      3. vv. 15-18
   D. vv. 19-29

Due to the modifying interpolations mentioned above, vv. 30-42 in the finished text now give reasons why Yahweh did not in fact carry out the well-deserved sentence.

The *rib* form probably stems from two ancient roots. First, it is reminiscent of the ancient Near Eastern practice whereby vassal treaty-breakers were arraigned before their Great King. It can be presumed that the prophets cast their preaching in this *rib* form, precisely at the annual festival where the renewal of Yahweh's covenant with Israel was celebrated.

Secondly, the *rib* form draws upon "divine council" imagery (see above on 13:1-5, 134). The prophets who claimed that their message originated in the divine council would assert that in their *rib* presentation they were simply repeating the charges against Israel which Yahweh had already laid "in council."

The distinctive feature of Deut. 32 is that, whereas the *rib* is traditionally sheer accusation (cf. vv. 1-25), here it is supplemented with the proclamation of forgiveness, restoration, and renewal (vv. 26-43).

In attempting to date the Song concretely, several factors come into consideration.

(1) The Song describes Israel's defeat at the hands of an enemy (vv. 19ff.). If the defeat was not a total "scattering" (vv. 26-27), then the reference may not be to the Exile but to some lesser disaster. Defeat by the Philistines (end of 11th cent.) is one possibility.

(2) There are archaic traits in the language of Deut. 32. But it needs to be asked whether these are endemic to the material or a trick of style used precisely to create a "Mosaic" atmosphere.

(3) There are also many similarities with the language of the prophets:

v. 1	Deut. 3:26; 4:39; 10:14; 11:21; Isa. 1:2-3; Mic. 6:1-2; Jer. 2:12-13
v. 3b	Josh. 7:19; Jer. 13:16
vv. 4, 15	Isa. 17:10; 26:4
vv. 6, 28	Hos. 4:11; Jer. 4:22; 5:21; 25:16
v. 10	Hos. 9:10; 11:1, 3; 13:5-6
v. 11	Exod. 19:4
vv. 13-14	Deut. 33:5; Isa. 44:2; Hos. 13:6
v. 20b	Hos. 2:4-5; Isa. 1:21
vv. 28-29	Jer. 5:21
v. 32	Isa. 1:10; 3:9; Jer. 23:16; Ezek. 16:46, 49, 53, 55
v. 34	Hos. 13:12
v. 41	Ezek. 21:3, 9-10; Jer. 25:16
v. 41b	Jer. 11:20

This factor also requires interpretation, however: was Deut. 32 directly influenced by the prophets, or did it and they draw on a common linguistic source?

These and similar considerations entitle us to date the Song somewhere between 900 and 600 B.C. Closer precision is not possible.

Opening of Moses' Song (32:1-6)

The calling of heaven and earth as witnesses (v. 1) belongs both to covenant ratification (30:19) and covenant *rib* (see above). At the same time the call to "give ear" is at home in the wisdom tradition (cf. 32:2-3, which also uses typical wisdom terminology). The description of "the Word" as coming like "gentle rain on pasture" recalls Ps. 72:6, where Yahweh's anointed, and Hos. 6:3, where Yahweh's self are described in the same terms. There is no sharp distinction between the word and the self: Yahweh's word is a mode of Yahweh's presence.

As frequently noted, "name" (Deut. 32:3) represents character or personality. To name Yahweh is not simply to pronounce the "sacred letters" but to focus on Yahweh's character (v. 4), on the generous favors which flow from that character (vv. 7-14), and on the obligation to grateful obedience which the disclosure of that character entails (vv. 5-6).

"Rock" (or "mountain"; v. 4) is used as a title for God throughout the Song (cf. vv. 15, 18, 30, 31, 37), as also in the Psalms. The usage has ancient roots in animistic thought, where mountains are the dwelling places of the divine, if not themselves redolent with divine power. The Assyrian deity Bel bore the title "Great Mountain," and Baal was known in Ugarit as "Mountain." Applied to Yahweh, the ancient title speaks of strength and constancy experienced amid the vicissitudes of history.

"Iniquity" (v. 4) is "crookedness" or "duplicity." A human example of "crooked" behavior is 25:13-16. There is nothing corresponding to this in Yahweh's dealing with humankind.

Some scholars have suspected that 32:5-6 is not an original part of its present context. Arguably, v. 5 breaks the logical flow of vv. 4, 7, and v. 6 switches from the grammatical third to the second person (not in itself a compelling proof of interpolation, certainly). If there is an addition, its purpose has been to strengthen the *rib* presentation.

As a "blemish" (v. 5) renders an animal unfit to be offered to God in sacrifice (15:21; 17:1), so Israel's behavioral blemishes make them unfit to be God's children.

Hebrew *gamal*, "requite" (32:6), is cognate to the Arabic *'amal*, used in Islam to indicate "good works" done out of gratitude and love for God. Here it is God who performs the "good work" of creating and caring; and the *'amal* offered in return is "corruption, perversity, and crookedness."

Only rarely is God called "father" in the OT (cf. Ps. 103:13;

Prov. 3:12, "like a father." Cf. Num. 11:12, "like a mother" (implicitly).

The word for "create" in this context is not Heb. *bara'* as in Gen. 1:1, but *qanah* — basically "get," and hence variously translated "give birth to" (Gen. 4:1), "buy" (Gen. 33:19), "purchase" (Exod. 15:16). All these shades of meaning color the picture of the Israel-God relationship presented here. The concept of the deity as "father" is ancient and has its reflections in paganism (cf. Jer. 2:27). In Israel, however, it is refined by the whole unfolding insight into God's character gained through experience of God's deeds, and knowledge of God's will (torah). The father's pain in face of the children's waywardness (Hos. 11:1-2; Isa. 1:2-3; Jer. 3:19-20) is central to the OT portrayal of God.

God's Saving Activity (32:7-14)

32:8 Deuteronomy 32:8 may reflect the old mythology of the divine council assembled at New Year under the tutelage of Elyon ("Most High") to determine the destiny of the nations for the ensuing period (see above on 13:1-5; cf. Ps. 82). In the demythologizing process, Elyon has become a title of Yahweh, who is alone supreme.

The intent of Deut. 32:8 is to set God's choice of Israel within the context of God's universal purpose. God "fixes the boundaries" not only of Israel, but of all nations. (Cf. Amos 9:7: God, who led Israel to their homeland, also led Israel's arch rivals, the Syrians and the Philistines, to theirs.) Israel is chosen not for favoritism but for witness, as an instrument for universal blessing (Gen. 12:3).

The boundaries are fixed "according to the number of the sons of God." In this reading the RSV follows the Qumran text, which is supported by the LXX and several other ancient versions. (The MT reads not "sons of God" but "sons of Israel." Because there were seventy "sons" of Israel [Exod. 1:5], Jewish exegesis deduced that there were seventy nations of humanity — all ruled by God's general providence.)

We may assume with most modern scholarship that "sons of

God" is the correct reading. Thus the picture is that Yahweh, as leader of the "divine council," at the beginning (and continuously throughout the process of history) allots each nation their territory and places each under the guidance of a "son of God," or angel (servant) of Yahweh. (The "gods" of ancient mythology are subsumed within Yahweh's sole rule, as Yahweh's sons/servants.) Yahweh's self, however, retains direct rule and responsibility over Israel (Deut. 32:9).

The old mythological picture, then, is used to underline two theological points:

(1) Israel's special role within the divine scheme of things is based on God's gracious choice.
(2) God's concern for the whole created world and for the whole human race is utterly certain.

It is striking that "Elyon," the Canaanite name for the head of the pantheon, was adopted with apparent ease as a title for Yahweh. In the adaptation the old name acquires new color and content, for henceforth it takes its basic significance from the record of Yahweh's deeds and words. Conversely, the use of the pre-Yahwistic title is a declaration that the spiritual reality for which the Canaanites were groping is present in Yahweh.

32:9-10 "Jacob is Yahweh's allotted heritage" — literally, "the measuring-string of Yahweh's heritage." Both land and people are described as "heritage." The one implies the other. Indeed, Yahweh's salvation is not a spiritual abstraction but a spiritual-socioeconomic whole. "Yahweh 'found' Israel in a desert land" (v. 10). The Samaritan Pentateuch reverses the letters of the Hebrew word for "found" *(matsa')* to read "strengthened" *('amats)* — possibly to soften the strangeness of the statement. For did Yahweh not "find" Israel in Egyptian slavery? There is, however, a strand in the OT which regards the wilderness as the cradle of the Yahweh-Israel relationship (Hos. 2:3, 14; 9:10; 13:5-6; Jer. 2:2; cf. also Ezek. 16:4-5). The wilderness is essentially chaotic. The "howling waste" recalls the "waste and void" (Gen. 1:2) which preceded Yahweh's original act of creation. There is something negative about "chaos" as being contrary to Yahweh's desire for being and order. It was easy then for Israel to envisage the wilderness chaos as the abode of malign spirits. Yahweh's election of Israel was therefore an act of creation, bringing order out of chaos and replacing their spiritual vulnerability with the protection of Yahweh's covenant presence.

The "pupil (RSV 'apple') of the eye" (Deut. 32:10; cf. Ps. 17:8) is perhaps the most precious part of the body. The Hebrew for "pupil" means literally "little man." Is it fanciful to suggest that there is a tiny mirror image of Israel reflected in Yahweh's eye? This image Yahweh guards with loving care.

32:11-13   On the picture of the eagle caring for its young, cf. Exod. 19:4. The "fluttering" over the young recalls the spirit's brooding over chaos at creation (Gen. 1:2). The undergirding of strong wings represents the educative process of learning to trust for manna and water in the desert, until at last the fruits of Canaan are tasted — milk and honey, wheat and wine.

"Riding on the high places" (Deut. 32:13), that is, swiftly traversing the territory and touching on its hilltops, may correspond to treading the borders and thus symbolically claiming the land as an inheritance (cf. 11:24).

Accusation (32:15-18)

"When you have grown prosperous, take heed lest you forget . . ." (8:11-18). "Jeshurun" (32:15) is a pet name for Israel, perhaps meaning "my upright darling" (Heb. *yashar,* "upright," picks up the first three consonants of the name *yisrael,* "Israel").

Yahweh's fervent hope is that the beloved "son" of Israel would "do right" (Heb. *yashar;* e.g., 6:18; 12:25; 13:18) because Yahweh's own nature is *yashar* (32:4). But the hope is frustrated. So, because the child spurns (literally, "kicks") the father's goodness (cf. 31:20), the child in turn is spurned (32:19). This spurning, however, stems not from vindictiveness but from "jealousy" (v. 16), which is the underside of love (4:24).

To "know" God (32:17) implies fear and blessing. It is to have trembled with awe before God's greatness (cf. Gen. 31:53: God was Isaac's "Fear") and to have grateful experience of God's benefits. But how can people worship "gods" whom neither they nor their forebears have "known" in this way?

Deuteronomy 32:18 resembles v. 6 both in content and in its use of the second person. Like v. 6, it is perhaps a reinforcing addition. The "parenting" language of v. 18 has both a masculine and a feminine connotation. "Begetting" can apply to either father or mother, but the Hebrew word translated "give birth" refers to labor pains, and is therefore uncompromisingly feminine in its imagery.

The total range of experience of human love at its highest is thus drawn upon in describing Yahweh's love — which is the source of both the father bond and the mother bond.

Sanctions against an Apostate People (32:19-25)

This section (and more generally the whole of 32:15-25) represents an expansion of the introduction to the Song in 31:16-22. The ironic "tit for tat" noted in that passage is elaborated here:

Israel spurned (despised) Yahweh (31:16)	Yahweh spurned Israel (32:19)
Israel provoked Yahweh (32:19, 21)	Yahweh provokes Israel (32:21)
Israel turns their face away (31:18)	Yahweh hides the face (31:17, 18; 32:20)
Israel stirs Yahweh to jealousy (32:21)	Yahweh stirs Israel to jealousy (32:21)

Deuteronomy 32:20 presents an awesome prospect: love ceases to be involved — a contradiction in terms! — and sits detached like Jonah under his vine (Jonah 4:5) to see what the end will be! What end but death can there possibly be for the covenant people cut off from the source of their life?

A "perverse" generation (Deut. 32:20) is an upside-down generation, pursuing goals which are diametrically opposed to their own basic existence. The gods ("idols," v. 21) they rely on are mere "vapor," "mist," unsubstantial as breath — in contrast to Yahweh, who is solid reality and the ground of reality.

Various attempts have been made to identify the "no people" (v. 21b) with whom Yahweh provoked Israel. Most likely the reference is to eleventh-century Philistine attacks. (If accepted, this of course would not be decisive for dating the Song.) It takes a "foolish nation" to bring a "foolish people" (v. 6) to their senses!

The fire burning at the roots of the mountains (v. 22) is reminiscent of the Horeb theophany — symbolic of Yahweh's awesomeness and akin to Yahweh's jealousy. Anger is the expression of that jealousy and the obverse of Yahweh's love (see above on 9:7-8).

Yahweh's "arrows" (32:23) may be the theophanic lightning (Ps. 18:14) or pestilence (Deut. 32:24) or enemy attack — or all three! The evils predicted in vv. 23-25 recall the covenant sanction curses from ch. 28 and elsewhere throughout Deuteronomy.

Loyal Love Prevails over Judgment (32:26-38)

As already suggested, Deut. 32:26-27 may be an addition, designed to ensure that the judgments pronounced in the remainder of the Song are applied not to Israel (as was probably the case in the original draft) but to Israel's enemies. The general thought of these verses recalls 9:14-15, 25-29. Cf. also Ezek. 36:20-32.

Viewed superficially, this portrayal of Yahweh may appear unworthy and egotistical: "Not for your sake, but for my own reputation." Two important theological points, however, are being made:

(1) Yahweh's salvation concerns are universal. It is vital that "the nations" recognize Yahweh's working, not for Yahweh's reputation, but for their own well-being — which is dear to Yahweh.

(2) Yahweh's fundamental stance toward Israel is grace. The logic of the conditional covenant would require that the apostate partner be obliterated. But loyal love bursts the bounds of logic — Yahweh is God and not humanity (Hos. 11:9; Mal. 3:6).

"We did it" (Deut. 32:27). Cf. Israel's similar boast at 8:17-18. No nation, covenant or noncovenant, may arrogantly deify themselves in this way. On Yahweh's working through the medium of military and political structures, cf. Isa. 10:5-7, 12-13.

In the finished text of the Song, the "latter end" referred to in Deut. 32:29 is the fate of the enemy (cf. Ps. 73:17). If the enemy could realize that God was in fact working in and through their activity, "common sense" would tell them that their national destiny must depend on the response they make to this universally-active God. Their reason should help them deduce ("judge," Deut. 32:31) that their military successes against Israel were possible only because Yahweh let them win in order to discipline Israel. (On previous occasions Yahweh had repeatedly granted Israel victory against them. Thus Yahweh had demonstrated both Yahweh's superiority over their national gods and Israel's special place within Yahweh's universal plan — the current defeat being the exception that proves the rule!)

Yahweh's disciplining of Israel will succeed when the realization of their own powerlessness brings Israel to acknowledge and embrace Yahweh's grace (v. 36). Then the arrogant obtuseness of the enemy will be rebuked (v. 35) and Yahweh's universal rule demonstrated.

Verses 32-33 are probably a reference to the sexual immorality inherent in the fertility cults as practiced throughout the ancient Near East. Good vines normally produce good fruit (Isa. 5:1-7). Conversely, the poisonous Sodom-like fruits of cultic prostitution and other such practices are an indication that the religious vine which bore them is in itself degenerate.

Israel may act contrary to nature and fail to produce the good fruit which possession of Yahweh's torah would indicate. The enemy, on the other hand, are running entirely true to the nature of their religion when they practice depravity.

Deuteronomy 32:37-38 forms a bridge to the clear statement of monotheism in v. 39. The tone is reminiscent of the anti-idol polemic of 2 Isaiah (Isa. 44:9ff.; 46:1-2). "Do they indeed eat and drink the sacrifices you offer them? Yet when Yahweh acts against your arrogance, these gods are powerless to protect you." It remains true: when God speaks, the gods fall silent.

Yahweh's Purpose Shall Be Fulfilled (32:39-42)

The monotheism implicit in Deut. 4:32-40 (see above) becomes explicit in 32:39. Cf. Isa. 41:4; 43:10-13; 44:6; 45:6-7, 22; 48:12.

That God "kills and makes alive" (i.e., has the power of life and death) was probably an everyday proverb (cf. 1 Sam. 2:6-8; 2 Kgs. 5:7). For a more theologized version of the same thought, cf. Isa. 45:7: "I form light and create darkness, I make weal and create woe." God's "wounding and healing" recalls Hos. 6:1. It is noteworthy that both in Deut. 32 and in Hosea the phrase is poetic, a worship expression and an affirmation of faith. By contrast, the same phraseology occurs in Job 5:17-18, only hardened now into dogmatic statement. One senses that the shift causes distortion. What is poetically true may appear one-sided and inadequate as dogma.

When human beings swear an oath, they raise hands to heaven (Deut. 32:40) as God's dwelling, thus asking that their faithfulness be checked against the Source of all faithfulness. But when the Source itself swears, what check is there? God here swears by God's eternally unchanging being. That admits of no checks, nor needs any!

In vv. 41-42 Yahweh is depicted as Supreme Warrior, imagery borrowed from the Yahweh's war tradition (cf. Exod. 15:1, 3, 6, 11, 21). The importance of the Yahweh's war tradition for the Deuteronomic school has often been mentioned. It is significant here that, after Israel have been punished for their apostasy (Deut. 32:19-25), the same hand which at the beginning led the nation into freedom is extended once more to restore their condition. So close is Yahweh's identification with the covenant people that their enemies are Yahweh's enemies (v. 41b). However, let the word be read as intended — an assurance of grace, not a cause for presumption!

The Yahweh's war language blends into the theophanic. The "glittering sword" (cf. v. 23) may represent the Horeb lightning. The God who met and chose Israel at Horeb is their faithful defender in every crisis of their ongoing history. This conviction is expressed by the application of Horeb language to wider and wider contexts (cf. Nah. 3:3; Hab. 3:11) till eventually it flows into apocalyptic.

"Long hair" (Deut. 32:42) also belongs to the ethos of sacral warfare, both Yahweh's war and sacral warfare throughout the ancient Near East in general. Along with newly-washed garments and sexual abstinence (Exod. 19:14-15), uncut hair was a ritual requirement for battle preparation. Cf. Judg. 5:2: "Warriors in Israel unbound their hair" (JB). The reference in Deut. 32:42 is of course to the enemies' long hair — their attempt to concentrate their mana-potential for their struggle against Israel. The import of the passage is, therefore, that no "sakti" (spiritual energy) generated by ritual sanctity, however potent, can withstand the might of Yahweh when Yahweh acts in judgment.

Conclusion of the Song (32:43)

The MT of 32:43 consists of four lines of poetry, compared with six in the Qumran text (4QDeut) and eight in the Septuagint. Compared with 4QDeut and the LXX, the MT appears to lack balance — one line of praise plus three of judgment, compared with two plus four (4QDt) and four plus four (LXX). The MT has therefore possibly been truncated. There is strong support for the view that the Qumran text is closest to the original and that the LXX is a conflation of two or more Hebrew versions. The Qumran text is as follows: —

> Shout for joy, you heavens, together with Yahweh
> And bow to Yahweh, all you gods.
> For Yahweh avenges the blood of Yahweh's children
> And takes vengeance on Yahweh's adversaries.
> Yahweh requites those who hate Yahweh
> And makes expiation for the land of Yahweh's people.

It will be noticed that lines 4 and 5 repeat Deut. 32:41b. 4QDeut, line 1, contains several words that are subject to variation from version to version. First, the final word of Deut. 32:43 is read *'immo* ("together with") by 4QDeut and the LXX and *'ammo* ("Yahweh's people") by the MT. Scholars suggest that originally both words were included: *'im 'ammo* ("together with Yahweh's people"). Second, is it "the heavens" (4QDeut, LXX) or "the nations" (MT) who thus join rejoicing?

To "make expiation" (4QDeut, line 6; Heb. *kipper*) is literally to "cover" (see above on Deut. 21:8). Here in 32:43 "land" and "people" are one entity which together forms Yahweh's heritage *(nahalah)*. The people's behavior has polluted the land: in "cleansing" (so the LXX translates "kipper") the land, Yahweh renews and restores the land-people totality.

Viewed as a whole, the impact of the Song is that "loyal love triumphs over judgment." The question arises as to whether this overall message is consonant with the Song's introduction in 31:16-22. There the mood is dark with unrelieved warning. At the least a marked change of emphasis occurs as we move from introduction to Song.

Interestingly it is the suspected additions to the Song (32:26-27, 30-31, 36, 43) which cause the change of mood. Was the Song originally unrelieved indictment of Israel — subsequently lightened by shifting part of the indictment onto the enemy and by so doing making room for a proclamation of forgiveness and restoration?

Moses' Final Advice (32:44-47)

In the LXX v. 44 begins with a summary of 31:30 (thus rounding out the presentation of the Song), and then continues with 32:44-47 as they stand in the MT, but making the whole passage refer to the torah (*torah* is read for *shirah* in v. 44a; see the introduction to ch. 31, 269). The MT makes the transition to torah at 32:45, which links back to 31:29.

As at 31:19, Joshua (32:44) is associated with Moses in publishing the Song. This is in keeping with the structure of ch. 31 as a whole, which as we have seen sets the Song within the account of Joshua's appointment.

The language of this section is typical Deuteronomic parenesis. The offer of "life" (32:47) in particular recurs frequently (4:1; 5:33; 8:1; 16:20; 30:16). "Life" and "length of days" are related, but not identical; "life" hints at the quality of living with which the days are filled. Bread and its concomitants may help to ensure length of days, but "life" depends on the words of God (which indeed subsume every material provision; 8:3). This torah in all its detail "is your life" — certainly so, because it is the recorded "voice of the living God" (5:26). Between the word and the God who speaks there can be no essential distinction. It is "life" to obey.

MOSES' IMMINENT DEATH (32:48–52)

As noted at 1:37-38, there are three strands of tradition in Deuteronomy concerning the death of Moses:

(1) The JE strand: Moses' death is the natural conclusion to a long and fruitful life (34:1-6a).
(2) The Deuteronomic strand: Moses dies outside the promised land as bearing the penalty for his people's rebelliousness (1:37-38; 3:23-29).
(3) The Priestly strand: Moses' death outside the promised land is punishment for his own imperfect obedience (32:48-52).

It will be seen that 32:48-52 reiterates Num. 27:12-14 (P). The repetition is obviously intended to pick up the account of Israel's travelings (from Horeb to the borders of Canaan; Num. 10–27) after the massive insertion of Moses' farewell speech (Deut. 1–32), and link that travel narrative with the Priestly account of Moses' death (Deut. 34:1b, 7ff.).

"That very day" (32:48) is the day on which the threefold speech has been delivered (cf. 1:3, also P).

"Breaking faith" (32:51) presumably refers to Moses' "lack of discipline" as recounted in Num. 20. God said "tell the rock . . . to yield its water" (Num. 20:8), but Moses "struck the rock with his rod" (v. 11) — thus exceeding his instructions, according to the Priestly interpretation (v. 12).

The Priestly theological aim in this is to inculcate in their exilic/postexilic contemporaries a great sensitivity to disobedience and its consequences. The Exile was seen as God's punishment on disobedience. Let Israel guard against a bitter repetition! In this Moses is an object lesson. If even the great pioneer-founder-leader of Israel was not exempt from punishment for going beyond what God commanded, let his lesser descendants take heed and discipline themselves to obey.

The theological point is heightened with a play on words: "Kadesh" (Deut. 32:51; cf. 1:2, 19, 46) means "holy": "You did not *revere me as holy* (Heb. *kiddesh*) at 'Holy-head.'"

THE BLESSING OF MOSES
Deuteronomy 33:1-29

As noted in the Introduction (24-25), by about the beginning of the 4th cent. B.C. Deuteronomy had been detached from the Deuteronomic history (the proposed unitary work comprising Deuteronomy – 2 Kings) and was attached to Genesis – Numbers to form the final volume of the Pentateuch.

We may assume that it was at this time that the Blessing of Moses was inserted into Deuteronomy, to strengthen the book's link with the rest of the Pentateuch. Concretely, Moses' blessing at the end of Deuteronomy parallels Jacob's at the end of Genesis (Gen. 49). The Blessing of Jacob was uttered in the context of a prophecy that the "tribes" of Israel would certainly return to the land of their forebears (Gen. 48:21). Moses' blessing has the familiar Deuteronomic double perspective. Within the "speech-of-Moses" context it is uttered on the threshold of the thirteenth-century occupation of the land. From the perspective of the exilic/postexilic redactor, it prophesies a lifting of the exile punishment and a fresh experience of Yahweh's grace.

According to ancient Near Eastern tradition, the deathbed blessing by a head of family is fraught with great "mana." That blessing settles the leadership succession and determines the family's future. Placing such a blessing on the lips of Moses ranks him with the patriarchs (Isaac, Gen. 27; Jacob, Gen. 49). Indeed, the Deuteronomic school presumably ranked Moses above the patriarchs, in that he mediated the definitive Yahweh-Israel covenant, of which the patriarchal covenant was the foreshadowing. So intimate, in fact, is Moses with Yahweh that in some sense his blessing is equivalent to Yahweh's own blessing.

Scholarly research tends to the conclusion that the Blessing of Moses was composed during the 11th century. The general tone is one of prosperity and optimism. The territorial expansion of Gad is complete (Deut. 33:20-21); Simeon has presumably been absorbed into Judah (cf. Judg. 1:3). The composition may have been written down somewhat later, perhaps during David's reign.

The Blessing proper (Deut. 33:6-25) is set within a hymnic framework, vv. 2-3 and 26-29, which was probably an original unity. (Verses 4-5 have been inserted subsequently.) This framework hymn is also appropriately dated to the reign of David.

It is striking that, in contrast to the preceding chapter, Deut. 33 allows of very little cross-referencing either with the language of Deuteronomy as a whole or with that of the prophetic writings. It has its own quite distinctive style and vocabulary. Most scholars suspect a northern (Elohistic?) provenance, but the evidence is tenuous.

On the identification of the twelve tribes, and the order in which they are mentioned, cf. 27:11-13. Two possibilities suggest themselves as to the arrangement in 33:6-25. (1) Perhaps a geographically-based listing is intended, proceeding from south to north (Gad is the only name that does not fit this pattern). (2) The tribes may be listed according to their eponymous "mothers": first the leading "Leah" tribes, then the "Rachel" tribes, followed by the lesser "Leah-ites" and finally (in mixed order) the "concubine" tribes.

The "Rachel" tribes are strikingly prominent in the center of the list. Does this support a northern provenance, since Rachel is the eponymous "mother" of "Joseph" (Ephraim-Manasseh) and Benjamin?

INTRODUCTION TO THE BLESSING (33:1-5)

The title "man of God" is frequently applied to northern prophetic figures throughout the books of Samuel and Kings, but only three times in the OT is it applied to Moses (Deut. 33:1; Josh. 14:6; Ps. 90 [heading]).

The poetic parallelism of the material indicates that "Sinai," "Seir," and "Paran" (Deut. 33:2a) together denote the mountainous terrain to the south of Judah traditionally regarded as Yahweh's ancient home, from whence Yahweh appears in theophany.

The text of v. 2b is disputed. The RSV follows the MT: "from the ten thousands of holy ones" (Heb. *meribebot qodesh*). The "holy ones" are probably heavenly attendants (less likely, the consecrated armies of Israel). Yahweh's coming "from" the holy ones would imply that the theophany is immediately from the southern mountains, but ultimately from heaven. Some scholars, sensing that this interpretation is rather forced, follow the Targum, LXX, and Vulgate, and emend "from" to "together with" (cf. NEB). Others conclude that *meribebot qodesh* originally read *mi-meribath kadesh* (i.e., "from Meribath Kadesh"; see above on 32:51) or "from the hosts of Kadesh." The JB version adopts this last possibility and translates "after the mustering at Kadesh," that is, after the clans had gathered for the proclamation of Yahweh's covenant-torah. The NEB solution is probably the most satisfactory: "with Yahweh were myriads of holy ones."

The text of 33:3 is also difficult, but a clear picture of Yahweh's "fiery love" emerges. The beloved people are "in Yahweh's hand" and "at Yahweh's feet," powerfully protected and obediently following.

On the pet name "Jeshurun" (v. 5), see above on 32:15. The first line of 33:5 reads literally, "Thus there was a king in Jeshurun." The NEB and JB take this as referring to the election of Saul or David, while the RSV refers it to the enthronement of Yahweh. If v. 5 did indeed once link directly with v. 26, the RSV interpretation is the more natural.

THE BLESSING OF THE TRIBES (33:6-25)

Reuben (33:6)

This blessing obviously reflects a situation where Reuben's numerical strength and influence were in decline — a decline presumably attributed to moral weakness like that of their ancestor (Gen. 49:3-4). By way of rebuke, Yahweh had permitted Moab to encroach on Reuben's territory (Judg. 5:15-16). Simeon has already disappeared (see above, introduction to Deut. 33, 294). The prayer of v. 6 is that Jacob's "firstborn" may yet be spared.

Judah (33:7)

In the situation reflected here, Judah is experiencing isolation from the other more northern tribes (v. 7a), through enemy incursions (v. 7b). Perhaps the setting is the eleventh-century Philistine threat. This blessing — or rather, intercessory prayer for Judah — contrasts strikingly with Gen. 49:8-12, where Judah is enjoying wide influence and prosperity (probably during the reign of David). A. D. H. Mayes has noted the similarity between Deut. 33:7b and 11b, and suggested that v. 11 once connected with v. 7 before being severed by the intrusion of vv. 8-10 (*Deuteronomy*, 404).

Levi (33:8-10 [11])

This saying also is more intercession than blessing, especially if v. 11 is indeed to be ascribed to Judah, as Mayes suggests (see above). (Other scholars, however — notably Frank M. Cross and David Noel Freedman, *Studies in Ancient Yahwistic Poetry*, 112 — argue a contrary position, that v. 11 is *the* original blessing on Levi in this context, and that vv. 8-10 are a later proselike interpolation.)

The warm positive assessment of Levi in vv. 8-10 (11) again contrasts sharply with the Blessing of Jacob, where Levi (and Simeon) are rebuked for their barbarity (Gen. 49:5-7).

Deuteronomy 33:11, if it belongs to the Levi blessing, indicates that the Levites were incurring resentment, presumably from original non-Levitic priests (cf., e.g., Judg. 17) who were threatened by the granting of exclusive priestly rights to Levi (Deut. 10:8-9).

Deuteronomy 33:9 implies that Levi won the right to priestly status by an outstanding display of loyalty to Yahweh at Massah ("Testing") and Meribah ("Disputing") — in contrast to the people in general, who (cf. Ps. 95:8) failed their test and displeased Yahweh with their faithless dispute. The other pentateuchal accounts of these incidents (Exod. 17:1-7; Num. 20:2-13) make no direct mention of Levi's role in them. Probably Deut. 33 has taken the details from a parallel oral tradition. We may surmise that the display of loyalty envisaged was similar to that described in Exod. 32:26-29, the golden calf incident, which clearly provides the background of Deut. 33:9.

On the Levites' functions, cf. Deut. 10:8-9. As suggested there, "Thummim" and "Urim" (33:8; cf. 1 Sam. 14:41; Exod. 28:30; Ezra 2:63) were almost certainly used in making priestly-legal "decisions" *(mishpat)* — "Is this the correct decision? Let the sacred dice answer 'Yes' or 'No.'" In the subsequent growth of Israel's theological understanding concerning torah as the expression of God's will, "keeping the sacred dice" developed in scope, depth, and sophistication, till it became "preserving the sacred traditions of torah." (According to the later Priestly source, the handling of Thummim and Urim was the special preserve of the high priest alone; here in Deut. 33 it is the right of all levitical priests.)

The word translated "incense" in v. 10b seems to have had the generalized meaning of "smoke" in the earlier literature, and only in the (post)exilic period developed the specialized meaning of "incense." Here, then, the reference may be to the "smoke of sacrifice" in parallel to "whole burnt offering."

Benjamin (33:12)

The title "Beloved of Yahweh" in fact translates the pet name "Jedidiah," applied to Solomon (2 Sam. 12:25). A suggested emendation produces the reading "Elyon encompasses him . . ." (see above on 26:19). This would clarify the following phrase, "he makes his dwelling between his shoulders." The reference is presumably to a Yahwistic sanctuary — perhaps the one at Nob (1 Sam. 21:1), situated among the hills ("shoulders") of Benjamin. Other scholars prefer the opposite interpretation: "Benjamin sits between Yahweh's shoulders" as the truly beloved child. Both interpretations are possible, but the first is probably to be preferred.

The calm atmosphere which pervades Deut. 33:12 contrasts strongly with the aggressiveness ascribed to Benjamin in Gen. 49:27: "a ravenous wolf, devouring . . . dividing the spoil." Character evolves with circumstances, and the word of God is never abstract, but concrete address in specific circumstances.

Joseph (33:13-17)

This lengthy blessing forms the centerpiece of the series, presumably pointing to the preeminent role of the Joseph tribes in Israel at the time the series was compiled.

A comparison of Deut. 33:13-17 with Gen. 49:22-26 shows several points of similarity, making it likely that the two versions stem from an ancient common origin.

At Deut. 33:13 MT reads "with the choicest gifts of the dew of heaven." Following several manuscripts, the RSV has amended this to conform with Gen. 49:25, "of heaven above." Possibly the original included both words: "the dew of heaven from above."

The "couching" (cf. Gen. 4:7) of the deep (Heb. *tehom*) is poetic language tinged with mythological coloring: the monster-filled depths paradoxically yield blessing at Yahweh's all-powerful behest. (The ancient mythology is indeed "Yahwehized" in the first Creation account [Gen. 1:2-3], so that *tehom* becomes the "deep" upon which Yahweh imposed creative order.)

"Ancient mountains . . . everlasting hills" (Deut. 33:15) is a favorite poetic parallelism (Gen. 49:26; Hab. 3:6) possibly taken into Hebrew poetry from Canaanite sources. As noted at Deut. 32:4, "mountain" in the ancient Near East could signify either a dwelling place or a title of the divine. Blessing of the mountain and hill means therefore the favor of creation's Author — favor marked by a durability which even the most permanent features of nature can only faintly symbolize.

If "the bush" (Heb. *seneh*, 33:16) is the correct reading, then the reference is to the burning bush, in which Yahweh appeared as "I Am" (Exod. 3:2, 14). It seems preferable, however, to read "Sinai" (Heb. *sinay*), that is, a reference to Yahweh's definitive theophany.

The "wild ox" (Deut. 33:17) was proverbial for its strength (cf. Job 39:9-12; Ps. 22:21). When combined with "horn," also symbolic of strength, the impression is of irresistible (because God-inspired) might. The historical reference is perhaps to Israel's wars against Midian (Judg. 6–8). In that case, the word of blessing is a powerful enablement, equipping Joseph to withstand and to conquer.

The older sources (Josh. 16:1-3 J) regard Manasseh-Ephraim as one undifferentiated tribe, whereas in the later Priestly source (Josh. 16:4-8; 17:1-10) they are regarded as having formed two separate units from the beginning. The change reflects Joseph's growth in numbers and influence in the intervening centuries between J and P.

Zebulun and Issachar (33:18-19)

The territory of these two tribes was in Galilee. The famous shrine of Mt. Tabor was on their border, with Issachar to the east and Zebulun to the west.

Zebulun "goes out" (Deut. 33:18) in trading contact with neighbors. In poetic contexts "rejoice" is often paralleled with "be glad" (Heb. *yasis*). It seems likely that this word has dropped out of v. 18b by haplography with the name of the second tribe: *yss ysschr* ("Be glad, Issachar").

The text of v. 19 is doubtful and can be translated only by somewhat forcing the Hebrew grammar. For some scholars the confused state of the LXX text at this point confirms their doubts. If v. 19 is authentic, however, "their mountain" will refer to Tabor. The "peoples" are trading partners come to share "the affluence of the seas" (the fishing industry, or the importing of goods from around the Mediterranean?) and "the hidden treasures of the sand" (the shellfish exuding precious purple dye, or the glass-making industry?).

Theologically significant is the religious tolerance described in v. 19a. Foreigners, attracted to the worship rites they discover at Tabor, ask permission to participate and find their offerings accepted. This acceptance contrasts with the exclusiveness advocated in 7:1-5. Another aspect of tolerance in these verses is the obvious acknowledgment of Tabor as a legitimate Yahwistic shrine in contrast to ch. 12's demand for strict cultic centralization. The verses therefore reflect a local tradition either prior to the Deuteronomic school or outside their sphere of influence.

Gad (33:20-21)

The Gadites were the strongest of the Israelite tribes living east of Jordan. Their fertile territory deserved the description "best of the land" (33:21). Gad's right to this pleasant heritage was based on their leadership role during the Conquest (3:18-20; cf. Num. 32:17).

The exposed position of the Gadite territory at the southeastern corner of Israel made them vulnerable to attack, notably from the neighboring Ammonites. Deuteronomy 33:20 (cf. Gen. 49:19) expresses confidence, however, that Gad will prove a match for the aggressors. Their strength in this is not entirely their own, but comes from Yahweh, who is Gad's "enlarger." (The RSV here follows the MT. Contrast the NEB reading, "blessed be Gad, in his wide [large] domain." The strength of the emendation is that it brings this blessing into line with all the others by making it refer to the tribe, rather than to Yahweh.)

Deuteronomy 33:21b as it stands may follow on (albeit awkwardly) from v. 21a. However, by a slight rearranging of the Hebrew letters, the first phrase of v. 21b becomes "when the heads of the people were gathered together" (cf. NEB). This is identical with the LXX text, and also with the second clause of v. 5. This congruity with v. 5 makes it highly likely that the whole of v. 21b belongs in fact not with the Gad blessing but with the framework (vv. 1-5, 26-29). Thus it is Yahweh, not Gad, who works righteousness *(tsedaqah)* and just decrees *(mishpat)* in Israel.

Dan (33:22)

According to Josh. 19:40-48, Dan originally occupied a narrow strip of land between Judah and Ephraim. However, because this was too confining they migrated north and captured Leshem or Laish on the southern slopes of Hermon, renaming it Dan (Judg. 18:29; Josh. 19:47).

Interestingly, Laish means "lion" (cf. Deut. 33:22: "Dan is a lion's whelp"). The blessing seemingly congratulates Dan on their successful resettlement. A difficulty with the MT (reflected in the RSV) is that traditionally Dan has no links with Bashan (east of the Jordan). Those scholars are probably correct, therefore, who

translate Heb. *bashan* as "serpent," and read the line as: (Dan)
. . . "who shies away from a serpent." The symbolism then becomes the same as in Gen. 49:17, though its use is different.

Naphtali (33:23)

The blessing reflects a period when Naphtali, originally confined
to the pleasant hill country south of Hermon (Josh. 20:7), had
begun to spread southward into even more fertile territory.

Hebrew *yam*, translated "lake" in the RSV, can also mean "sea"
(NEB, JB) or more generally "west." The "lake" would be Chin-
nereth (Galilee), the "sea" the Mediterranean. Whether Naphtali
ever reached the seaboard is doubtful. In any case, however, the
point is that Naphtali's progress is by Yahweh's blessing and
enablement. The same expansion and fertility is also the theme
of Gen. 49:21, though under different imagery.

Asher (33:24-25)

Asher means "blessed" — a fitting name for the "favorite" son.
(Probably this ascription of "most favored" status is not based on
historical fact, but simply read out of the etymology.)

The "oil" is from the olives which thrive in the area.

Deuteronomy 33:25 probably constitutes a promise that Asher
will always be enabled to protect their holdings from the greed
of envious neighbors.

Reviewing the blessing series as a whole, it is noteworthy that
these are not generalized expression of goodwill, but concrete
promises attached to specific situations. In this, the passage is a
miniature of the entire history of Yahweh's dealings with the
covenant people. The word of God is always concrete; it may
become a paradigm, but never a philosophical abstraction.

THE CONCLUSION OF MOSES' BLESSING (33:26-29)

On Yahweh as cloud-rider (v. 26), cf. Ps. 68:4, 33; Isa. 19:1. The
description has been borrowed from Canaanite literature, where

Baal-hadad, god of storms, is depicted as charioted on the storms. In taking over such language, Israel is declaring that Yahweh whom they have known as Controller of history is also Controller of nature — Giver both of political victory and of natural prosperity.

The same "arms" (Deut. 33:27) which are experienced as gently supportive (Hos. 11:3) of the covenant people are also conceived as bared implacably against the people's enemies — "thrusting out and crying 'Destroy'" (cf. Deut. 7:15). There is surely a mixture of insight and obtuseness in these words. It is a true insight that the arm of God is gentle toward human weakness and strong against human arrogance. But are we not judging rashly when we too quickly assign the weakness to ourselves and the arrogance to others?

A similar "naïveté" appears in 33:29. An exuberant reveling in the free grace of God (v. 29a) couples with a triumphalistic enjoyment of the rival's discomforture (v. 29b). How "human," that the grace we claim for ourselves we deny to our opponents! God is indeed a God of judgment: is it not safer to apply this to ourselves, rather than to others?

The idyllic picture of security and plenty (v. 28) reminds us that the heart of the covenant promise is glad possession of the land, which is at once Yahweh's "inheritance" and Israel's. The language recalls the blessing on Joseph (vv. 13-16) and the glowing descriptions of the inheritance in 8:7-10 and elsewhere.

Having acknowledged the rather regrettable triumphalism that shows through these concluding verses — and perhaps having been tempted to excuse it as an understandable compensation for exilic sufferings — it remains true that the convictions about ultimate good expressed here are a tremendous statement of faith. The covenant curses (ch. 28) have fallen, yet God remains God. "Who is like Yahweh?" (33:26). From this basic conviction, the compiler still dares to draw the consequence; "Therefore, who is like the covenant people whom Yahweh has chosen?" (v. 29).

302

THE DEATH OF MOSES
Deuteronomy 34:1-12

This concluding chapter is composed of material from various sources. Most scholars assign 34:1aα, 7-9 to P; vv. 1aβ-6 to the Deuteronomic source; and vv. 10-12 to a post-Deuteronomic writer.

It will be seen that v. 1aα connects with 32:48-52 (P). In both the "mount of viewing" is named Nebo, whereas the Deuteronomist prefers the name Pisgah (34:1aβ; 3:27; 4:49).

On the other hand, 34:1aβ-6 connects back to Deuteronomic material in 31:23-29, and forward to Josh. 1:1ff. These verses (Deut. 34:1aβ-6) are thus the core of ch. 34. The author has obviously employed inherited JE material in his account.

Representative(s) of the Priestly school later expanded the basic narrative by the addition of vv. 1aα, 7-9 as noted. This would have happened at the time Deuteronomy was disjoined from the Deuteronomic history and incorporated as volume 5 of the Pentateuch.

Finally, another author added vv. 10-12 as the definitive assessment of Moses' role. He obviously regarded this assessment as a fitting conclusion to the whole Pentateuch — the core of which is Yahweh's torah-word as mediated by Moses.

MOSES SIGHTS ISRAEL'S INHERITANCE (34:1-4)

"Yahweh showed Moses all the land . . ." (v. 1), so fulfilling the promise made at 3:27.

Several commentators have remarked on the parallelism between 34:1-4 and Gen. 13:14-17. According to some of the ancient legal codes the transfer of land was ratified by the two parties together officially sighting the land, with its features and boundaries. In these two texts Abraham (Gen. 13) and Moses (Deut. 34) are invited by Yahweh to stand and sight the land, with Yahweh's faithful intention to hand the heritage over to the covenant people.

As regards Deut. 34, modern witnesses confirm that Mt. Hermon, at a distance of about 160 km. (100 mi.), can indeed be seen from the top of Pisgah. (The city of Dan is on Hermon's slopes.) Ebal and Gerizim, the twin heart of Ephraim-Manasseh, are also clearly visible. Only Judah and the Negeb are partially obscured by an intervening mountain range.

The author envisages Moses standing with Yahweh on Pisgah, and having his gaze directed north along the east side of Jordan right to Hermon, then back down west Jordan through Naphtali, and on through Ephraim-Manasseh to Judah in the south and the Negeb in the deep south. Then the gaze is shifted to Jericho at the north end of the Dead Sea and due west of Pisgah, and from there runs right down the east shore of the Dead Sea to the southernmost extreme. Thus the whole land is sighted.

Once again (v. 4; cf., e.g., 1:8; 6:10; 8:1; 9:5) the Horeb-Moab covenant is presented as fulfillment of centuries-old promises made to the forebears. Thus the enduring faithfulness of Yahweh is stressed.

On "You shall not go over there" (v. 4), see above on 1:37 (cf. 3:27; 4:21).

THE DEATH OF MOSES (34:5-9)

The title "servant of Yahweh" (34:5) recalls the similar title "man of God" at 33:1. "Servant of Yahweh" (Heb. *'ebed-YHWH*) occurs frequently in the Deuteronomic history, Chronicles, Psalms, and in 2 Isaiah — applied variously to Abraham, David, Jacob, Joshua, and the prophets, but most frequently to Moses. 2 Isaiah uses the title frequently both of Jacob-Israel the servant people (Isa. 42:19; 41:8-9; 44:1-2, 21; 45:4), and of the Servant (49:5-6; 42:1; 49:3; 52:13; 53:11) who epitomizes the complete servanthood to which Israel aspired but failed to attain.

We noted earlier (Deut. 1:37) that 2 Isaiah's portrait of the ideal Servant is very probably founded on, or at least influenced by, the Deuteronomic picture of Moses as innocent punishment bearer. The use of *'ebed-YHWH* in 34:5 and throughout the Deuteronomic history as a title for Moses tends to confirm that conclusion.

"According to the word of Yahweh" is literally "by the mouth of Yahweh." In the rabbinic tradition this has been rendered unscientifically but movingly "by the kiss of Yahweh." Moses' dying, like his living, was characterized by intimacy with Yahweh.

Moses is buried "in the valley . . . opposite Beth-peor" (v. 6), that is, in the spot where he had just delivered his farewell speech (3:29). There is an air of purposefulness about this. The task is complete, and the messenger withdraws forthwith.

The "he" who buried Moses is Yahweh. The Samaritan text and the LXX read "they buried him," presumably to avoid the anthropomorphism. But the MT is clearly correct, explaining as it does the concluding phrase "no one knows the place. . . ." Moses was buried not by any human being, but by God. He left behind him not a place of pilgrimage but an example of faith and obedience and a definitive word to follow.

On Moses' age (34:7), cf. 31:2. That "his eye was not dim, nor his natural force abated" seems at odds with 31:2b, "I am no longer able. . . ." The Priestly writer (34:7-9) wishes to stress that Moses' surrender of office was not from old age but from Yahweh's decision.

The normal mourning period (v. 8) in OT times was seven days (Gen. 50:10; 1 Sam. 31:13; 1 Chr. 10:12). The outstanding exception was Joseph, who was mourned seventy days, perhaps because foreign (Egyptian) mourning customs applied in his case, which puts him out of the reckoning.

Moses and Aaron were both mourned thirty days (Num. 20:29; Deut. 34:8). That Moses (and his associate) were mourned not a week but a month is a sign of the foundational character of his (their) ministry.

For the Deuteronomist, "wisdom" (v. 9) resides not in the leader but in the torah (4:6). Solomon is the first leader to whom wisdom is ascribed (1 Kgs. 3:9). This contrasts with the Priestly tradition, which frequently, as here, ascribes wisdom to outstanding persons (e.g., Exod. 28:3; 31:3, 6). It is noteworthy too that in Deut. 34:9 Joshua is "ordained" by the laying on of Moses' hands, whereas according to the Deuteronomic writer (perhaps a century earlier) he is commissioned by the direct, unmediated word of Yahweh.

Verse 9, with its emphasis on the respect accorded to Joshua, provides a link with the book of Joshua (cf. Josh. 1:16-18).

ASSESSMENT OF MOSES' ROLE (34:10-12)

"No prophet since . . . like Moses" contrasts with Deut. 18:15: "The LORD will raise up . . . a prophet like (Moses)" (see above on 18:15ff.). As mentioned in the introduction to ch. 34, the two passages are from different sources.

In any case, the contrast does not amount to a contradiction. In ch. 18 the accent is on the contemporization of "Mosaic" torah in each succeeding generation. Here, however, attention is focused rather on (1) the unique intimacy existing between Yahweh and Moses and (2) Moses' primacy as standing at the beginning of the prophetic line — the pioneer in whose footsteps all the prophets follow.

Deuteronomy speaks several times of the people "knowing Yahweh" (see above on 11:28; 29:26). In 34:10, on the other hand, it is Yahweh who "knows" the person (Moses). This "knowing" on Yahweh's part implies a strong concern (Ps. 103:13-14) which is expressed in choosing (Jer. 1:5), controlling (Amos 3:2), protecting (Nah. 1:7), preserving (Ps. 1:6), and understanding the subject in depth (Ps. 139:1-6, 23-24). The Bible in general stresses that our knowledge of God is grounded in God's prior knowledge of us (1 Cor. 13:12b; Gal. 4:9).

Yahweh knew Moses "face to face." The phrase is symbolic of deep intimacy (see above on 31:17-18). The same phrase occurs at Exod. 33:11: "face to face, as a person talks to a friend." Cf. also Num. 12:8: "With (Moses) I speak mouth to mouth . . . and he beholds the form of Yahweh." Here is "knowledge" at its most intimate.

According to Deut. 5:4, Yahweh had spoken "face to face" with the people at Horeb. However, there was a difference between their experience and Moses'. They still required a mediator, to spell out for them the significance of what they had heard and experienced in that divine encounter. Moses, however, directly apprehended the detailed meaning of what he heard — and recorded it as torah. This then is the essence of Moses' uniqueness: his intimacy with Yahweh consisted in his apprehending and expressing Yahweh's definitive word.

This would imply that intimacy with Yahweh is not to be attained via the mystic pathway, but through hearing and obeying Yahweh's word. "Intimacy" and "obedience" are closely intertwined.

It is interesting that 34:11-12 cite "signs and wonders" as evidence of Moses' greatness. By contrast, 13:1-4 has sounded the warning that signs in themselves may deceive. Only as ancillary to the word are they dependable. This is of course the presumption of the present context.

That is why no direct reference is made, in this final assessment of Moses' contribution, to the torah which he mediated. (Contrast the prophet Muhammad whose proof of apostleship is in the book he transmitted.) Torah is word, and word is implicit in the intimacy which Moses experienced with Yahweh.

"No prophet since . . . like Moses"? The first friends of Jesus sensed in him an obedient sensitivity so complete that the accompanying intimacy with God was perfect, and in that intimacy the divine word was apprehended in all its purity. They sensed a "face-to-face"-ness so direct as to reflect God's nature (2 Cor. 4:6). Thus the conviction came across to them from Jesus: "If we have seen Jesus, we have seen Yahweh" (John 14:9).

SELECTED BIBLIOGRAPHY

Baltzer, Klaus. *The Covenant Formulary* (Philadelphia: Fortress and Oxford: Blackwell, 1971).

Cairns, Ian J. "The Role of Theophany in the Formation of Scripture in Early Israel and the Qur'an" (Dissertation, Edinburgh, 1970).

Cross, Frank Moore, Jr., and Freedman, David Noel. *Studies in Ancient Yahwistic Poetry*. SBL Dissertation Series 21 (Missoula: Scholars Press, 1975).

Hamlin, E. John. *Inheriting the Land: A Commentary on the Book of Joshua*. International Theological Commentary (Grand Rapids: Wm. B. Eerdmans and Edinburgh: Handsel, 1983).

Hertzberg, Hans Wilhelm. *I and II Samuel*. Old Testament Library (Philadelphia: Westminster and London: SCM, 1964).

Kraus, Hans-Joachim. *Worship in Israel* (Richmond: John Knox, 1966).

Lohfink, Norbert. *Das Hauptgebot: Eine Untersuchung literarischer Einleitungsfragen zu Dtn 5–11*. Analectica Biblica 20 (Rome: Pontificio Instituto Biblico, 1963).

Mayes, A. D. H. *Deuteronomy*. New Century Bible Commentary (Grand Rapids: Wm. B. Eerdmans and London: Marshall, Morgan & Scott, 1981).

Mendenhall, George E. *Law and Covenant in Israel and the Ancient Near East* (Pittsburgh: Biblical Colloquium, 1955).

Nielsen, Eduard. *The Ten Commandments in New Perspective*. Studies in Biblical Theology, 2nd series 7 (London: SCM and Naperville: Allenson, 1968).

Noth, Martin. *The Deuteronomistic History*, rev. ed. Journal for the

Study of the Old Testament Supplement 15 (Sheffield: JSOT Press, 1988).

————. *Exodus*. Old Testament Library (Philadelphia: Westminster and London: SCM, 1962).

————. *The History of Israel*, 2nd ed. (New York: Harper & Row and London: A. & C. Black, 1960).

von Rad, Gerhard. *Deuteronomy*. Old Testament Library (Philadelphia: Westminster and London: SCM, 1966).

————. *Old Testament Theology*, 2 vols. (New York: Harper & Row and Edinburgh: Oliver & Boyd, 1962).

————. *Studies in Deuteronomy*. Studies in Biblical Theology 9 (1953; repr. London: SCM and Naperville: Allenson, 1961).

Stamm, J. J. and Andrew, M. E. *The Ten Commandments in Recent Research*. Studies in Biblical Theology, 2nd series 2 (1967; repr. London: SCM and Naperville: Allenson, 1970).

Teilhard de Chardin, Pierre. *The Future of Man* (New York: Harper & Row and London: Collins, 1964).

de Vaux, Roland. *The Early History of Israel*, 2 vols. (Philadelphia: Westminster and London: Darton, Longman & Todd, 1978).

Weinfeld, Moshe. *Deuteronomy and the Deuteronomic School* (Oxford: Clarendon, 1972).

Welch, Adam C. *The Code of Deuteronomy* (London: J. Welch, 1924).

Wellhausen, Julius. *Prolegomena to the History of Ancient Israel* (1885; repr. Magnolia, Mass.: Peter Smith, 1973).

Wenham, Gordon J. *"Bᵉtûlāh* 'A Girl of Marriageable Age,'" *Vetus Testamentum* 22 (1972): 326-348.

Wolff, Hans Walter. "Hoseas geistige Heimat," *Theologische Literaturzeitung* 81 (1956): 83-94; repr. *Gesammelte Studien zum Alten Testament*. Theologische Bücherei 22 (Munich: Kaiser, 1964), 232-250.